"Through extensive interviews with the victims' families and friends, Kolker creates compassionate portraits of the murdered young women and uncovers the forces that drove them from their respective hometowns into risky, but lucrative, careers as prostitutes in a digital age." —*The New Yorker*

"A gothic whodunit for the Internet age . . . nearly unputdownable . . . a horrific, cautionary tale that makes for a very different kind of beach read." —*New York Times Book Review*

"Terrific . . . vivid and moving. . . . Grade: A–" —*Entertainment Weekly*

"Hard to put down. . . . Kolker's convincing takeaway is both an indictment and a challenge." —*Boston Globe*

"Humane and imaginative. . . . [Kolker] shows the dented magnificence and universal sorrow within ordinary lives and makes you realize how much more they are worth." —Laura Miller, *Salon*

"Kolker is a careful writer and researcher . . . [he paints] a far more nuanced picture of each young woman than any screaming headline could." —*Miami Herald*

"Robert Kolker's *Lost Girls* is reportage at the highest level; it's miss-your-bedtime storytelling. . . . It's a wonder." —Darin Strauss, author of *Half a Life*

LOST GIRLS

ALSO BY ROBERT KOLKER

Hidden Valley Road: Inside the Mind of an American Family

LOST
GIRLS

AN

AMERICAN MYSTERY

THE LIVES OF THE VICTIMS OF THE
LONG ISLAND SERIAL KILLER

ROBERT KOLKER

HARPER ● PERENNIAL

NEW YORK ● LONDON ● TORONTO ● SYDNEY ● NEW DELHI ● AUCKLAND

The epilogue to this edition was first published, in a slightly different form, as "The Botched Hunt for the Gilgo Beach Killer," in the *New York Times Magazine*, October 19, 2023, updated November 3, 2023.

First Harper Perennial international mass market printing: May 2025
First Harper Perennial paperback printing: February 2020
First Harper hardcover printing: July 2013

Print Edition ISBN: 978-0-06-346653-1
Digital Edition ISBN: 978-0-06-341111-1

Cover design by Amanda Kain
Cover photograph © Andrew Gombert/EPA/Shutterstock
Designed by William Ruoto
Maps designed by Springer Cartographics, LLC

25 26 27 28 29 BVGM 10 9 8 7 6 5 4 3 2 1

For Kirsten

AUTHOR'S NOTE

Lost Girls is a work of nonfiction about five women connected to the same criminal investigation—the case of a suspected serial killer or killers operating on Long Island from 1996 until the present day. The narrative is based on hundreds of hours of interviews with the victims' friends, family members, acquaintances, neighbors, and members of law enforcement. No scenes were invented. All events and dialogue not witnessed firsthand are based on personal accounts and published reports. For reasons of privacy, the names of some children have been changed, as have the names of four adults: "Blake," "June," "Teresa," and "Jordan."

CONTENTS

LIST OF CHARACTERS

Maureen Brainard-Barnes
(disappeared 2007) (working name: Marie) (from Norwich, CT)
- Mother: Marie Ducharme
- Father: Bob Senecal
- Younger sister: Missy
- Younger brother: Will (died 2009)
- Daughter: Caitlin
- Son: Aidan
- Friend: Jay DuBrule
- Friend: Sara Karnes (working name: Lacey or Monroe)

Melissa Barthelemy
(disappeared 2009) (working name: Chloe) (from Buffalo, NY)
- Mother: Lynn Barthelemy
- Mother's boyfriend: Jeff Martina
- Grandmother: Linda
- Grandfather: Elmer
- Aunt: Dawn
- Younger half-sister: Amanda
- Boyfriend: Jordan
- Friend: Kritzia (working name: Mariah)
- Boyfriend/pimp: John Terry (working name: Blaze)

Shannan Gilbert
(disappeared 2010) (working names: Sabrina, Madison, Angelina) (from Ellenville, NY)
- Mother: Mari Gilbert

- Younger sister: Sherre
- Younger sister: Sarra
- Younger sister: Stevie
- Boyfriend/former driver: Alex Diaz
- Driver: Michael Pak

Megan Waterman
(disappeared 2010) (working names: Lexi, Jasmine, Tiffany) (from South Portland, ME)

- Mother: Lorraine Waterman
- Father: Greg Gove
- Mother's boyfriend: Bill
- Older brother: Greg
- Grandmother: Muriel
- Aunt: Liz Meserve
- Daughter: Liliana
- Boyfriend/drug dealer: Akeem Cruz (working name: Vybe)
- Friend: Nicci Haycock
- Police officer: Doug Weed
- Pimp: Banks

Amber Overstreet Costello
(disappeared 2010) (working name: Carolina) (from Wilmington, NC)

- Mother: Margie (died 2005)
- Father: Al
- Sister: Kim (working names: Mia or Italia)
- Friend: Melissa Wright
- Owner of Coed Confidential: Teresa
- First ex-husband: Michael Wilhelm
- Second ex-husband: Don Costello
- Chaperone/roommate: Dave Schaller
- Chaperone/roommate/boyfriend: Bjorn Brodsky (Bear)

Suffolk County Law Enforcement

- Police Commissioner, 2004–2011: Richard Dormer
- Chief of Detectives, 1972–2011: Dominick Varrone
- Chief of Department, 2012–2015: James Burke
- District Attorney, 2002–2017: Thomas Spota
- Police Commissioner, 2015–2017 / District Attorney, 2018–2021: Timothy Sini
- Police Commissioner, 2018–2021: Geraldine Hart
- District Attorney, 2022–present: Ray Tierney
- Police Commissioner, 2022–2023: Rodney Harrison

PROLOGUE

To most travelers, the barrier islands of Long Island are just a featureless stretch between Jones Beach and Fire Island—a narrow strip of marsh and dune, bramble and beach, where the grassy waters of South Oyster Bay meet the waves of the Atlantic Ocean. The main artery of the barrier islands, Ocean Parkway, is long and straight and often empty at night—a drag racer's dream. A driver can see little more than the beach heather or bayberry tangled thick and high on the shoulders of the highway. Fifteen miles of darkness surrounds passing vehicles like a tunnel, and the headlights of other cars are visible for miles down the straightaway. You can tell when you're alone.

Late on a warm night in May 2010, just after one A.M., Michael Pak weaved his black Ford Explorer around the traffic circle surrounding the elegant brick spire marking Jones Beach and shot out the other side on Ocean Parkway. From Manhattan, he was heading east on the straightaway, passing right by the best-kept secret of the barrier islands, Gilgo Beach: a surfing mecca in the sixties, until erosion ruined the waves. Just before he reached the Fire Island turnoff, his GPS guided him off Ocean Parkway and down an unlit, unmarked side access road. The sign on the turnoff read OAK BEACH. In the backseat sat a young woman with chestnut hair streaked blond. Her name was Shannan Gilbert.

They moved slowly now in the dark. The narrow road was overgrown with Virginia creeper and shining sumac and poison ivy. Outside, the air was spongy and salty, and the hum of the car was drowned in the whir of insects. Through some pine trees on the left, they both could see the rushing glow of cars speeding by on the highway. Through the brush on the right were the lights of a house—the only indication that anyone lived at the end of the road.

After half a mile, Michael pulled up to a white gatehouse decorated with a wooden model of a lighthouse and, a few yards beyond the gate, a blue wooden sign that read OAK ISLAND BEACH ASSOCIATION EST. 1896 in the kind of gold cursive lettering you might find on the side of a sloop. Where the gatehouse once had an attendant was now a metal box with a keypad. Michael didn't know the code. Neither did Shannan. Michael dialed a number on his phone and, a moment later, another SUV—this one white—approached the gate from the other side.

The driver's door opened. Out stepped a middle-aged man with a potbelly and a wavy mess of dark hair. The man waved, jogged a few feet up to the gatehouse, and punched in four digits, smiling over at them.

The gate swung up. The Explorer rolled through, and Michael waited for the man to get back in his car before following him down a path he hadn't seen, back toward the house with the light.

Gus Coletti is shaving. He is eighty-six years old, a grandparent, long retired. He and his wife, Laura, are up early in their small wood-frame house in Oak Beach to head upstate to a car show. He hears pounding on his front door. He opens up and sees a girl with chestnut hair. In her hand is a cell phone.

The girl is shrieking. The only word Gus can make out is "help." Those who have heard the 911 recording say it sounds as if Gus never let her inside, though he will later insist that he did. In any case, all it takes to send her running away is Gus saying he's going to call the police.

The girl trips down the porch stairs. Gus heads outside, staying on the porch, watching as the girl beats on a few more doors, then finds a hiding place behind the small boat just outside his house. Both he and the girl see the lights of a truck coming down the Fairway toward them. When the car stops, he can see it more clearly—a black Ford Explorer with a young Asian driver.

The SUV slows to a stop. Gus comes down from the porch to talk with him. As soon as the girl sees that the driver is distracted, she bolts out past the headlights, across the road, and into the darkness.

Gus's driveway is just a few dozen yards from the Oak Beach gatehouse. The way out of the gated community is just yards away, plain to see, but the girl doesn't head in that direction. Instead, she runs down another road, Anchor Way, to knock on another door—that of Wanda Housman—but again, there is no answer. She keeps on running, a hundred more yards, to a street called the Bayou. Barbara Brennan hears the knocking, and she even sees the girl, notices her frantically fiddling with her cell phone. She calls out, but the girl doesn't respond, and Brennan doesn't open the door. Instead, like Gus before her, she calls 911. The girl runs.

When the police finally arrive—about forty-five minutes after Gus Coletti's and Barbara Brennan's 911 calls—the officer talks to the neighbors but doesn't get much of anywhere. It isn't the least bit clear what has happened here or what is to be done. Both the car and the girl are gone.

Seven months later, over three rainy days in December, police uncovered the bodies of four women in the bramble on the side of Ocean Parkway on Gilgo Beach, three miles from where Shannan Gilbert disappeared. Detectives thought at least one of them had to be Shannan. They were wrong. There was Maureen Brainard-Barnes, last seen at Penn Station in Manhattan three years earlier in 2007, and Melissa Barthelemy, last seen in the Bronx in 2009. There was Megan Waterman, last seen leaving a hotel in

Hauppauge, Long Island, just a month after Shannan in 2010—and, a few months later that same year, Amber Lynn Costello, last seen leaving a house in West Babylon, Long Island. Like Shannan, they all were petite and in their twenties. Like Shannan, they all came from out of town to work as escorts. Like Shannan, they all advertised on Craigslist and its competitor, Backpage.

It had seemed enough, at first, for some to say the victims were all just Craigslist hookers, practically interchangeable—lost souls who were dead, in a fashion, long before they actually disappeared. There is a story our culture tells about people like them, a conventional way of thinking about how young girls fall into a life of prostitution. But that story, in the Internet age, is quickly becoming outmoded. Shannan, Maureen, Melissa, Megan, and Amber took part in a modern age of prostitution in which clients are lured with the simple tap of a computer keyboard rather than the exhausting, demeaning ritual of walking the streets. The method is easier, seductively so, almost like an ATM—post an ad, and the phone rings seconds later—but also deceptive about its dangers. They each made the decision to have sex for money for intensely personal reasons: acceptance, adventure, success, love, power. They kept working, often, for reasons even they didn't comprehend. And they traveled in worlds that many of their loved ones could not imagine.

When they disappeared, only their families were left to ask what became of them. Few others seemed to care, not even the police. That all changed once the bodies were found on Gilgo Beach. Then, a few miles from where Shannan had last been seen alive, the police flailed, the body count increased, the public took notice, and the neighbors began pointing fingers. There, in a remote community out of sight of the beaches and marinas scattered along the South Shore barrier islands, the women's stories finally came together, now all part of the same mystery.

BOOK ONE

I.

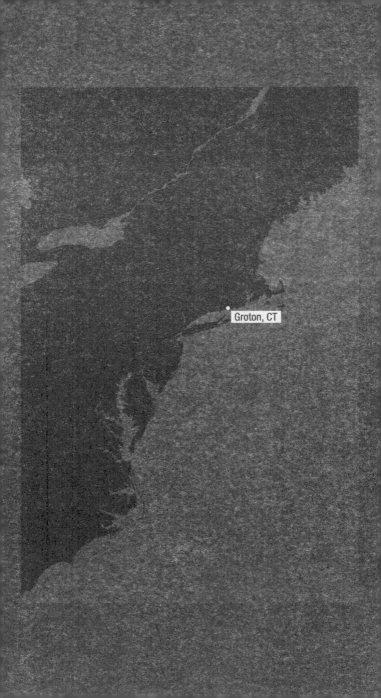
Groton, CT

MAUREEN

Hi! I'm Maureen! I'm calling from Atlantic Security! We have an offer right now—this is not a sales call—we're offering a free month for a demo, a free in-home estimate . . .

Maureen Brainard-Barnes was winsome and girlish, with porcelain skin, dark tousled hair, and green eyes that shifted to blue and gray and back—depending, it seemed, on her mood. Sara Karnes was blond and plump, with a dimpled chin and intense green eyes of her own. As employees at the same telemarketing company, they clicked right away—jabbering with each other over the cubicle walls, getting yelled at by their boss about how they were supposed to be making calls, and snapping back: "We *are* making calls! The computer makes calls for us. When we hear a pickup, we shut up!"

Groton, Connecticut, is an industrial port town of forty-five thousand on the Thames River and the northern reaches of the Long Island Sound, once known for manufacturing submarines and now better known for the nearby Indian casinos. Atlantic Security's office of ten cubicles was housed away from the water, in a storefront in the middle of a shopping strip on what the locals called Hamburger Hill—a spur of Route 95 with Burger King, Wendy's, and McDonald's. Sara had been working there for a few weeks when Maureen arrived, right before Christmas in 2006. After Maureen's first few days making cold calls, chirping from

5

a prepared script about protecting your family and safeguarding your property, Sara decided that she was different from the others. Maureen might not have been happy there, but at least she wasn't actively hostile. She didn't act like she was risking her soul on the outcome of her calls. She smiled.

Sara soon learned that she and Maureen had a lot in common. They were the same age, twenty-four, and had gone to the same high school in Groton, Robert E. Fitch. They didn't remember each other. Sara had gone there only briefly, transferred there after being expelled from a Catholic school for playing a minor prank. Maureen, only a little less wild, left when she was sixteen to have a baby and never went back. She had two children now, each with a different father. The job had come in the nick of time: Unable to afford a place of her own, Maureen had crashed at the home of her little sister for a few months, then moved into a place in Norwich paid for by her son's father. Maureen told Sara she didn't like being so dependent on her ex. She complained about her roommate, who Maureen assumed had been asked to keep an eye on her. In this respect, too, Sara saw something of herself in Maureen. Both women were a little irresponsible and unself-conscious and more than a little annoyed by those who would hold them down.

As precarious as Maureen's situation seemed, it was far better than Sara's. Sara and her boyfriend were staying in a hotel room paid for with the two hundred dollars a week Sara made at Atlantic Security. When they couldn't afford food, they made the rounds at soup kitchens and food banks. Still, Sara had one thing that Maureen didn't: a car. Sara drove a '93 aqua pearl Chrysler LeBaron GTC, a gift from her mother. Carved into the driver's-side door was the word *whore,* a message to Sara from one of her boyfriend's bitter exes. Maureen thought that was funny. So did

Sara. Soon after they met, Maureen, not wanting to bum rides from her ex any more than she had to, asked Sara for a ride home after work in the whore-mobile. Sara said yes. From then on, Maureen had transportation every night.

Both women had been told that Atlantic Security offered seasonal work only; full-timers, of course, would have been entitled to health benefits. Sara was let go shortly after New Year's. A month or so later, Maureen was let go. Maureen and Sara kept in touch. Sara started working at McDonald's, but the money she made didn't cover her room. Sara's boyfriend moved in with an aunt, and Sara moved in with her McDonald's boss and his girlfriend. She was an inch away from homelessness. That was when Maureen stepped in with an offer.

"I need a driver," she said. "This guy wants a massage."

"You're a masseuse?" Sara asked.

Maureen smiled. "Yeah."

Take the Long Hill Road exit off of 95 in Connecticut and curl south toward downtown Groton and you'll find, not far from Atlantic Security, each of the places, still standing, that briefly employed Maureen Brainard-Barnes. There's the Blimpie not far from the T. J. Maxx and the AutoZone and the Stop & Shop. And Cory's gas station, where she worked behind a Chester's chicken counter, making the JoJo's—what the locals call potato wedges. And the Groton Shopping Plaza, with the Groton Cinema 6 where she picked up discarded snacks from the carpet in exchange for free admission and a bag of popcorn.

Before the mid-nineties, when Foxwoods and Mohegan Sun came to this part of Connecticut, Groton was a two-company town. There was the navy submarine base—where, depending on the geopolitical situation of the moment, Tomahawk missiles would roll in and out after dark, for nights on end—and there was Pfizer. Scientists filled the wealthier suburbs like Mystic, home of the upper middle class, or "stuck-up rich people," as Maureen's family put it. They avoided Mystic much of the time, just as they avoided the town on the other side, New London, where the gangs lived. Groton was in the middle—and in Groton, if you weren't navy, you didn't have anything.

Maureen grew up in a three-bedroom apartment in a federally subsidized housing development called Poquonnock Village. Each day her mother, Marie Ducharme, would walk two miles to clean rooms at a motel on the side of another highway off of 95; she would have driven, but the car almost never started. Maureen knew her father, but Bob Senecal, who stayed with them only from time to time, was just like Maureen—mellow though a little immature, not one to take life too seriously, quick with the Beavis and Butthead imitations. Bob worked in lumber, mostly, and a little as a mechanic. He was the one the kids would turn to if they had a question about Middle Earth. Marie, meanwhile, was short-tempered—understandably so, considering the whole family's fate rested on her shoulders. Bob treasured solitude, and he liked to go on long walks that gave him the chance to think. It was on one of those walks that he died a few years later, in 2003, on Maureen's twenty-first birthday. He was walking on a train trestle late at night, tripped, and drowned in the shallow water where he had fallen.

Maureen's mother stopped cleaning motel rooms when she became one of the first employees of Mohegan Sun. A new job as a slot attendant helped her afford the down payment on a car, a tan Ford Taurus, which allowed her to drive to a second job cleaning offices. From that point on, she was almost never home. Maureen and her younger sister and brother, Missy and Will, would take care of one another. Each week their mother bought a new stack of frozen meals, Ellio's pizza, and chicken cutlets that the children would heat up for dinner. They were left on their own to explore the woods behind the apartment complex, to pick berries and walk on railroad tracks when they weren't supposed to, to run from the police when they were spotted. Some evenings, Maureen would sneak Missy and Will into American Billiards to shoot pool and drink, or they would play with an old football in the big field right next to the apartment building. In warmer weather, they would climb on top of the sheds filled with lawn-maintenance equipment and just sit there staring up at the sky.

While her sister and brother spent a lot of time playing sports, Maureen looked inward. She would remember her dreams and scribble them down in a marble-covered notebook, and she used her MySpace page to let others know of moments when she sensed things happening before they happened: the death of her grandmother, a friend scorching herself with a cigarette lighter. She felt somehow anointed, in touch with things that others couldn't see. Her writing helped her arrive at some central questions: *Is heaven a physical place or just a state of mind? Tell me what you think.* She turned to certain books for answers. The book of Revelations fascinated her for a while. Later on, *The Da Vinci Code* became a sacred text for her, along with anything about the Illuminati. From there, she moved on to anything about the supernatural. Maureen believed that the answers to most of life's mysteries were attainable to anyone who sought them out. She told Missy and Will about what she read and learned, lecturing and making connections right before their eyes. Sometimes they believed, too.

Although school was easy for Maureen, she would rather read all day than be there. That changed when she started getting attention from boys. Maureen had never been a makeup-and-accessories girl, but she developed curves and breasts early. She didn't need makeup to be noticed, and by the time she started at Fitch High School, she was reveling in the attention. Where she once was pensive and introverted, now she was impetuous and needy. If she walked into a room, friends said, she made sure the boys knew it, and she ignored the girls. Jealous girls targeted her, and when they started fights, she withdrew again. She stopped going to school for a while, long enough for her mother to make an issue of it, and the two of them fought. Maureen left school for good when she was sixteen, as soon as she learned she was pregnant.

She had been with her boyfriend, Jason Brainard-Barnes, for just six months, but they were in love. He asked her to marry him, and she said yes. A justice of the peace performed a brief ceremony at a courthouse in 1999, after Maureen delivered their daughter, Caitlin. They moved into Jason's grandparents' place in Pawtucket, and then they went south for two years when Jason enlisted in the army. Shortly after they returned, the marriage fell apart, but there were no fights and no lawyers. Without drawing up papers, they decided that Caitlin would live most of the time at her father's place in Mystic, where the schools were better.

Maureen moved in with her sister, Missy, and her children in a low-income housing development in Groton called Branford Manor—once considered a grand experiment in suburban public housing, but by then another anonymous project in a struggling town. The three of them were reunited—Maureen, Missy, and Will, grown up, each with children of their own. As their mother receded from their daily lives, Missy hosted Thanksgiving and Christmas; she was younger than Maureen but had always been more grounded, more practical. At least once a week, Missy cooked large dinners to lure Will and his kids over. Will had been a Fitch High School football star and now was working as a mechanic at Midas. He became the family's protector and pater-familias. If Maureen ever complained to him about a boyfriend, she knew the conversation would end with her brother attacking whoever had caused her to worry.

Maureen was the one everyone loved—the dreamer, the artist, the romantic. One morning she brought two stray kittens in from the rain. When Missy noticed they had fleas and told Maureen to kick them out, her sister went on about about how heartless she was, went shopping for the right shampoo, and came back and bathed them, even though they scratched her to pieces before it was done. The real world still stumped her sometimes. Her most promising job, as a card dealer at Foxwoods, ended in under a year when she started calling in sick too often. Delivering pizza or running the register at the ShopRite failed to capture her imagination. More and more, she left her daughter with Missy while she went out. Sometimes Missy would lose patience, and the little sister would lecture the big one, and Will, the peacemaker, would try to calm Missy down. These confrontations made Maureen feel guilty, and she'd spend whatever she earned to make amends—presents for Caitlin, a lobster bake, or pizzas for Missy and her kids.

Still, when Missy thinks of their time together now, all she can remember is a family idyll: Maureen reading Shel Silverstein aloud to Caitlin and, later on, Missy's children; Maureen playing dress-up with Missy's daughter and the cat; the whole crew heading out together to get grinders and sit in the park; Maureen filling her stacks of marble composition books with poetry and rap lyrics. The apartments were almost like townhouses, each with a yard out back. All weekend long in good weather, the grills would be going, the neighbors would come out, and the children ate and played. Maureen would bring Caitlin there, too, when she could;

Maureen never seemed more at ease than when she was barefoot and in a sundress, running free in the backyard, smiling broadly.

It took a while for the situation to become strained. By 2003, Maureen was twenty-one with a four-year-old daughter, no steady job, and no place of her own to live. Another person might have resigned herself to the limitations that bound her life—no diploma, no job good enough to support her daughter—and never even tried. But Maureen wouldn't make the same choices that Missy did. For Maureen, the possibilities lay ahead, the breaks this way and that of a life she had barely begun. She remained flexible and curious. Who knew what luck would find her? Maybe she'd be a rapper, maybe a model. The plan always changed. If nothing else, Maureen always had a plan.

The following year, Maureen stopped by her friend Jay DuBrule's place, almost giddy with excitement. She'd brought Caitlin, then five, and directed her into another room to play with Jay's daughter, who was a year older. "Oh, look!" Maureen said before the kids ran into the other room. "I had the photo shoot!"

Jay was living down the hall from Missy at Branford Manor when he first met Maureen. He worked for a time doing remote broadcasting setups for a local radio station. Maureen interned for him once, but when they asked her to wear an elephant suit, she wasn't feeling it, and she quit before the shift ended. Since then, Jay had been laid off from that job and was working two others—delivering paint for Sherwin-Williams and delivering pizza. They had grown close. She could talk to Jay about anything. They slept together now and then, though neither of them talked about what that might mean. Better to be friends forever instead of ex-boyfriend and ex-girlfriend someday.

Maureen saw plenty of men, but recently, she had left Missy's and moved in with the one she was most serious about. Steve ran a pawnshop in Norwich. Tall with a mustache and beard, Steve was white but dressed and talked ghetto. He never wanted to be around any of Maureen's friends or family, not even Missy and Will. Their relationship seemed strained almost from the start. One friend remembers Steve talking about Maureen as if she were a child who couldn't be relied on to do anything. Maureen would say that was his way of saying he wanted her to stay home. Jay's place had become another refuge for Maureen, the way Missy's place had been. She and Jay wouldn't always hook up. Sometimes she'd come there to share some weed or go online. Jay always had a few different computers lying around. Being at Jay's place to tinker with her MySpace page was always better than using the computer at the public library. Other times they would hang out, watch their daughters play in the yard, watch a video, or write a new rap together.

Maureen talked more and more about writing for a rapper one day, or better still, becoming one herself—like Lil' Kim, she joked, only hotter. Her approach was different—less playful and more grave, like Three 6 Mafia. Where Lil' Kim wrote with coy, self-aware swagger about money and sex, Maureen wrote indignantly about coming up in hard times.

> *There's too many people walking around with plastic faces*
> *Too many children hanging in the wrong places*
> *Too many dirty cops controlling ghetto blocks*
> *Too many fistfights ending in shots*
> *Too many girls taking to wrong paths*
> *It's not too late to do the math*

Jay thought she was nothing short of a poet. Missy thought so, too. But Maureen was twenty-two, and her music wasn't getting the attention she'd hoped it would. The photos were her solution—a stepping-stone. She had been using MySpace to market her music and network with other rappers when she noticed ads for modeling there. Those ads led her to a site called Model Mayhem.com, which invited her to send in a portfolio that bookers could reference. She'd found a friend to take some photos for free, as long as he got to keep the negatives. The pictures she showed Jay that night weren't provocative—just Maureen smiling from head to toe, wearing a few different dresses and one that would be considered lingerie, a red nightgown. Jay thought she looked adorable.

She was open to anything: catalogs, magazines, music videos. When she enrolled on the site, she started getting dozens of e-mails from places purporting to be modeling agencies that, after a few clicks, turned out to mean nude modeling and sometimes escorting. She wasn't exactly surprised. What surprised her was the money. Clicking some of the links, Maureen saw how escorting was made to seem like webcam stripping, only in person, with no sex involved. From there, it was easy to see how much money she could make if she did have sex. As far as she could tell, the only major catch was having to sign on with an escort service. Maureen had no interest in sharing her money or being an employee—trading, essentially, one dependency for another.

But there was another way to make the same amount of money completely on her own. On Craigslist, Maureen saw women posting ads right in Groton, earning a living without leaving their homes, and not having to share what they made with anyone—not a pimp, not a service, not a boyfriend.

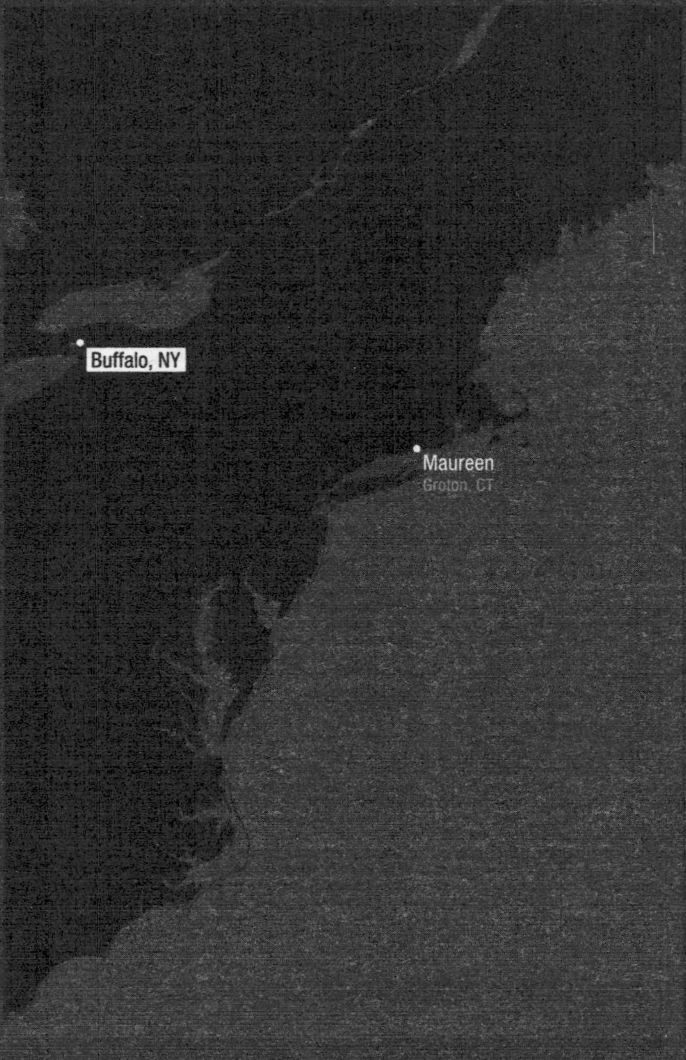
Buffalo, NY
Maureen
Groton, CT

MELISSA

The black walk-ins at the Continental Beauty School were pay-ing about an eighth of the normal price to get their hair styled. So they couldn't say a word, not one of them, when they saw that the girl who was about to work on their weaves and extensions was white.

As the customers mouthed silent prayers, Melissa Barthelemy went to work—smiling, confident, almost unnaturally relaxed for a stylist-in-training entrusted with kinks that she had never known herself. She'd comb through the hair first, making a neat part, and grab a very small section as close to the hairline as pos-sible, pulling tight without sending the woman into hysterics. Using her hand as a pitchfork, she'd divide that tiny section of hair into three puffy strands that she held between her middle and index fingers. Next came the twist, from left to right, and finally the tuck. The twist was nothing without the tuck—grabbing the free hair left underneath and moving it into the braid. The under-neath catch, followed by another twist, was what was so hard to remember each time, and even harder to get right without having to start all over. *Braid, tuck, and twist, braid, tuck, and twist, braid, tuck, and twist.* Melissa never slipped.

The cornrow designs weren't just a snap for Melissa; they were a pleasure. She had spent years practicing, not only on her friends but on her half sister. Amanda was nine years younger than Melissa; her father, unlike Melissa's, was black. On countless afternoons, Amanda would squeal as Melissa tugged and pulled and braided and twisted and experimented. Yet Amanda probably would have preferred white-people hair. She shopped at American Eagle and Abercrombie. Melissa, meanwhile, wore tight braids herself for a time, listened to nothing but hip-hop, and dated black guys almost exclusively. Sometimes their mother, Lynn, thought her daughters had been born in the wrong bodies. Amanda, in her heart of hearts, wanted to be white. And Melissa, for as long as anyone could remember, wished she had been born black.

Lynn Barthelemy had known before she bought a pregnancy test. She never missed her period. She told Mark the results. Mark, proud of himself, proposed marriage. That only upset her more— she didn't already have enough to worry about?

It was September 1984. Lynn was sixteen, beginning her sophomore year at Seneca Vocational High School in Buffalo. Mark was two years older, a senior on the track team. He was from a Polish family in Kaisertown, the German-Polish section of South Buffalo. She was from the North Side, a neighborhood called Kensington-Bailey, a leafy section of town with large houses and wide, quiet streets. They had been together for a year. Mark used to join Lynn's family on picnics to Emery Park and the beach at Port Colborne, just across the border in Canada. The pregnancy posed a problem.

She thought about marrying Mark and what that might be like, and she drew a blank. Mark was so meek. He let his family run his life, and whatever free agency remained, he ceded to Lynn. She couldn't see spending the rest of her life that way. She thought about abortion, but that scared her. Mark was against it, too. They both came from Catholic families. Lynn had trouble processing the idea of giving a baby away. Whenever she thought about it, she'd start to cry.

For two months, she kept the pregnancy a secret. Finally, in October, she told her mother, Linda. The news was a shock; usually, it was Lynn's little sister who misbehaved, while Lynn was the one who had always performed well in school and followed the rules. Lynn was too afraid to tell her father, Elmer, so her mother did it for her. When he heard, he punched a hole in the bathroom door. They didn't speak for months. Her mother told Lynn not to worry, he'd get over it. Meanwhile, Lynn had a decision to make.

Lynn's grandmother offered her wedding rings for a ceremony, if that was what Lynn wanted. At the same time, she tried to be candid. "Don't marry him just because you're pregnant," she said. "You make sure you love him." When Lynn decided to say yes, her grandmother didn't let up. "Why don't you live together for a few months?" she suggested. Mark moved in with Lynn and her parents and sure enough, Lynn learned how he really was. He didn't dote; he hovered. If she got up off the couch to go to the bathroom, Mark would say, "Where are you going?" If she took a phone call, he wanted to know who was calling. She was about seven months pregnant when she told him the wedding was off.

Her parents feared for her. "You're going to have to get a job," Lynn's mother said. "And you're going to have to pay for day care." Lynn agreed to do both.

Lynn was offered a spot at a different school, one for teenage mothers. She said no. She wanted to stay at her school and graduate like everyone else. Her swollen belly drew catcalls from the boys as she walked the halls. She got into fights. When the instructor in her church's confirmation class started talking about abortion and locking eyes with her, Lynn walked out and told her mother the bitch was lucky she didn't slap her in the face. That spring, when she went into labor at a nearby Catholic hospital and the nun in the room tried to quiet her through her pain, Lynn, as furious as she was terrified, cursed her out: "Shut up! You probably haven't even *had* sex!"

Lynn's baby entered the world on April 14, 1985, after eighteen hours of labor, weighing seven pounds, nine ounces, with a stubborn head that needed coaxing out with forceps. A few weeks earlier, Grandma Mary had died during an epileptic seizure. Lynn named the baby Melissa Mary Barthelemy.

Lynn went back to school six weeks after Melissa was born. After the baby's three-month checkup, Lynn got a job washing dishes after school at the Manhattan Manor nursing home, a twenty-minute walk from her parents' house. Lynn didn't know it then, but she would keep that job for the next twenty-five years.

Linda and Elmer agreed to help with child care. Melissa spent most of her childhood in their house, a three-bedroom clapboard colonial on Stockbridge Avenue in the neighborhood of Kensington-Bailey. The family had moved there in 1978, when Lynn was in third grade. Elmer had paid nineteen thousand dollars for the place, putting down 10 percent, saving the money from his four-hundred-a-week salary working nights in industrial maintenance—first at Freezer Queen, a meatpacking company on the waterfront, and later at Wonder Bread. Both were union jobs; that was when Buffalo still had enough blue-collar work to go around. The neighborhood was warm and welcoming back then. Elmer, a reformed drag racer who served as an air force mechanic during the Vietnam War, tore the house apart room by room and restored it, adding a fourth bedroom up top. Black and white mingled well in the neighborhood; Buffalo had one of the least painful forced school integrations of any big city. Only in looking back did they notice how the conversations with their white neighbors had changed from "Isn't this a nice place" to "Let's get out before our house isn't worth anything." By the time Melissa was growing up on Stockbridge Avenue, the ice-cream and candy shop on the corner was gone, as was the big Rite Aid, victims of Buffalo's great rust-belt decline. A pizzeria was destroyed in a fire, and the movie palace also burned down. The crime rate was rising, people were leaving, and the new black neighbors frightened some of the older whites. Elmer thought the new people were decent, but their kids were trouble. He guessed it was jobs: They didn't have any. Both Freezer Queen and Wonder Bread had left town, around the same time that Buffalo lost Bethlehem Steel and Westinghouse and the auto plant that had employed their neighbor. Elmer found non-union work mowing lawns at an assisted-living community. In the end, it wasn't just a question of black or white. The whole middle class seemed to be fleeing Kensington-Bailey, the same way Elmer's parents had fled the East Side a generation earlier.

Lynn was too busy working to pay much attention to where Melissa went or who her close friends were. With no one person to answer to, Melissa was left to police herself—or not, if she didn't feel like it. The other kids growing up in Kensington-Bailey were the kids of laid-off union workers—most not interested in finishing school the way Lynn had, and some in gangs. As a little girl, Melissa was adorable, and smart in school with lots of friends, just like Lynn had been. Despite her pixie looks, she was formidable—quick to shout down someone twice her size for looking at her the wrong way. That reminded everyone of Lynn, too. Lynn was kind of glad her daughter was feisty, as she'd been. Her only rule for Melissa was never to hit first.

Lynn never thought she would live in Kensington-Bailey forever. Melissa was just three when Lynn got an apartment with a boyfriend about ten miles away in South Buffalo. About a year later, Lynn came home early from work, and he was in bed with another woman. She and Melissa moved back to Elmer and Linda's house. A few years later, Lynn met Andre Funderburg, and they had Amanda, Melissa's little sister. Andre worked lots of different jobs, from nursing to telemarketing. Though he was black, Elmer and Linda never raised that issue with Lynn. Amanda was born when Melissa was nine. Andre got along well with Melissa, and for a time, the four of them were a family, living in the north end of town. When Andre cheated on Lynn, too, she came to live with Elmer and Linda again, this time with the baby.

By her early teens, Melissa had boyfriends, although years of long talks about how young Lynn was when she got pregnant seemed to successfully dispel any of Melissa's romantic notions about having a child. But as Melissa got older, the tough girl Lynn had seen so much of herself in was doing things Lynn had never done—leaving at night and staying out late with friends, then skipping school the next day. Lynn decided something needed to change. She tried sending Melissa to a Friends school for a time, and a teacher told her, "You don't belong here." Only when Lynn met one of her daughter's boyfriends did she start to panic. Jordan was tall and rail-thin, with pitch-black skin. That wasn't an issue—Amanda was black, Andre was black, most of the neighborhood was black now—but Lynn worried anyway. "He was like a hoodlum," Lynn said. "He was into dealing drugs, things I didn't want her to be around. She didn't agree. She was like, 'Aw, Mom, he's my friend.'" Lynn was running out of ideas, and now she felt she was running out of time. She had worked so hard to graduate from high school, even with a baby at home; her daughter didn't seem to care about going to school at all.

Melissa was about sixteen when Lynn thought of a Hail Mary maneuver. She called Melissa's father, Mark. He had recently moved to Dallas, where he and his wife had relocated for his wife's job. Mark agreed to take his daughter in. The reunion failed almost from the start. Melissa called Lynn every chance she could, complaining: "There are cockroaches as big as cows!" She and her stepmother fought. Lynn secretly liked hearing that they hadn't hit it off, though she knew she might not be hearing the whole story. Maybe Mark's wife tried to be more like a mother to her, and Melissa fought back. Maybe Mark didn't know how to deal with Melissa. Plenty of people didn't. She stayed two and a half years in Texas until she acted out in a way that couldn't be ignored. Melissa stole her father's work van and drove it around without a license. She was so tiny—four feet, eleven inches and ninety-five pounds—that the police pulled her over, thinking there was no way she could be old enough to drive. Melissa was sentenced to community service. Her dad got a fine and, soon after, presented his daughter with a plane ticket home for Christmas. The trip was supposed to be just a visit. Mark hadn't told Melissa that she wasn't welcome back, leaving that part for Lynn. On the phone, Melissa told her father that his wife must be keeping his balls in her purse.

Melissa was relieved to be back until she saw how much had changed while she'd been away. With two thousand dollars left on the mortgage, Elmer and Linda had sold the house in Kensington-Bailey to a single mother, African-American, who installed bars on all the doors and windows the second she moved in. Melissa's grandparents bought a new place in a suburb of Buffalo called Alden—basically farmland, a world away from Kensington-Bailey. Lynn and Amanda had moved there with them. For Melissa, Alden was almost Dallas all over again. "It's so *boring* here!" she'd moan. Her new school didn't change her mind. Alden was more white than the schools she'd attended in Buffalo.

She was a senior, with one more year to go, when she announced she was moving out. There was a fight, but Lynn had very little leverage. Melissa was almost eighteen, and Lynn had Amanda to think about as well. Little by little, Lynn started to ease up. Lynn's sister, Melissa's aunt Dawn, lived in the same part of South Buffalo where Melissa wanted to move. They were close in age and becoming confidantes. Maybe Melissa could get what she wanted and the family could keep her close. Not that she ever stopped worrying. She was convinced Melissa would never finish school. "You're not going to get a job without a degree," Lynn said. What went unsaid was what kind of future Melissa could expect in Buffalo even if she did graduate.

Melissa surprised Lynn. She found a roommate and got a job working at a pizzeria to make her half of the rent. She re-enrolled at South Park High, the school she most likely would have attended if her family had stayed in Kensington-Bailey. After a few months of not speaking, she and Lynn started going out to dinner. Melissa seemed upbeat to Lynn, trying to get her life together. She kept in contact with Jordan, but not all the time. She seemed to be outgrowing him, or so Lynn thought. She kept little notebooks, jotting down how much it would cost to have her own apartment, how much she would have to make, how much she could save.

She graduated with A's. Lynn came to the ceremony with Elmer, Linda, and Amanda. Lynn felt like a weight had lifted—her daughter was back on track; she would be the person Lynn knew she could be. Not long after graduating, Melissa decided she wanted to go to beauty school. She grabbed a financial aid form from Continental and filled it out. She needed Lynn to co-sign the eight-thousand-dollar loan. They went to the bank together; half the debt was in Lynn's name and half was in Melissa's. Melissa went to school every day. If she missed a class during the week, she made it up on Saturday. She thought maybe she could own her own business someday—just like Lynn's new boyfriend, Jeff Martina, who was opening a diner on Bailey Avenue, not far from the beauty school.

Melissa quit the pizzeria and worked a few shifts for Jeff after classes. Since she still didn't have her driver's license, Lynn would pick her up at the apartment she was sharing on the West Side and drive her to classes, and Jeff would drive her home at the end of her shift at the diner. Practically every day, her hairstyle changed. She even dyed it red for a time. Melissa still kept mostly to herself; Lynn never met her roommate. But Melissa and Lynn had spent enough time away that they were ready to feel comfortable with each other again. Each day in the car, Lynn would listen to Melissa make plans from the passenger seat, doodling in her notebooks, figuring out how much it would cost to open her own hair salon. She seemed scared straight—maybe, Lynn thought, after seeing how little she made at the diner and pizza place. On one of those drives, Melissa talked about watching Lynn work so hard as a single mom and how that had affected her. She said she didn't plan on getting married or having kids until she was thirty-five. Lynn had seen enough of the inside of a nursing home, Melissa said. She didn't want her mother to end up in one herself. "I want to take care of you and give you things you never had," Melissa told her. "I want to walk into a store and not worry about a price tag. If I like it, I want to buy it."

Melissa was the only white face at the Continental graduation ceremony. She was beaming. But when the time came for her to cash in on all her work, the best job she could find was at Supercuts. At the location in Williamsville, a northeast suburb of Buffalo, she had to sit at a mall for two hours every night after closing just to catch a bus home. After a year, she moved to a Supercuts in a yuppie neighborhood near the zoo. Her customers at both locations were mostly white. Melissa tried to stay diverted with dye jobs and French braids. She was losing patience.

She hooked up with Jordan again and got mad at Jeff and Lynn when they disapproved. "We hope you're not going out with that monkey!" Jeff would shout as Melissa was on her way out the door. The race thing was a peculiar subject for all of them. Everyone in the family would toss epithets around with perverse familiarity. Even Andre, Amanda's father, in touch from time to time with both Amanda and Melissa, went out of his way to warn her: "You're just this little pretty white girl, and they want to use you."

Jeff would say it a little more crassly: "You're their trophy."

Melissa would only smile and say, "They're nice to me."

In 2006, Melissa and Jordan took a trip to New York together. "Jordan's uncle owns a recording studio," Melissa told Lynn and Jeff. They came back a few days later, then turned around and went to New York a few weeks after that. Upon her return, she announced that she and Jordan were going to move there.

"I met this guy," Melissa said. His name was Johnny Terry. He had offered her a job, she said, cutting hair.

Lynn tried to talk her out of it, but she'd been in this place with Melissa before and had less influence on her now. Part of Lynn felt defeated, as if everything she'd done to stop this from happening had been in vain. She felt like she had seen this moment coming all along. So her protests were perfunctory, thin. "Are you sure? It's not as easy as you think. The rent is high. It's so far away."

The conversation was over before it started. "I can handle it," Melissa said. "The guy has a place set up for me."

Melissa
Buffalo, NY

Ellenville, NY

Maureen
Groton, CT

SHANNAN

Someday I'll step on their freckles
Some night I'll straighten their curls . . .

When she was in eighth grade, Shannan Gilbert took the stage in her middle school's production of *Annie*. She had hoped to play the little orphan herself—for the past six years, she had more or less been living the part, shuttling through several foster homes—and she was crestfallen when she was told she was too tall. Still, the teachers could tell that Shannan had a beautiful voice—booming and R&B-ready—not to mention a lush, round face with wide doe eyes. So they offered her the part of Miss Hannigan, the boozing, scheming head of the orphanage.

It took a little while for Shannan to see that this was the flashier role—the only truly funny grown-up character, the one part with any hint of sexuality, ideal for a teenage ham. Nerves carried Shannan through the rehearsals, but on opening night, she killed. Vamping her way through Miss Hannigan's solo number, "Little Girls," Shannan ranted, merrily and nastily, about how Annie and the other orphans were all that stood between her and the life of her dreams.

Little cheeks, little teeth
Everything around me is . . . little
If I wring little necks
Surely I will get an acquittal . . .

Shannan had never been in front of so many people, and the applause had a profound effect on her. One person in the audience mattered more than everyone else—a woman whose undivided attention Shannan had been fighting to capture almost her entire life. Onstage that night, as Shannan browbeat each of the little orphans into offering up fealty—one by one, saying, "I love you, Miss Hannigan!"—anyone who knew her mother, Mari, wouldn't have found it hard to guess whom Shannan was channeling. From then on, performing would be all that she would want to do.

From on high, the village of Ellenville, New York, seems preserved in time, the steeple of a church poking up above the trees, with glimpses of what once must have been a cozy main street nestled in the foothills of the Shawangunk Ridge in the Catskills. When Mari Gilbert and her family arrived there in 1991, the village was emptying into a ghost town, down to a ShopRite, a few banks, and some dollar stores. A nearby state prison was turning Ellenville into a village of transients: Relatives of inmates would come to town, rent an apartment for a few years, then turn around and leave. Many of Shannan's old friends from Ellenville say that half of their classmates are dead, in jail, or on drugs.

Mari had the same bright eyes as her oldest daughter, Shannan, only with long, wild blond hair and a raspy, lived-in voice. She'd grown up in Lancaster, Pennsylvania, the youngest of five children. Mari's father was a brickmaker who drank hard on the weekends. Her mother was a restless woman of faith, changing churches constantly. If religion was Mari's mother's response to a chaotic world, Mari came up with one all her own. In her view, life was combat, and no savior would change the fact that the next fight was looming just around the corner. She never saw a point in pretending that wasn't the case. "I can't be plastic," Mari often said, and she warned her daughters to be real, too, or deal with the consequences. "If you run your mouth about something, be ready," she'd tell them with a steady glare. "You're gonna have to fight the person, because they're either going to be mad you told the truth or mad you lied. So watch what you say. If you can't defend yourself, either you're gonna get your butt kicked, or you better get ready to kick somebody's butt."

About two years before coming to Ellenville, Mari left her husband and moved away from her hometown to upstate New York, bringing their three daughters with her. Shannan was five, Sherre four, and Sarra three. When they were older, Mari told the girls that she'd left him because he was using heroin. Though none would see their father again, all three girls had inherited his cara-mel complexion. After she left, Mari and the girls stayed briefly with Mari's mother, who had left her husband and moved to Rockland County, before heading off on their own. Mari worked as a manager at Sears and Dunkin' Donuts and an assistant teacher at an after-school program, then later on at an Ames gardening-supply warehouse and, for many years, a Walmart in Middletown. She was determined to raise her daughters alone—without her family, without the government, and without friends. "I didn't need anybody else coming into the house telling me this, saying this, giving me advice. I had enough to deal with. I had work, I had the kids, I had my life, I had my troubles."

Her troubles started with a man named David, who fathered Mari's fourth daughter, Stevie. Shannan's sister Sherre, about five years old at the time, remembered huge fights after Stevie was born; she and Shannan cowered under the kitchen table as plates of spaghetti crashed against the wall. When Mari's mother found out what was happening, she called the police. David went to jail, and all four of Mari's girls were placed in foster care. Mari was furious at her mother for involving the state. Mari didn't get her girls back for close to two years. Soon after they were reunited, Mari settled them all in Ellenville, hoping for a new start.

Mari called Ellenville "a very small town where there's more rumors than people who live there." The rumor mill about Mari wasn't very complimentary. People spoke of her as a gruff, checked-out mother who never seemed that attentive to her children. "Shannan and I, we kind of ran the streets together," said an old friend of Shannan's, Erica Hill. "It didn't seem to matter to Mari what happened to Shannan. When Shannan would run away, I never saw anyone say, 'Hey, has anybody seen Shannan?' And her mother never came looking for her."

She might not have known, because Shannan wasn't always living at home. Shortly after they arrived in Ellenville, Shannan, then about seven, entered the foster-care system again. For six years, until the year she appeared in *Annie,* she lived nearby in a series of foster homes, by all accounts decent places run by well-intentioned, caring women. Every day at school, Shannan walked the same halls as her sisters, ate the same food, and hung out with a lot of the same people—she just didn't sleep under the same roof. Not a lot of people knew about the arrangement, though those friends who did said that Shannan was devastated by it. More than once, she ran away *to* home, back to Mari and Sherre and Sarra and Stevie. She rarely stayed long. To outsiders, Mari never explained why Shannan couldn't live at home. Only years later, after the world learned Shannan's name, would Mari say that the problem had been Shannan herself—that she was not only independent-minded and willful but unstable—"a lot of mood swings, a lot of overeating, a lot of binge-and-purge." When she was twelve, Shannan would be diagnosed as bipolar, though she never took her medicine, complaining about its side effects.

As Mari would tell it, foster care was the best option for a daughter she had trouble controlling. She took pains to explain that Shannan went back and forth on whether she wanted to be at home, sometimes asking to live apart. A blowup with Mari would cause her to call the state for placement in another foster home. Just as quickly, Shannan would change her mind. "She'd say, 'I want to come home.' I'd say, 'Well, call your case worker and say you changed your mind and want to come home.' The grass is always greener on the other side."

The story was different when others told it. While Shannan was deliberately vague, telling friends that her mother cared more about her boyfriends than she did about her children, Sherre was more specific, saying that Shannan's exile from the family had to do with a certain boyfriend who moved in when Shannan was seven. According to Sherre, Shannan and the boyfriend didn't get along, and Shannan was sent away because of him. The irony was that living elsewhere spared Shannan further exposure to the boyfriend, who Sherre said went on not just to clash with Shannan's sisters but to physically abuse them. Sherre said that Mari was oblivious to the abuse and learned of it only when the girls spoke up years later. Mari supported the girls when they accused him, and the boyfriend went to jail, dying a few years after that. Mari, for her part, has refused to discuss him. "I told my kids what happens in the house stays in the house," Mari said. "That's, like, a basic given rule."

It was possible that both accounts were true. Maybe Shannan and the boyfriend did clash, and maybe Mari found herself ill equipped to parent a daughter like Shannan. But if Mari described Shannan as a smart but troubled girl, plagued by emotional problems, her friends never knew that girl. Their Shannan was popular, bright, energetic, talented, and beautiful. To those who were closest to her during her teenage years, Shannan's biggest problem—maybe her only problem—was that, from a young age, she felt locked out of her own family.

The year Shannan appeared in *Annie*—her eighth-grade year—was supposed to be her big homecoming. Mari and the state had agreed that she could come home, and she lasted longer than she had before. It would turn out to be her only year as a teenager when she would live full-time with her mother and sisters. Sherre said the problems began when Shannan, still oblivious to the abuse, tried to play peacemaker between Mari's boyfriend and the other girls, and both the boyfriend and her sisters pushed her away. Shannan was crushed. She thought that too much time had passed with her out of the house; that her sisters didn't seem like sisters anymore. What she couldn't have understood was how much her sisters envied her: At least Shannan had a way out, a way not to live there. The closest Sherre came to talking about the abuse was to say that Shannan was the lucky one—that she was better off living anywhere but in that house.

Shannan wouldn't accept that. "Yeah, but *you* don't understand," she said. "I *want* to be here. This is where I *want* to be."

After eighth grade, Shannan knew she couldn't stay any longer. The state found a placement for her with a foster parent in New Paltz, a more affluent town about a half hour from Ellenville that had much better schools. Jennifer Pottinger was relatively young for a foster mother, and Shannan liked her. When Shannan talked about wanting to be on her own one day, Jennifer encouraged her to dive into classes with enough dedication to graduate a year early. Shannan was thriving, or seemed to be.

It was Mari's turn to feel rejected. As a mother, she might have been distant, but she could also be possessive and easily threatened. As Shannan moved swiftly toward graduation, Mari made noises about how her daughter was being exploited, made to work for Jennifer at the day-care center she ran. Mari would never get over how drawn Shannan was to the things at Jennifer's house—name brands like Tommy Hilfiger—that obviously hadn't come from Walmart. "She was born wanting to be beautiful, wanting to have the latest, wanting to have everything that she felt that my income, at the time, I could not give her," Mari said. "Something was in her that she wanted nice things in life."

Through performing, Shannan found a way to deal with whatever dissatisfactions and sadness she buried within. During high school, she developed a soulful voice that gave some of her friends chills and made others cry. They could feel every note, every riff, every ripple. Her poetry and essays seemed to tap into a deep well of pain, too—sharp and emotional, accessing the same damaged part: *I take on armor every time I walk out the door / But that's just what life's all about, right? / I immerse myself in the moment, and I will enjoy it.*

Even as she did well in school, curfews had no hold on Shannan, and most evenings she'd find her way back to Ellenville. While her sisters welcomed her, the wild card on those nights was Mari. In difficult moments, Shannan's mother would seize power any way she could: sometimes by leaving the room, sometimes by temporarily writing people out of her life. Once, after Shannan got into a fight during a party at her friend Anthony's house, Mari ordered Shannan never to speak with Anthony again. It was startling how, almost randomly, Mari would decide to step back into Shannan's world and issue orders—as a way of reminding everyone she was still the mother, the most important person in

Shannan's life. Their confrontations invariably ended with Shannan in tears. However the argument started, Shannan brought the subject back to the same place. "You don't want me," she'd say, crying. "You don't raise me, but you raise my sisters." When she heard that, Mari would turn cold. She wouldn't argue. She would just turn and leave.

After graduation, Shannan spiraled away from Ellenville for longer and longer stretches. She lived for a time with her grandmother and enrolled in nursing classes. She worked at a hotel, an Applebee's, and a senior center, as a secretary at a school. Within a year, she dropped out of college and quit the secretarial job, saying it bored her. She left her grandmother's house after being reprimanded for staying out too late. She had a boyfriend whom the family met only once or twice before she said she had left him and was planning to move to New York City.

She was too old to run home anymore. She had something more ambitious in mind, a new role. She would audition for singing jobs, do whatever she could to make money. She would build a life that her sisters and her mother could only dream about. She would become an entrepreneur, a self-made woman. She would have the best of everything. She would become their benefactor. And they would be grateful to her. And they would love her.

Portland, ME

Melissa
Buffalo, NY

Shannan
Ellenville, NY

Maureen
Groton, CT

MEGAN

Happy Wheels is tucked away in a bland stucco building off an access road in an industrial section of Portland, Maine. The roller rink, with a wood interior barely updated from the early eighties, is built for wear and tear. The pop music blares. For generations, Happy Wheels has been a reliable Saturday and Sunday destination for working families from Portland, including the struggling section of Congress Street downtown, where Megan Waterman lived. The prices have barely changed in twenty years. Even now, admission on a regular night is just $5.50, and skate rentals cost two dollars.

Far and away the most popular event at Happy Wheels—more popular than the roller derby nights—is the monthly twelve-dollar All-Night Skate. Parents all over town, particularly struggling families on a budget, know of Happy Wheels as a safe space where they can take a much-needed night off, dropping kids off at eight P.M. and not coming back until six A.M. Even as young as ten or twelve, Megan was determined never to miss an All-Night Skate. Moon-faced and bubbly and blond, she cut loose on the floor and sang with unique abandon. She never seemed to care what a soul thought of her, and a lot of the other children envied her for that. Few people there knew much about her mother, Lorraine, who had lost custody of Megan when she was a baby. All they knew was that Megan was being brought up by her grandmother.

Part of Happy Wheels's appeal—for parents, at least—is its

strict no-fight policy. If you're caught misbehaving twice, you get a Happy Wheels rap sheet: Your name ends up on a pink piece of paper in a loose-leaf binder in the front office, and you're sent home for the night. Get in a fight, and you're out for longer: a thirty-day suspension for the first offense, whether you started the fight or not. The second offense is six months. The third is a year. The fourth is permanent. Most of the kids who roll through Happy Wheels never learn about the binder, and the staff never learns their names. But Megan, they knew. Her young life was detailed practically week by week in the binder. The trouble tended to flare out of nowhere, usually over some teenage drama: "Your hair's purple, I don't like it" or "I don't like the way you look at my boyfriend."

Still, the staff had a soft spot for Megan. They marveled at the way she could pivot from rage to charm in an instant, working her deep brown eyes to make anyone forgive whatever she'd done. And they always thought fondly of her nana, Muriel, who stood out from all the other parents in how passionately she'd defend Megan on charges of misbehavior—appealing any ejection while standing right beside her, acting like her chief counsel. The people behind the counter never thought the worse of them for trying to sidestep the rules. *What kid isn't wild sometimes?* they'd think as Megan walked out the door, fuming. Good for her nana, everyone thought, for going the extra mile for her granddaughter.

Muriel Benner brought her six children up more or less on her own in downtown Portland, first on the bustling main drag of Congress Street and then in a townhouse-style condo just off Congress at 16 Avon Place. This was low-income housing, built on an intimate scale—a safe street with no through traffic and just twenty or so families who all knew and looked after one another.

Muriel was tan and impish, shaped like a dumpling, and managed to date and have as much fun as she could. The children remember a parade of men through the house, and lots of leftover drinks for them to sip from the coffee table the next day. Lorraine's favorite had been Allen's coffee-flavored brandy.

Muriel was the sort of mother who tended to separate her kids into little files in her head: a tempting enough thing to do if, like Muriel, you had so many. Kathy, Liz, Ella, and Eli—they were good. Lorraine and Ricky, they were trouble. Early on, she had branded Lorraine—Muriel's first child with her second husband, Ricky Waterman—as something more than bad. She had been the family dissident, never satisfied, forever outraged.

Then Lorraine got pregnant, and Muriel held her breath. The problem wasn't the baby. Lorraine was twenty, and she wasn't the first of Muriel's children to have children of their own. The problem was Lorraine.

A year earlier, Lorraine had moved out of her mother's house and found a room at the YWCA in downtown Portland. She had been working for a small company that cleaned the airport and offices, and she spent her off hours trying to get her GED. She moved out because her mother let her hold on to only fifty dollars a week out of her paychecks. *Why am I working just to give her all the money?* she thought. So she left. Lorraine had been on her own for a month when she met Greg Gove. He was the first boy to come up and talk to her since she'd left home. He was tall and skinny. He was only four days older than she was, and like her, he hadn't finished high school. He was from Wilmington, Maine. His aunt had kicked him out because he didn't want to work, and now he was doing odd jobs.

They went out to eat at a Bonanza steak house by the Maine Mall, the mammoth shopping center in South Portland. They had nothing in common, but Lorraine had never had a boyfriend; within a month, they were living together. They rented a room together on Sherman Street in a rough section of Portland. It was full of cockroaches, so they left. Then they stayed at the Days Inn in Westbrook, renting a room by the week.

Lorraine drank a lot after meeting Greg. Coffee brandy was still her favorite. In no time, the relationship darkened. Lorraine's memories of her time with Greg were Gothic, filled with abuse, though Greg, now married with a large family and living several hours from Portland in northern Maine, recalled that things turned violent on both sides. Within months, though, she was pregnant. Lorraine left Greg but returned in time to have their first baby—a boy, also named Greg. They broke up again when she was eight months pregnant with their second child, Megan. As the pregnancy advanced, she quit her most recent job, at Burger King, and went on welfare. Lorraine was sure she was done with Greg for good this time. To her surprise, he turned up again, this time with a new girlfriend named Karen. Greg and Karen offered to help Lorraine with both babies if they could all crash in the apartment that Lorraine was paying for with her welfare check.

Lorraine said yes. Lorraine and little Greg slept in the bedroom. Big Greg and Karen slept in the living room on the floor. This was the home Megan Waterman was born into, on January 18, 1988—a rented room occupied by her mother, her father, and her father's new girlfriend. And this was when Muriel reentered Lorraine's life and took her children away from her.

Muriel and everyone else in the family heard the stories: The baby would not be changed all day; Lorraine would smack little Greg; someone saw little Greg toddling around next to an open oven with gas heat pouring out of it; someone else saw little Greg eating cereal off the floor. Muriel hadn't liked the father, big Greg, much to begin with, and then she found out that little Greg had a bruise on his nose. One of her other daughters told her that big Greg and a friend were tossing little Greg around the room, and one of them was too close to the door casing and spun around too quickly, tagging little Greg right across the bridge of the nose. "That," Muriel said, "was when I started telling the state."

Together with Lorraine's sisters, Liz and Kathy, Muriel worked to start a file on Lorraine, writing down what they saw happening with the baby. When she was accused, Lorraine's response was achingly familiar to Muriel. When she couldn't deny, she shifted blame. Nothing was her fault. The bruise? Little Greg had a vein visible under the first layer of skin—a dark smudge everyone only thought was a bruise. The cereal on the floor? Little Greg would never eat milk in his cereal, Lorraine said, so she'd put cereal in a bowl, and he'd walk around with it and sit down in the kitchen and dump it on the floor. And the oven? Big Greg, the father, would turn the oven on and open up the door for heat, and Lorraine would always shut the door for safety. "I was shutting it!" Lorraine said.

When Megan was born, she had an abnormal blood test—nothing serious, just something that needed to be monitored. Lorraine was supposed to bring the baby back for a follow-up test, but she kept dodging the social workers, going elsewhere on the days when home visits were scheduled. Muriel became alarmed that the state couldn't seem to track Lorraine down, even though they received state aid. Finally, Muriel discovered that Megan was in the hospital with respiratory distress. That was when Muriel said she applied for custody.

The state had foster care ready for emergency situations, and when Megan left the hospital, she, along with little Greg, were taken from Lorraine and placed directly in foster care. While Muriel's custody application drifted through the system, Muriel and Doug would drive every Sunday morning to visit the babies in Naples, an hour north of the city. Lorraine was supposed to go with them, but Muriel said they could never find her. Muriel, meanwhile, began to bond with the children—more, she suggested, than Lorraine ever had. Small as they were, she thought the babies anticipated her arrival, getting up early on their own. Little Greg was talking now. Some of his first words, Muriel said, were "Nana coming!"

In a crusade she looks back on with pride and satisfaction, Megan's nana started gently campaigning to take the babies for a day here, a day there—rising at three A.M. on a Saturday after working five days at a watch shop, grabbing coffee to stay awake, driving to Naples and back, and doing it all again that evening. Muriel befriended the foster family and asked for more time: "Can we take them all weekend?" The family said yes. All the way back on Sunday night, Muriel would cry. Her boss at the watch shop took pity on her, because she often couldn't do her job until Wednesday. Friday night couldn't come fast enough. Muriel wanted them all the time. Finally, three months into the fostership, the family let Muriel keep the babies all week—unbeknownst to the state.

Lorraine came around from time to time, but her visits started to grate on Muriel. She found her daughter too cavalier, as if she didn't realize how much the babies needed a mother. Sometimes, when Lorraine reneged on a visit, Muriel would swear that Megan and little Greg felt jilted. After a while, she told Lorraine, "If you're not here within ten minutes of when you say you'll be here, don't bother coming."

Lorraine had her suspicions. She thought she knew what Muriel's bid for custody was really about. Eli, Muriel's youngest, was turning eighteen. The nest was emptying. And without a child at home, Muriel and Doug wouldn't qualify anymore for their federal welfare subsidy, Aid to Families with Dependent Children. Without a child, Muriel would have to leave Avon Place. Without a child, her mother would be homeless.

Soon her inkling became a deeply felt conviction. Could it really have been a coincidence that Muriel started calling the state on a regular basis just a few months before Eli's birthday? "She knew what she was doing," Lorraine said. "It was constant income."

If the accusation seemed a little too convenient—another case of Lorraine shifting the blame—it also happened to be true, at least in part. While Muriel genuinely loved the children, Lorraine's sister Ella has acknowledged that government support did play a part in Muriel's decision to take them in. One of the first things Muriel did when the kids came to her house was to apply for AFDC funding. Still, Ella said, Muriel was the only one who seemed to be actively trying to secure the well-being of the children. "It was my mother who had done all the work," Ella said, "like fighting to get them." Lorraine's three sisters all came to the same conclusion. What Lorraine may have overlooked—or been willfully blind to—is the fact that no matter why Muriel wanted the children, her mother was still a better bet than she was.

Lorraine fought for custody at first. She got an attorney. So did Greg Gove. The day they went into court, Muriel took Lorraine aside and delivered an ultimatum. She said if Lorraine signed the children over to her, she would still be able to see them; if she didn't, she wouldn't be able to see them at all.

There was no third option. Lorraine had no way of disproving the case. "We threw in the towel," Greg recalled. They signed away custody. Lorraine's lawyer, once he turned up, said, "You should've never done that, Lorraine."

Lorraine stared at the lawyer in anguish. "What was I supposed to do?"

Muriel raised Megan and her brother as if they were her own. Greg Gove visited the children for a few years before leaving town. Lorraine saw them, too, but only when Muriel had the patience to allow it. That turned out to be just enough exposure to earn Megan and Greg's unbridled resentment and anger. Many of Megan's closest friends didn't even know she had a mother, and those who did knew that Megan despised her. Greg felt the same way. "My grandmother was like my mother," he said. "My grandfather was the only father I knew. They gave me all my Christmases and all my birthdays. My mom will blame it all on my grandmother till she's blue in the face. But no, we'd never see her. All we had was us."

■

The social worker never forgot the day she met Megan: She stood a few feet from the breakfast table and watched as Megan and Greg got into a fistfight right in front of her over a piece of toast. Megan was nine and Greg was ten, but they were evenly matched. They raged at each other, no holds barred, hitting, pulling hair, screeching.

Jo Moser had come to 16 Avon Place as a parenting coach. She saw how worried Muriel was about the children. Their volatility was rattling her: children who would scream "Fuck you!" to anyone they wanted, even running out on the street and yelling it to the whole neighborhood. Muriel knew she was in over her head. Doug had heart trouble and couldn't work as many hours driving a truck, and Muriel, now in her fifties, was a softie, hard on Megan and Greg one minute and then giving them anything the next. Moser remembered a lot of chaos in the house—friends, family, and acquaintances filing in and out. She remembered a household in a constant state of anxiety over money, a family living from check to check. When Moser started taking Greg and Megan to the all-you-can-eat buffet at the China Wall, near the Maine Mall in Portland, the kids couldn't stop eating.

In the first few years, she saw the children two or three times a week, for a few hours each time. Megan resisted until Moser told her that if she didn't want to meet, she might not get to live with Nana. Megan agreed, and over the course of a decade, Moser came to adore Megan, even if she was hell on wheels, or maybe because of it. Greg mouthed off, ditched school, got into fights, stole money. The social workers saw kids like him all week long. But Megan was one of a kind. She always felt that she ruled the house, and she did. She could talk her grandfather into pretty much anything, and she ran hot and cold on Muriel—from "I don't care anything about her" to crying about how much she needed her. What Megan wanted most of all was freedom, and Muriel lacked the resolve to contain her. The word Moser wrote in her notebook over and over was *defiance*.

At Reiche Elementary School in Portland, Megan was more hostile and threatening than her brother. Four or five boys would gang up on Greg after school, down at the bottom of the ramp, and when Megan started down the ramp, they took off. She had the police called on her for the first time in first grade. There was a bridge connecting the buildings, thirty feet above the sidewalk, and she climbed over the railing and wouldn't come back. By second grade, there was, courtesy of the McGeachey Hall Mental Health Center in Portland, a diagnosis: attention deficit hyperactivity disorder. She lasted at Reiche Elementary until fifth grade, when she was transferred to a school for troubled kids called Prep, where some of the students were afraid of her. She was finally removed from public school when she tried to dunk a kid's head underwater in the school's swimming pool. She wasn't trying to drown him—just trying to get a reaction, to make people laugh. What scared the school was that Megan didn't seem to realize how dangerous it was.

Even when she was at her most extreme, watching Megan could be exhilarating. "Megan was what I called honestly stupid," said an old friend, Lashonda Gregory. "I say that in the most loving way, because it was the best thing I loved about her. She was so carefree. It wasn't that she sought out dangerous stuff. It was more like she was an adventure seeker." In summertime, Megan and her friends would swim at a hotel pool behind McDonald's, not far from their house. Megan would do everything the other kids wished they had the nerve to do—dives, cannonballs, flips— then jump out of the water and dare the others to do it, too, until she was running laps around the edge of the pool, imploring the others: "Come on! Just run around with me!" Once, Megan's bathing suit strap kept sliding, and a man sitting on the edge of the pool made a crack about it: "She might as well be naked!" Megan looked at the man and took off her suit, then jumped in the pool, completely naked. She was twelve.

The vulnerable side of Megan was hard to notice. Jo Moser believed that Megan's bravado was a façade, but she saw how the girl could seem threatening. The cousins and friends who spent the most time with Megan all knew what she was capable of. What provoked her the most was hearing the word *no*. The refrain of Megan's teenage years was pretty consistent: "I don't care, I'm going anyway" or "You can't make me" or "I'm going to go back to school and beat the shit out of so-and-so." By the time she reached her teens, many people believed Muriel was simply too frightened to rein her in. Everyone heard the threats: "I'll kill you in your sleep! I'll stab you to death!"

"I honestly think they were scared of her," her cousin Jessica Small said. "If she wanted something, she'd be like, 'I want this,' and they'd hand it right to her." Muriel would hear Megan pitching a fit and try to put her foot put down, but Megan would get really mad and throw something at her, and then Muriel would say, "Megan, I don't have the money, but take my last five dollars!" What appalled her aunts and cousins the most was how Megan was rewarded for bad behavior. No matter what, she always got an allowance. Megan's aunt Ella remembers asking Muriel, "Why do you pay her to be bad?"

It wasn't hard to draw a line from Megan's recklessness to the pain she might have felt about Lorraine. Moser didn't think so at first—she thought Muriel was well ensconced in the mother role, and Megan almost never brought up Lorraine when they talked. But after close to ten years, Moser reconsidered. What struck her was how little the girl had changed. Megan was an unfulfilled child, still angry, still wounded, still feeling like she wasn't getting what she deserved in life. She grew up to become a romantic, looking for love—somebody who accepted her with all her flaws—and her grandparents weren't enough. Indulging her only made her more insecure, more needy. "In some ways, she had both inferiority and grandiosity going at the same time," Moser said. "Those were the two elements: *I can do anything I want,* and *I'm a piece of shit.*"

Scarborough, Maine, is about two square miles, with a population of just under twenty thousand people. Along the ocean, east of Route 1, are the million-dollar homes in spots like Prouts Neck, where the Bushes and Oprah and Billy Joel and Paul Newman have spent their summers. To the west is farmland that, over the last few decades, has been developed into lots of McMansions. That's the allure of Scarborough: The newly rich can build their dream homes in the woods and still be nestled right in between everything they would ever want, a half-hour drive from Portland, the ocean, and Sebago Lake.

At about the time Megan was finishing junior high school, Muriel and Doug moved the family from downtown Portland to Scarborough. Greg didn't make the move; he went on to a series of group homes and relatives before living on his own. Muriel and Doug had a trailer on the western border of town, as far from the ocean as you can get without leaving Scarborough—a single-wide mobile home, fourteen by seventy feet, with three bedrooms, an open kitchen, a small living room, putty-gray siding, and a little brown deck with room for a couple of chairs. The Crystal Springs trailer park housed only ten trailers on this road, and woods surrounded them on all sides.

Scarborough is a commuter town, a bedroom community. But for Megan, compared to Avon Place, it was the middle of nowhere. She thought most of the people in Scarborough were snobs, and most people in the Crystal Springs trailer park shared that opinion. Almost the second she walked into Scarborough Middle School, Megan was marked as white trash. She started in regular classrooms but soon was sent to special ed. When she started Scarborough High the following year, she was placed in the alternative part of the school for troubled kids, a place the students called the Basement. It was an open campus for troubled kids; Megan could come and go as she wanted. But she had her share of envy: She saw other kids walking around Scarborough High in designer sneakers and backpacks that weren't in her family's price range.

The police in Scarborough know all about Crystal Springs. They get domestic calls there a lot, as well as some drug cases: dealers, people with outstanding warrants, people trying to blend in, to fade away. On various occasions, they caught Megan in town, shoplifting from Walmart—cosmetics, usually—and she ended up in the Youth Center, a jail for young offenders. Though the kids were rowdy there, it wasn't designed to feel like a grown-up jail; more like a group home where you happened to be locked up. Greg called it Kiddie Camp. When Megan was sent there, Muriel's first reaction was relief, and then leniency kicked in; she went from "Yes, Megan should be there" to "Well, maybe she deserves another chance."

Her arresting officer, much of the time, was Doug Weed, a married father of five who had grown up in Scarborough. He first met the girl when she was fourteen, in October 2002, when he got two calls from a girl accusing Megan of stalking her. The two had been feuding, as he remembered it, and the matter fizzled in time. But he would see Megan again. For a few years, you couldn't be on the Scarborough police force without running into Megan. There was the neighbor she tangled with in 2004 who asked for a restraining order. Then there was the time in June 2005 when she got caught carrying drug paraphernalia, most likely a marijuana pipe, which forced her into juvenile rehab. There was the time, the following November, when she dashed out of the rehab and back to Muriel's place. Muriel called the police to come collect her.

Weed was conservative politically, and before he had kids, he had a tendency to write off as drains on society some of the people in town whom he was supposed to be serving and protecting—to just say, *You're a waste, you're a piece of shit, I don't care.* After becoming a father, he noticed how a lot of his childless colleagues couldn't stand teenagers. If they saw a group of them hanging out, they'd walk the other way. Officers like Weed were more likely to give the kids a mulligan, thinking, *Okay, you're sixteen years old. You're an idiot.* Sometimes, as he did with Megan, Weed went a little further. He saw they didn't have what his kids had. They didn't have a father there to keep them in line—to tell them what to do, to help them when they had those questions all kids have. Weed decided that it depended. If kids were receptive to what he was trying to do and how he was trying to help, then he would go out of his way ten thousand times to do anything he could. If kids weren't receptive—if they weren't willing to help themselves— then he wouldn't bother.

Weed found he was one of the few cops who could actually talk to Megan, because he'd given her breaks now and then. He would catch her with cigarettes: "Megan, come on, seriously, you're sixteen years old. You know you can't do that. Put them away. Let's go home." Or he'd find her out late at night: "Let's go back to Muriel's house, Megan." He'd drop her off himself. He gained her trust. And he liked her. He noticed she was angry a lot. Weed wasn't sure where that anger came from. He didn't know who her mother and father were. But when he met Muriel and saw a sixty-year-old woman struggling to control a fifteen-year-old girl, that was all he needed to know.

When Megan was seventeen, she stopped going to school.

She continued to live at home with Muriel and work odd jobs. She was picked up more often, usually for shoplifting or alcohol; once, her cousin Desiree said, she blew a 1.25. She and her friend Lashonda Gregory got arrested when they picked up a credit card a customer left behind at Mr. Bagel, where Megan worked briefly, and went shopping for Lashonda's baby shower.

Despite everything, Officer Weed decided to be optimistic about Megan. He saw someone who didn't have the support that he'd had as a child, and he felt he could help her. At the very least, letting Megan know she could come to him with any problem would be better than doing what everyone else seemed to do—write a summons and then kick a kid loose. Why not take a chance on people? Otherwise, he figured, he was just a robot who locked people up. She had his phone number and called all the time, leaving long voice mails. He heard from her when she needed to vent, even to say her grandmother was in the hospital. The fact that she reached out led him to believe that Megan knew she needed stability, someone to rely on other than Muriel, someone to whom she felt comfortable talking. Even if his return calls were five minutes—"I got your message, tell your grandmother I'm thinking of her. You doing good? You staying out of trouble?"—Weed felt the conversations calmed Megan down, made her feel a little more secure.

She never brought up boyfriends with him, and he never asked. But Megan did tell him when she found out she was pregnant. The father was a DJ, about thirty-two, with one child already in New Hampshire. Megan met him at a club in Portland—a bathroom hookup, nothing more. "I don't know what I'm going to do," she said softly.

Officer Weed told her it was a blessing. He had five children of his own. Children, he told Megan, helped you understand why you were here—and help you start living for someone other than yourself.

With Muriel's consent, a judge in the youth court that had sent Megan to rehab ordered Megan to stay in St. Andre's, a home for unwed mothers, for the length of her pregnancy. Megan spent her time there in a panic, watching the state take away other new mothers' babies as soon as they delivered. When Muriel tried to convince Megan that they wouldn't take her baby—that every mother's situation was different—Megan was too angry with Muriel to listen. The staff couldn't convince her, either. Megan couldn't get away from the sense that history was repeating itself. She thought about how her own mother had lost her and what it had done to her. She couldn't let that happen to her child.

When Lorraine heard that Megan was expecting a baby, she tried harder than usual to stay in touch. Since losing custody of Megan and Greg, Lorraine had drifted in and out of the family's orbit, sometimes falling out of contact for years at a time. She quit drinking for almost a year, then married, then divorced, then started drinking again. When she had three more children—Allie a year after Megan, and twins named Bethany and Stephanie a few years after that—the state took them away from her, too, arguing that her living conditions weren't acceptable. Lorraine had relinquished those children rather than allow the state to move them all into a state-run family shelter—something she vowed never to do to her kids. That never ceased to appall Megan. "She couldn't even take care of us," Megan would say. "How come she had more kids?"

Her rift with Muriel had long since separated Megan from the rest of her family. But this would be Lorraine's first grandchild— and for the first time, Megan was living away from Muriel, receptive to Lorraine in a way she'd never been. When her due date approached, Megan contacted her caseworker and asked if she could leave St. Andre's and stay with Lorraine. Lorraine jumped at the chance to take in Megan when Muriel would not.

For two weeks, Megan was able to experience her mother for the first time without Muriel filtering everything she saw. Lorraine was sober now, in her late thirties, with dark circles under her eyes that revealed her years of hard living. After a few years in Florida, she had moved back to West Portland. She was working at a Domino's managed by her boyfriend, Bill, whom she credited with keeping her from falling off the wagon. Lorraine seized the chance to tell her daughter everything she'd wanted her to know. She railed against Muriel and the injustice she believed had been done to her—to them both, really, and to Greg, she said. She talked about how horrible a mother Muriel had been to her when she was younger, and how Lorraine and Megan had been separated for no good reason. Megan's eyes widened as she listened. She seemed to sympathize. Lorraine held out hope that she did. Of course, Megan had a lifetime of longing to remind her who had stayed with her all those years and who hadn't. Two weeks wasn't nearly enough to persuade Megan that she had been brought up by the wrong person.

Megan delivered a healthy baby girl in the summer of 2006. She named her Liliana. By then she had left Lorraine's; now she returned to Scarborough, taking the baby with her. Her choice stung Lorraine. In time, she would decide that Megan couldn't handle the truth—that she had been poisoned against her mother. Still, a door had been opened; she and Megan would stay in touch, even if they felt like strangers. And something about meeting her mother and having the baby seemed to chasten Megan a little. When she finally came home to Crystal Springs, she seemed determined to do things differently. Megan could tell herself she had it all now—she'd never be lonely again—and that as long as she lived, nothing would come between her and Lili.

Motherhood became Megan. In the beginning, she was never anything other than ecstatic about the baby and gentle toward her. The same people who'd been cowed and intimidated by her were in awe of how happy she seemed with her daughter, how peaceful and free of anger. Gone were the histrionics, the temper, the volatility. "Megan loved her daughter," Greg said. "Liliana was everything to her."

But Megan began to feel some new pressures. The four hundred dollars a month she received from the Maine Department of Health and Human Services wasn't enough to feed and clothe her and Lili, at least not the way Megan would have liked. The girl who once demanded the best of everything, who shoplifted makeup to compete with the rich kids of Scarborough, was looking at a life very much like her mother's and Nana's, living on government checks. Megan felt a need to deliver for her daughter and secure her future while also securing something more for herself—a life apart from the baby, one that promised success. No matter how much she loved Lili, that love did nothing to cure her of the elemental loneliness she'd always had.

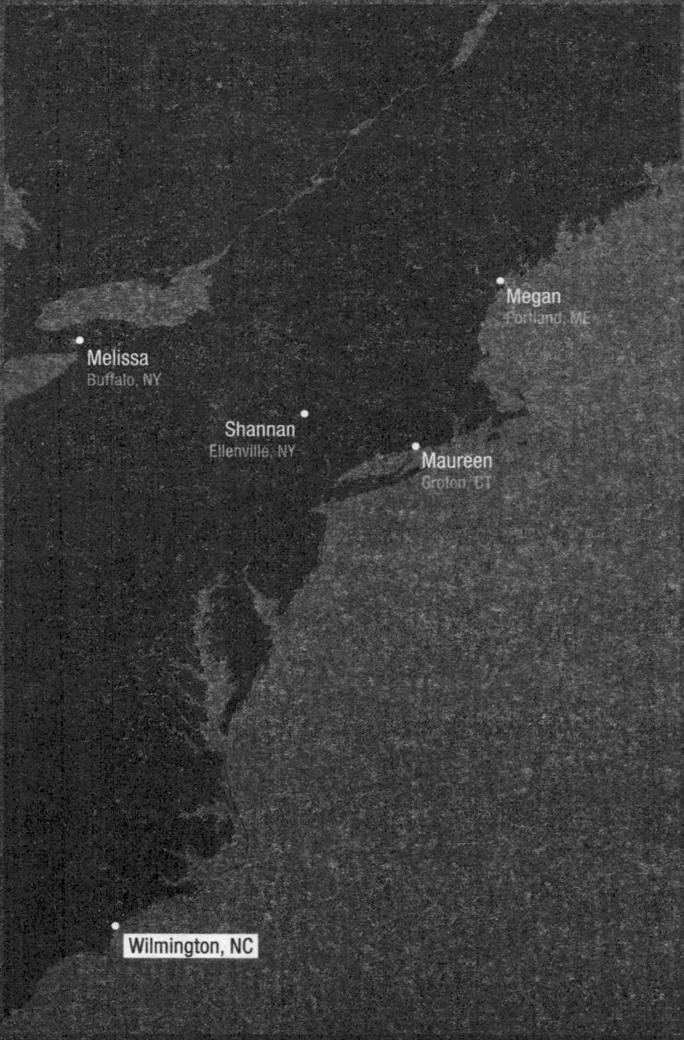

Megan
Portland, ME
Melissa
Buffalo, NY
Shannan
Ellenville, NY
Maureen
Groton, CT
Wilmington, NC

AMBER

Kim and Amber were both tiny and skinny, with the same long nose that had a little bulb on the tip. The Overstreet sisters were born six years apart in Pennsylvania—Kim in 1977, Amber in 1983. Kim may have been the firstborn, but Amber was Margie's baby: Everything about her was cute; anything she wanted, she'd get. Even Kim, who resented her sometimes, used to tell her that her legs looked like meaty drumsticks. When Amber grew up, she weighed a hundred pounds soakin' wet, as her family put it, and stood four-eleven. Their dad, Al, liked to rib her that she was a half inch short of qualifying for disability payments as a little person. "Why don't you take your shoes off?" he told her. "You'd get a check every month for the rest of your life."

Al had grown up in Wilmington, North Carolina, where his father had been a farmer. Bakery work sustained Al for years. He made rolls for Oroweat, and for the Federal Bake Shop, and then for Donut Town in Bristol, Pennsylvania, fifteen minutes outside of Philadelphia. That's where he met Margaret Ann Sassy. She was a waitress at a seafood restaurant, four years younger than Al, and attractive, with dark hair, like Amber's would be. Margie had a much more comfortable childhood than Al. Their daughters, looking at photos years later, would decide their mother's side was just plain rich, and she'd gone and run off with a bad boy from the wrong side of the tracks. To Amber and Kim, at least, it was a grand love story.

Shortly after Amber was born, the family moved from Pennsylvania back to North Carolina. Al reconnected with his father for the first time in years, and Kim remembers family dinners with a bunch of cousins she never knew she had. At first they lived several hours away from Wilmington in Gastonia, then a tough working-class town next to Charlotte, where Al had found work in the knitting mills nearby in Dolford.

Gastonia was where the first tragedy of Amber's life took place. She was five years old. Through all that came afterward, Al and Margie stayed close to their daughters. If all four of them ended up suffering from the same affliction—addiction was, it seemed, the Overstreet family business—they each did so privately. Call it pride or denial, but to them, it was how they expressed their love.

The tragedy happened at home. Amber's family was renting the garage apartment of another family's house. According to Kim and Al, a twenty-six-year-old neighbor named James would take Kim and Amber and another girl to play tennis at the local park. Amber would retell the story in different ways to different friends over the years, but a few of the same details always came up: that James grabbed Amber and took her to the bushes . . . that Margie caught James and Amber in bed together nude . . . that Margie couldn't pull him out of bed, since he weighed too much . . . that Margie called the police.

What came next was mixed up in everyone's memory. Kim always thought that James went to jail and Al went to jail for shooting him. But Al said he bought a shotgun and threatened to blow James's brains out and the police intervened before he could. No formal charges were filed. No arrest record for the incident appears to exist today, suggesting that everyone decided to walk away.

The Overstreets moved immediately. The entire family fell to pieces. Kim said that Amber went on to blame her mother, and

Margie blamed herself, too. Margie was hospitalized with a nervous breakdown, and when she got out, she remained separated from Al, moving with Amber to Charlotte and later Wilmington, bunking in an aunt's house. Kim stayed with Al, except when he served a jail sentence after racking up too many DUIs; then she stayed for a short while with a friend's family. The rape scarred Amber physically as well as emotionally. Several friends and family members said that she told them she couldn't have children because of what James had done to her. But the years eventually papered over what happened, and when Amber was in junior high school, they all settled together—first in Wilmington, then in Florida, then back in Wilmington.

The family lived for a year in Carolina Beach—the redneck Riviera of Wilmington—and then in a housing project called Nesbitt Courts. The 216-unit development was whites-only when it opened in 1940, and it held on to its reputation for being the only project in Wilmington that housed whites. Kim's first baby, a girl named Marissa, was born when they lived at Nesbitt Courts. Amber and her friends would race home to play with her. Kim was almost twenty when Marissa was born. The father was a kid from the neighborhood named Mootnie. She'd have two more children with him, though another boyfriend would end up raising all three.

Life was about as stable for the Overstreets at Nesbitt Courts as it ever would be. Al worked at Krispy Kreme. Margie worked part-time managing properties and looked after Kim's baby. By then Amber's mother had become an almost ghostly presence around the house. Slender, with shoulder-length hair that had turned prematurely gray, she kept cases of Olde English in the pantry and would sip from the warm forty-ounce bottles bright and early in the morning. Amber earned A's and B's, smart enough that if she had to get a teacher's note signed by a parent because she cut class, she'd trick her mom into signing it by setting up her little desk and pretending she was playing school: "Ah, yes, yes, Mrs. Overstreet, could you sign this?" Margie, watching TV, would sign anything.

Amber and Kim had just one fight that Al knew of—a knock-down, drag-out brawl that they wouldn't let him break up. They told him that he had better get out of the way or he might get hurt. More often, they looked after each other. One time a member of the Crips gang came to the house looking for Amber; Kim, pregnant at the time, came out with a baseball bat. When the sisters clashed, it would be because Amber felt entitled to everything of Kim's—her clothes, her perfume, anything sitting around her room. Kim would see her sister wearing something of hers and tell her she couldn't, and Amber would act like Kim hadn't said a thing. Their lives were symbiotic. What was Kim's, Amber always thought, was rightfully hers.

Teresa didn't look like a madam to Kim. She had red hair and green eyes and freckles—not exactly a knockout but pretty, with a boob job that brought her up to size D. Unlike Kim, Teresa had her life figured out. She had a husband who was in the military, based in another town, and rarely home. He was, if anything, a junior partner in the business. Teresa was the boss, and a successful one.

When they met, Kim was nineteen and a sophomore at the University of North Carolina Wilmington, studying sports medicine and paying tuition by waiting tables at two different restaurants—Bojangles' and Freddie's Italian-American Grill. Kim and Teresa were in a psychology class together; Teresa was a year ahead and a few years older. She didn't keep her living a secret. Coed Confidential advertised in the local paper, promising "entertainment" for men: solo appointments, bachelor parties, massages. But Teresa didn't talk about herself at first. Instead, she listened as Kim talked about how her own life was unraveling.

At the start of the school year, Al and Margie had been rocked by back-to-back health setbacks. First, Al had gone to get a hearing aid, and the MRI had revealed tumors on his acoustic nerve. After surgery, he was at home in bandages when Margie collapsed with a perforated ulcer. She, too, was rushed into surgery. Amber was just thirteen, so Kim became the nurse for both parents. What little sports-medicine training she had came in handy as she repacked her mother's bandages and bathed her, and then turned around and rebandaged her dad, too, minding the staples in his head. Kim was holding on, but the financial pressure was mounting. Waiting tables wasn't going to cover it.

Teresa kept listening as with each class, Kim became more despondent, losing heart. Then one day Kim said she'd seen an ad for amateur night at a strip club. She was thinking of trying to win the five-hundred-dollar prize.

Teresa shook her head violently. "You're not gonna make shit there. You won't make half of what we make."

"I'm not gonna have sex," Kim said.

"That's not what it is," said Teresa. "It's about the show." And then she proposed a half-measure. "Why don't you come answer phones for me?"

The rate depended on location. Calls within reasonable driving distance of central Wilmington were $150 an hour, cash only. The dancer collected $100, and the rest went to the house. Calls from farther away charged more—Carolina Beach was maybe twenty minutes away, and that was $200 an hour per girl—but since they were the ones driving there, the girls kept the extra money. The girls were making $800 a night or more, just like that, while their friends were working eight or ten hours a day at places like Bojangles' for ten dollars an hour.

When a guy called Coed Confidential, he would give his address and directions. During a normal appointment, the girl would come in, take the money, and go in the bathroom or bedroom to get changed. The client was supposed to give the girl adequate time to fit into her outfit—no pounding on the door, no shouts to hurry up. About thirty minutes later, Teresa would call to let the girl know how long she'd been there. The rule was no longer than an hour, unless the customer was paying more. The phone call from Teresa was a sort of safety valve: If she couldn't get ahold of the girl, she'd know to be concerned. There were other security provisions: Girls couldn't go alone to a party; more than one guy necessitated the hiring of more than one girl.

Kim had no trouble perfecting her delivery of the script: *A girl comes out, she models lingerie, she dances for you topless, she ends up nude. Some girls offer massages, but if she's rubbing your back, she has to be dressed. Tipping is optional.* Sex, or "full service," was never officially part of the deal. Inevitably, guys would ask, and the girl working the phones had a stock answer: *No, that's against the law. They will be topless, and they give you a massage as long as they have bottoms on.* The girls were allowed to keep all tips, which was tacit encouragement to do more than dance, provided a client was willing to tip big. Teresa made a big show of not wanting to hear about any side deals. "Do what you want to do to earn the tips," she said, "but just know that we don't condone it." She also covered herself. Each girl signed a form drawn up by Teresa's lawyer, declaring that she worked as an independent contractor and that Teresa was not employing her to do anything illegal.

Those early years, it was all about fun, and in some ways it was innocent. They weren't prostitutes, at least on paper, and at times they didn't even feel like escorts. They were best friends. Shortly after Kim started, Teresa moved to a breathtaking plantation-style house: eleven hundred dollars a month in rent for four bedrooms, hardwood floors, a grand staircase, huge living rooms on the ground floor, an antique rug, and a big Jacuzzi in one of the bathrooms. All the girls who worked for her kept extra clothes there. It was like they were college kids, crashing together in the same stunning dorm.

Teresa made it easy to work for her. If you wanted to go on a call, you did. If you didn't, you didn't. When you made what you considered enough money, you had the rest of the day to do whatever you wanted. The big-money calls were at resorts like the Bald Head Island golf club off the coast of North Carolina. Those jobs were ideal: Guys on golf getaways, wives left at home. The girls would dance and spend the rest of the time doing a bunch of coke, playing poker, and negotiating side deals for sex. At the end of the weekend, they'd come home with a few thousand dollars each. For many of the girls, working for Teresa was about more than the parties—it vaulted them into a life of affluence, with all the trappings. Lending practices were so loose that the girls could pick up a car-loan application form at OfficeMax and have Teresa fill it out with whatever amount the girl wanted, and in no time, she would be approved.

Even answering phones, Kim was making enough to forget all about waiting tables. Teresa was kicking twenty-five dollars of her own commission over to Kim for every call, which translated into hundreds of dollars a night. Kim poured herself into the job, working nights and days, skipping classes. Before long, she sat in on interviews for new girls. One night, when a few of the girls were hired to perform during a bachelor party at the Beau Rivage, a golf club in Wilmington, Kim decided to go and observe. The guests were a bunch of doctors and lawyers from New York and New Jersey, about seventeen in all. Kim watched as the girls brought in suitcases with black lights and glow-in-the-dark body paint. One girl brought vibrators to play with while she stripped. Another brought Ping-Pong balls with which to perform the crudest, most notorious bachelor-party trick. They were all just stripping and dancing, no full service, and still Kim saw how the money—the tips—flew. One girl gave a hand job. Kim had never watched someone do that before, and she was a little stunned to be right there in the room while it happened. The takeaway for Kim was more than powerful. It was seismic. For just two hours of work, each girl made five hundred dollars plus tips. She figured they each came home with close to nine hundred dollars.

On her first call, Kim used the name Mia. The john was a guy named Vinnie who owned a backhoe service in Raleigh. He was nearly twenty years older than Kim, and she was scared to death. But when he opened the door, he seemed nice, so she danced and stripped to the music she played on a boom box. He was a gentleman and tipped her and kept her an extra hour. She walked out with hundreds of dollars and a regular customer.

Once she signed, Kim became part of a little sorority of full-timers. Kim already knew a couple of them from school. June's working name was Cameron. Crystal's was Mocha; she was one of the few black escorts working consistently in this part of Wilmington. Like any sorority, they threw a great party: a DJ for one part of the house, a band for the other. Once they took aluminum foil, poked holes in it, and covered the TV screen like a Lite-Brite. They turned the volume down on a cartoon, threw on the Doors and Pink Floyd, and sat there, high, staring at the light shining out of the holes, laughing. Another time they filled a bathtub with purple Jesus—vodka and grape juice and whatever else was around—and guys came by and dipped their cups. A guy who was seeing one of the girls brought ecstasy. Someone else's boyfriend walked around administering acid directly into people's eyes with a dropper.

Kim became fixated on making more. Her family was a parade of tragedy, and Kim was the one who always had to fix it. Now that she was making real money, she felt empowered. She learned tricks to maximize revenue. Even though the fee was $175, the guy usually had $200, and if by chance you couldn't make change, that was an automatic $25 tip. Sometimes she'd lift a john's credit card. Other times a watch would disappear, or some checks. One look at her parents, frail and declining at home, and Kim could justify anything.

Just as it was for all the other girls, Kim always made a show of not offering full service, at least to anyone who asked. When it was Amber's turn, she wouldn't bother drawing that line.

Some survivors of childhood sexual abuse turn their back on sex altogether. Others turn the tap on full blast, trying in vain to trivialize it even as they reopen the wound over and over. By the time Amber was a teenager, sex had become meaningless to her, even as it came to define her. Even before she worked for Teresa, Amber tried to make money for herself as a free agent in and around Nesbitt Courts. When she was sixteen, Amber charged some neighborhood boys for sex. Her first trick, according to an old neighbor named Carl King, earned her seventy-five dollars.

Carl eventually lost his virginity to her—for free, or so he says—and so did a friend of his. "She didn't care what people thought about her," Carl said. "She really didn't. It was kind of her thing, and I always admired her for that."

Not everyone was quite as warmhearted as Carl. A promiscuous white girl in Nesbitt Courts was a hot topic, and Amber got a reputation. A rumor went around that Amber was spreading gonorrhea. Amber never cared what anyone said. Her sister was more famous around Nesbitt Courts than she would ever be.

Everyone saw that Kim had a car, cash, and clothes. Practically everyone except their parents knew where Kim was working. She had made up a cover story for Al and Margie that held for a while. She said she worked for the Hilton in Wilmington, driving a limo to the airport to pick up VIPs. All her cash, she said, came from tips. She waited to tell them the truth until she was sure there was nothing they could do about it. They needed her. They were too frail to work, and Kim was paying their bills.

When Amber finally joined Kim at Coed Confidential, both sisters were mindful enough not to throw it in their parents' faces. Privately, Margie told Al that she hoped the girls were working their way through a phase. The girls were young, she said. Their stories weren't over yet. Al tried his best to be philosophical. Kim was a hard worker, ambitious and powerful, stronger than he was. Amber, though, was a special case, more sensitive and vulnerable. Al saw how much Amber needed to be close to Kim, but he also saw her wrestling with her decisions. What gave him the most hope was the way Amber would allow herself to be overtaken by a deep and chaste religious fervor, at least sometimes. That, in Al's estimation, had always been the biggest difference between the sisters: While Kim never believed in anything except herself, Amber never stopped searching for something bigger.

They'd seemed so alike to the other girls at Coed Confidential—both skinny little chatterboxes, brash and sassy—that it took a while for everyone to notice how different Amber was from Kim. Kim ran cooler. She was less affectionate and more self-reliant and mercenary. Amber was the sweet one. She had an endearing daffiness, a genuine innocence. She couldn't even drive.

For Amber, the work didn't seem to be as much about the money as the chance to connect with the people at Teresa's house—to be a part of a family. She wanted the money, but more than that, she wanted to make an impression, to fit in. If you asked her to pick up a dime bag of weed, she would come back with a quarter bag or a twenty and try to shrug it off: "Here, I got you some extra, I didn't know if you wanted it or not, but what the hell." "She'd yes you to death," June remembered, telling you anything you wanted to hear if you would only be her friend.

Once, the boyfriend of a girl named Chastity got busted buying pills, and she couldn't afford a lawyer. Amber wanted so badly to help that she made an offer: "I'll just dance for the lawyer. How about that?" After Amber walked out of the office, whatever had happened inside, Chastity's boyfriend had adequate legal representation.

Teresa's parties were getting bigger—so big that they upstaged the business. Where they'd once lasted all weekend, now they started earlier in the week until it seemed like every day offered a chance to cop. Teresa moved seamlessly from pot to acid to ecstasy, then coke, then crack, then heroin, then meth. She'd order enough for everyone, as if ordering pizza. The ecstasy parties always got a little mystical. Crystal thought ecstasy opened her third eye. Once Crystal was giving Teresa a massage and started seeing a flash of light in Teresa's back, and then she started seeing visions of what seemed to be Teresa's life. Teresa went ballistic, screaming, "What the fuck!" After that, everyone wanted a reading.

Kim's first pull on a crack pipe happened at one of Teresa's parties. Teresa had been the first to try it, as usual. Then she kept taking June's coke and cooking it into crack, and June—the stuck-up one who used to say, "Crack, that's the poor people's drug"—eventually went all in. Then came Crystal and, finally, Kim, who fell in love. "I could work all the fucking time," she said. One gram would last Kim for two days. She could work an entire weekend without crashing. The only problem with crack was how miserable you got when you started to come down. All the girls experimented with Xanax and other pills, anything to help them sleep off the hollow feeling.

Whom Teresa liked best often depended on who did the drug she liked at the time. When she was into coke, she and Kim were best friends. When she moved on to crack, she and June were best friends. And when Teresa started on heroin, it was Amber's turn. Amber wanted only crack at first—like her sister—but heroin snuggled up to her and held her tight. It numbed her, zoned her out. She started when Teresa had made a new connection, a dealer who would go to New York and bring back pills. One day the dealer showed Teresa and Amber how to shoot up. Heroin brought the parties to another level. The dealer went into convulsions once, and they stuck a wallet between his teeth so he wouldn't bite off his tongue. When the dealer's girlfriend started OD'ing once, they had to do the same thing for her; for a little while, as they watched her shake, they considered dumping her at the ER and driving away.

By then the drugs had fully upset the familial atmosphere at Coed Confidential. Kim was scooping up whatever coke was floating around at the parties and selling it on the side. Crystal left Teresa altogether and started a rival agency called Sensual Pleasure, specializing in happy-ending massages. And Amber was forced out by Teresa after too many complaints about her ripping off the johns—taking the payment and any drugs and just walking out.

With nowhere else to go, Amber worked a little for Crystal. One night she went by Crystal's place at the Governours Square Apartments, near Carolina Beach, and they smoked crack. Crystal performed a reading on Amber, looking into her past and seeing that she had been through something terrible. They talked about the rape and cried together. Crystal thought the drugs must have been to help ease the pain. She could relate: She didn't want to deal with the stuff flashing in her head all the time, either.

By dawn, the crack was gone, and they didn't have anything to help them come down. Amber started crying again. She wanted to go out and get more. Crystal said they should stay there. Amber kept crying, so Crystal held her like a baby. Then Crystal started praying for her, telling her it was going to be okay. "Have you ever prayed before?" she asked Amber.

"Yeah," Amber said. "I pray sometimes."

"Well, are you saved? Are you a Christian?"

"I think I am, but I don't know."

"Let's just be sure," Crystal said. She said the Sinner's prayer— *Heavenly Father, I know that I have sinned against you and that my sins separate me from you.* Amber repeated it after her and received Jesus Christ.

Amber stopped crying. She smiled a big smile and gazed upward, weeping gratefully, praising God, praising Jesus, praising and praising until her voice was a hollow whisper. Crystal sat and watched her, thinking how fucked up it was, coming down off a crack high and praising the Lord.

II.

Maureen Marie
Groton, CT
Oak Beach, NY

MARIE

New Year's had come and gone, and so far, for Sara Karnes, 2007 had been a disaster. The telemarketing job had ended, as had the job at McDonald's. Things with her boyfriend were strained. They fought as much as they slept together, and they hadn't lived together since losing the hotel room. The only bright spot was Maureen.

Sara said she hadn't known what her new friend was really doing at the massage appointments. Later on, she would chalk that up to gullibility. Even if she had suspected something, Sara might not have brought it up, for fear of ruining a good thing. Maureen was throwing Sara fifty dollars just for driving her to the appointments. Most of the time, she would dart back out in ten or fifteen minutes; if she stayed the full hour, Sara got a hundred. Being paid for sitting and waiting seemed like a good deal to Sara. Moreover, every time Maureen got in the car, she filled the gas tank.

It took a while for Sara to realize that life wasn't going that well for Maureen. The red tape of Maureen's life seemed exhausting: Sara got tired just watching Maureen juggle custody of two different kids with two different dads. Some days she had Aidan, other days Caitlin, other days both, other days neither. If she had the children and a massage appointment, the kids went to Missy's, which sometimes prompted an uneasy negotiation. Despite the money she was making, Maureen's life seemed to be closing in on her. She and her roommate had been a month or two behind on rent for a while. By spring, they were being threatened with eviction. She was constantly worried about Steve calling social services and arguing that their boy should live with him. Maureen knew he was waiting for a reason to try.

Maureen couldn't find a regular job, and not for lack of trying. She had answered want ads for receptionist positions, for a job greeting shoppers at Walmart, but wasn't hired. Again and again, she turned to Sara and her car to make enough money to pay the rent. Their lives intertwined. Sara's boyfriend did some dealing, and Maureen became a customer, buying ecstasy and pot and sometimes coke to stay awake. He was good to Maureen at first, charging just forty dollars for a gram of coke and allowing her not to pay up front. Maureen would give him her food-stamp Electronic Benefits Transfer card as collateral. That arrangement worked only as long as Sara and her boyfriend were together. As winter turned to spring, Maureen accused him of trying to take extra money off of her EBT card while he waited for her to pay. Sara didn't believe Maureen at first, but he couldn't hide what he had done forever, and when Sara learned the truth, she left him.

That left Sara homeless for real this time. Maureen came to Sara's rescue again, inviting her to stay on the couch at the apartment in Norwich. She didn't charge Sara rent and even paid for all the groceries. Sara couldn't believe it, though she soon learned that being a friend of Maureen's meant being on the receiving end of an almost embarrassing amount of generosity. Turning a blind eye to whatever financial pressures she was under, Maureen had taken in other friends, including a girl named Penny. When Sara started thinking that Penny might be using Maureen, she realized she couldn't talk, since she was freeloading, too.

They all needed money, not just Maureen. As summer approached, no great solution seemed to be presenting itself. Sara wasn't sure how much longer they all could stay together. It took until June for Sara to learn that Maureen had a plan. Both of their birthdays were coming up. Sara turned twenty-five on the eleventh, Maureen three days later. With whatever money she had made from appointments, Maureen booked a hotel room at Foxwoods and threw a party. The room overflowed with friends Maureen had made over the years at the casino. Sara got drunk, and not long before the sun came up, she and Maureen went back to the apartment. They were alone for the first time all night, and Sara noticed how Maureen's expression had changed. She seemed serious—completely sober.

"I need to talk to you. It's important."

"What?" said Sara.

"You like to have sex. Why don't you get paid for it?"

Sara had always liked to think of herself as an operator—someone who could talk anyone into anything. Now she realized that Maureen was in a whole other league. She fell silent as Maureen explained that before Aidan was born, she'd been going to New York for a few days at a time, but only every now and then, when she needed the money. She wanted to start again, with Sara as her partner.

"Do you like it?" Sara asked.

Maureen told her it was fine. In New York, she was a different person.

Maureen had posted her first ads on the Eastern Connecticut/ Adult Services page of Craigslist three years earlier, not long after she had showed her friend Jay DuBrule her photos. She had used her mother's name, Marie—a choice that she never explained to anyone who knew enough to ask. The replies had been instantaneous. She asked Jay if he'd come with her. He drove her to a few people's houses. She taught him the procedure: She goes in the house, and Jay calls her five minutes later; no answer means trouble. If she answers and says everything's fine, that means he paid her and she's good. "Then I'll be out within the hour," she said. And out she'd come, a hundred dollars richer.

The sex itself she insisted she could handle, but the johns were too close for comfort. Many of them were men who lived in Groton and the surrounding towns—guys whom she easily might run into later at ShopRite or Cory's or Wendy's. And the money wasn't quite what she had hoped, or at least not as much as she knew she could make a short distance away, at the casinos. Though Mohegan Sun was out of the question—her mother still worked there—Foxwoods was wide open. Maureen waited until Caitlin wasn't visiting from Mystic and booked a few nights in a hotel room at the casino. Before her first outing, she taught Jay how to freshen her Craigslist ad, editing it every now and then while she was out so the ad would bump up to the top of the list. The casinos brought Maureen to a different class of john— out-of-towners, from all over New England and New York and beyond, with more money and willingness to pay for what they wanted. They treated girls like entertainers, like professionals. This felt more like a business now, and Maureen preferred that. She met a few other girls, including one named Chrissy—a boy dressed as a girl, really. Missy later told friends that it was Chrissy who invited Maureen on her first trip to New York.

Manhattan was the ultimate moneymaker, Chrissy said— filled with tourists and businessmen and bored rich people. If she got a hotel room and posted an ad, she could make a thousand dollars or more every night. Maureen's initial trips there were brief, just a day and a night, with Chrissy at first and then alone. She asked Jay to drive her, but he declined. He had two jobs and custody of his daughter, and truth be told, he didn't feel quite as bold about going to New York as Maureen did. When she came back, Maureen had talked with all her friends in bright, breezy tones about her experiences. She spun it as an adventure: The men she met were all young and good-looking and nice to her. The hotel was luxurious. The city sparkled. She was exaggerating, but the money, at least, was real—piles of bills that she nonchalantly stacked high on her dresser. Some of her closest friends, as well as Missy, would say later that what Maureen was doing didn't satisfy her soul—that the spiritual, cosmically curious Maureen had nothing to do with this. But it wouldn't have been difficult for Maureen to be open to the possibilities. After so many years of depending on others, she could leave responsibilities at home and become another person for a while—all under the pretext of making money so she could be a responsible parent. And the attention: Seen the right way, the job was one where people were so eager to see her that they were willing to pay money. For the length of a call, she would be desired—a star, famous, loved, rich.

The logistics weren't ideal. She had to give Steve a story to explain her time away; since he hated talking to Maureen's family, she said she was staying with them. She managed to keep Will out of the loop, too—that was necessary; he was too volatile and protective to allow it—but not Missy. She needed her sister to know where she was; otherwise, she'd have nowhere for Caitlin to stay when she wasn't with her father in Mystic. By then the sisters' relationship had become tense. Although the trips to New York had upset Missy, there were limits to what she could tell her older sister to do and not do. She was too afraid of alienating Maureen to talk about it. Caitlin was old enough to overhear Maureen making her plans. When she was within earshot, Maureen called them "modeling trips." Around Jay, Maureen was less discreet. The work demanded something other than romance—something sharp-edged and practical. When she talked about the work with Jay—managing Craigslist postings, fielding phone calls, meeting strangers—he thought for the first time that his friend was more than whimsical and mystical and lighthearted. She was tough. Not that she would fight, but that she would never let anything get to her. To do what she did, and in New York, of all places, took a certain fearlessness.

There also were hidden costs—anxieties that Maureen couldn't tamp down. On July 5, 2004, the year she started traveling to New York, Maureen had another premonition, which she dutifully recorded on her MySpace page:

> Having serial killer dreams again . . . Love is hemorrhaging in my head, fading away with every beat. Maybe all it takes to keep alive is smoking it to death.

For Maureen, the money also promised freedom from Steve. But when she became pregnant with her second child, a boy named Aidan, she and Steve grew closer. Maureen had used condoms as an escort; there was never any doubt in her mind that Aidan was Steve's child. Steve wanted the baby, and part of Maureen did, too—another baby to care for, now that Caitlin was growing up and living mostly with her father.

The pregnancy brought the New York trips to a halt, and when Aidan was born, in 2005, Steve was a devoted father. Maureen went searching for work, never keeping a job for long. It took a year for the relationship to fall apart, and for Maureen to go off on her own with Aidan. By then, Steve was paying all the bills, and Maureen had next to nothing of her own. When the telemarketing job at Atlantic Security didn't pay enough, the massage appointments began.

Now, with Sara as her new protégée, Maureen was ready to go back to New York. The city presented the solution to everything all at once. The money would help Maureen support both Caitlin and Aidan, prevent her eviction and keep a roof over her head, and maybe even liberate her from Steve once and for all.

They hadn't even left for New York yet, and Maureen had become a different person—all business. "I'm gonna hook you up with Vips," she told Sara. He was her guy in New York, the one who could almost guarantee a successful and profitable trip to the city. While Craigslist was still free—the website wouldn't start charging five dollars per Adult Services listing until 2008—Vips, or Vipple, had a JavaScript program that would keep posting and reposting your ad so it stayed at the top of the list, never getting lost in the shuffle. Vips charged a flat fee of $150 a day for his services, and he spent a good chunk of his spare time trolling modeling websites to offer his services to girls thinking of getting into the game. That, Maureen said, was how she met Vips. From the start, she had built Vips's fee in to her overhead, along with a hotel room. Even with those expenses, Maureen told Sara that if she did anywhere from five to seven calls a day, she could walk away with one to two thousand dollars for every day she worked.

Sara called Vips from Groton. He had an Indian English accent. He told Sara he wanted to meet her. She and Maureen were talking about going down to the city that weekend anyway. They left the next day, taking the train instead of Sara's car. Maureen said Manhattan parking-garage fees would be an added expense—sixty dollars a day to park was money they could be spending on cabs for outcalls.

Maureen was seasoned enough to have developed some rules. She started sharing them with Sara on the Amtrak ride into the city. Rule number one was always follow your instincts: If it doesn't feel right, don't do it. Maureen said some of the johns were cool, but some of them were shitty. No amount of money can save your life. Rule number two was to view all outcalls suspiciously, but if she ever agreed to one, stay in Manhattan. Don't go to Queens. Don't go to Brooklyn, even if it's just over the bridge in Williamsburg. Staten Island, no. The Bronx, no. Only some parts of Manhattan were allowed. Unless it was a regular call, Morningside Heights was a no, as were Washington Heights, Harlem, and Alphabet City. Sara spent a lot of those first days with a city map in front of her.

The Maureen issuing all these directives was different from the carefree girl Sara had met six months earlier at the telemarketing company. This new sense of seriousness seemed to Sara like an unintended consequence of the escort life. Maureen would explain that, too: You got onto Craigslist to make more money than you could ever make at a real job, but sooner or later even that started to feel like a grind.

The first order of business in Manhattan was to meet Vips and see about getting Sara onto Craigslist. They left Penn Station and checked in to a hotel on West Thirty-seventh Street, a few blocks away. Maureen, who had posted on Craigslist already, told Sara she had a call. They walked a few blocks to the Marriott Marquis in Times Square and got in one of the glass elevators. Before the doors closed, in walked an Indian guy with a port-wine birthmark that covered a good part of his face. As the elevator glided upward, soaring over the hotel lobby, Maureen introduced Sara to Vips.

The view from up high in the Marriott elevator left Sara spellbound. When it came to a stop, Maureen got off but told Sara to head back down. "Just go with Vips," she said. "I'll call you when I get out."

The two went down and walked around Times Square while Maureen worked. Sara learned a little bit about Vips—that he was indeed from India, and while he wasn't technically a pimp, it was something to which he aspired.

With Sara, Vips kept things light. "Look, there's Samuel L. Jackson!" he said, pointing, and Sara, distracted by her first time walking past Madame Tussauds, just nodded. On their second time around the block, she realized he'd been pointing to a statue.

"Ha!" Vips said. "I got you!"

Sara laughed. "Can we go in there?"

"No," he said. "It's mad expensive."

Vips agreed to post Sara's ads for the usual fee. Later on, through Maureen, Sara met a few of Vips's associates. There was Tony, a producer of porn movies who worked out of the Film Center Building on Eighth Avenue, and there was Al, a big Italian guy who made noises about being connected but seemed to work mainly as an associate of Tony's—a "modeling agent" for adult films. Vips was the low man on the totem pole—an Internet troll, a wannabe pimp and porn producer—but he was the only one Maureen seemed to know well. Tony and Al were guys Maureen had been hoping to get to know better, guys who might help her stop doing this one day. She had told her friend Jay DuBrule that porn was legal and safer and easier than what she was doing; it resembled a legitimate entertainment career and was one step closer to the life she dreamed about.

Sara was heavier than Maureen, but she was a definite type—busty and sultry, like Anna Nicole Smith or Jessica Simpson. In need of a working alias, she chose Monroe, a nod to Marilyn. Vips had set up Sara's ad using someone else's picture. Sara was appalled when she saw it. The girl looked older, with the same blond hair, but fatter, with her leg propped up all the way in the air near her shoulder. Sara couldn't believe how little the picture looked like her, though later on she felt like that got her more tips—guys saying, "Oh, you're so much prettier in person!"

Next, Sara learned Maureen's rules for security. The person who comes with you—and someone always has to come with you (another important rule)—doesn't have to stay in the room during the call; too many guys check closets and bathrooms for lookouts. But the chaperone does have to stay on the block. If there's a restaurant across the street, the chaperone sits and takes a load off for an hour. The escort phones or texts when inside to say all's well. The calls were all business for Maureen. If a john paid for an hour and he finished in five minutes, Maureen was done, too.

As a trial run, Maureen set Sara up with a regular of hers named Patrick. He was Asian and young, about Sara's age, and he lived in a pretty apartment not far from the old Studio 54, which blew Sara's mind. His place was nice, but when he said he was paying a thousand or two a month for the one-bedroom, Sara's jaw dropped. "It's location that you pay for," Patrick told her. They spent the better part of the afternoon together. He'd brought coke, and now he had "coke dick," so he took a long time to perform. Sara got into it. She was fine with giving head under regular circumstances and didn't see any reason not to like it now.

Five and a half hours passed before Maureen burst in, furious. "We're leaving! Now!" Patrick gave them all the cash he had and wrote a check for the rest made out to cash. Maureen said that they normally couldn't take checks because johns could cancel them (another rule), but Patrick was a regular and a friend. On the way out, Maureen snapped at Sara, "I couldn't do all these calls, because *you* were too fucking busy."

The whole train ride home, Maureen was angry, and not just about Patrick. That weekend, nearly all the calls had been for

Sara—not for *Marie,* but for *Monroe.* Maureen was a little jealous but mostly indignant. She felt like she had absorbed a financial loss for introducing Sara to the profession. Toward the end of the ride, Maureen asked for a 20 percent commission of everything Sara had earned that weekend.

Sara flipped out. "Fuck that!"

"Well, I introduced you to Vips," Maureen said.

"You shouldn't have taught me how to post, then! I can break off from you right now, and you can't say shit to me! I'm not giving you shit!"

Maureen dropped it. But Sara, fully empowered, went back to New York the following weekend. She brought a friend with her, a guy named Matt, as a chaperone. Vips, noticing that Maureen wasn't with her, took the liberty of squeezing her for more money, raising his rate to $250. Sara decided to post her ads herself. To avoid Vips, she changed her Craigslist name from Monroe to Lacey. She switched hotels, too, to the Super 8 on Forty-sixth Street.

The following week, Friday, July 6, 2007, Maureen was back in town. All was forgiven. Sara and Maureen were friends again.

Keeping New York Plan B and not Plan A was another one of Maureen's rules. "You don't want to make it a full-time job," she said. Maureen had told Sara that she'd worked as an escort practically full-time before she got pregnant with Aidan. That was when she learned that you needed the break. Otherwise, the sex could make you jaded. Ninety percent of her clients were married. Some of them didn't take off their rings. The calls could feel like an assembly line to Maureen—like work. That was the worst. That was why Maureen's demeanor changed in New York. She was on guard.

But Sara was still infatuated. Everything about the work was fun for her—the sex, New York, and especially the money. While Maureen was gone, Sara made twelve hundred dollars over just a few days—more money than she had ever made in such a short time—and she held the bills in the air and told Matt, "See? Take a picture." Then she saw the look on his face, his eyes blazing, and Sara felt something shift—in him and in her—that she liked. "I'm never coming back to Connecticut!" she said.

By now, she knew almost as much as Maureen did. In her weeks at the Super 8, working independently of Maureen, she had seen a lot of ethnic men with heavy accents—straight off the boat, it seemed to her; Asians and Middle Eastern men—waving lots of money around. They came in seconds. Hiring an escort was less about sex, she thought, than the chance to show some power. She also saw three police officers, all of whom swore they were off-duty, and to whom Sara refused service as politely as she could. (That was yet another Maureen rule: Always ask if they're cops. They can't lie, because that would be entrapment.)

The problem was that the money never lasted. After weeks in the city doing calls, Sara had held on to practically none of what she'd made. It went to hotel bills, shoes, and clothes. It went to makeup from Sephora, including twenty-three dollars for what turned out to be, essentially, ChapStick. It went to Sara's new prized possession—a $160 fitted Yankees cap from Lids in Times Square, decorated with sterling silver and cubic zirconium.

When Sara and Matt went to meet Maureen at Penn Station, they saw that she had brought a chaperone: Brett, her roommate. While Brett was friends with Maureen's ex, Steve, he had a vested interest in Maureen making money. In just a few days, they were due to appear in eviction court—on Tuesday, July 10. Maureen knew if she couldn't pay their back rent and the eviction went through, Steve would make a play for custody of Aidan. That weekend Maureen had come to New York on a mission. She needed eleven hundred dollars or she would lose her home and her son.

Sara and Maureen tried posting together, without the assistance of Vips, on Matt's laptop—*two girls, snow buddies,* which meant they did coke. From the start, they ran into a problem. Almost as soon as they posted the ads, they were flagged as "offensive content" and pulled from the site. They tried it once more, and the same thing happened again and again. Someone had to be monitoring the Adult Services page and flagging the ads. Clearly, Vips was being vindictive.

All through Friday night, Maureen and Sara couldn't make a dime. They hung out in one of the hotel rooms and smoked a blunt and started talking about what Maureen might do if she did get kicked out of her apartment in Norwich. Maybe fate was telling her to stay in New York. With nothing better to do, they fantasized about a whole summer in the city as business partners, doing incalls and outcalls from their own apartment. Maureen surfed a different corner of Craigslist, responding to an ad for a sublet on the Upper West Side. The rate was $749 a week, a bargain compared to the Super 8. Maureen smiled dreamily just talking about it. Sara felt she saw her friend coming back—the real, warm Maureen shining through.

Vips must have grown bored flagging the ads. They got a few calls the next day, so they didn't really see each other. They worked Sunday, too. But later that day, their ads were getting booted again. They'd made just $700. Maureen was $400 short. There was nothing left to do but have some fun. They decided they needed new pictures for their ads. Sara needed a fresh look to go with her new name, and Maureen hadn't changed her photo in three years. The occasion called for a full makeover. Sara got her nails done and her eyebrows waxed. She went back to Sephora and spent two hundred dollars in an hour, buying all kinds of colors that would look good with her eyes, plus glitter. Sara also sprang for outfits. Maureen came with her to Macy's, on Thirty-fourth Street, and all Sara could think as they walked in and went up the narrow wooden escalators was *Oh my God, I'm in Mecca.* When she saw the women's shoe department, Sara practically collapsed.

For decent photography, Maureen called a friend she'd made in the city, a graffiti artist of some renown. When they arrived at his place, Maureen and Sara told him they wanted him to do their makeup, too. Maureen had her face done up as an old Hollywood glamour queen, and Sara had hers done all crazy, with green, blue, and purple eye shadow and some sparkles. Their hair was done to match, sprayed in place to fend off the smallest imperfections. He took Sara's photos first, then Maureen's. They hung out there for a while and then walked back to their hotel through Times Square, the city lit up on a hot summer night. They had on jeans and T-shirts, but from the neck up, they were impossible to ignore. Random guys in the street were hitting on them both. Sara's original makeup design got a lot of attention. "Is that a tattoo on your face?" someone asked. Sara snorted. "No, it's not a tattoo—it *sparkles*."

The longer they stayed out on Broadway, the more exhilarated they felt. Sara imagined they were supermodels, or princesses, or goddesses. She felt like nothing and no one could touch them. Maureen seemed happy, too—lighter, for once. Of all the moments Sara shared with Maureen, this was the one she would revisit the most—spending all night walking through Times

Square, the center of attention, not a care in the world, the rest of the summer laid out just for them. For years afterward, she wouldn't remember a happier time in her life.

Back at the hotel, they saw that they weren't the only call girls staying there. Standing outside smoking a cigarette, they met a guy with dreads. "Are you guys working?" he asked. "Where's your pimp?"

Sara sneered. "We don't *have* one," she said. "We aren't owned. We're each other's."

Midtown Manhattan. July 9, 2007.

Monday morning arrived sooner than they'd hoped. The plan had been for them to go back to Connecticut—Sara to see a friend, Maureen to face the music in eviction court. But they were still thinking of changing the plan and staying another day. It was only Monday; an extra night would give Maureen more time to make the money she needed. Maybe she could wire it to Brett in time for court on Tuesday. She had heard back about the Upper West Side sublet and had made an appointment to see it the next day, assuming they were in town.

Sara went up to the sixth floor to tell their chaperones to head back without them. Brett couldn't believe it, and neither could Matt. As the three of them argued, Matt was especially persuasive—he simply didn't want to leave them alone. It wasn't safe. Sara saw the look of concern on his face and went back down to the fourth floor.

Maureen was lying in bed, the TV on, the curtains drawn. They both had been up all night, and Maureen was finally crashing. She looked up at Sara. "Where's your stuff?"

"Matt doesn't want us to stay," Sara said. "I'm going back. You need to come back, too."

Maureen shook her head. "I'll just stay here in the hotel room."

Their roles had reversed. Sara was the responsible one now. She'd feel guilty about going back alone.

"Please stay," Maureen said. "Please."

Sara went back up to Matt's room on the sixth floor. "I'm gonna stay. We're just gonna stay in the hotel room."

Matt flipped out. He wanted Sara to come with him, with or without Maureen. Sara pushed back. "I'm not your *girl*," she said.

Matt softened. "Yes, I know," he said. "You're my friend. And as a friend, I'm telling you I do not like that idea."

Sara thought of Maureen's first little rule: Always follow your instincts. If it doesn't feel right, don't do it. She went back to Maureen. "Look, man, I'm not trying to have this argument. Get your shit, and let's go."

Maureen didn't move. "No," she said, "I'm just gonna stay here. I'll wait for you." She looked at Sara and tilted her head. "You *are* coming back on Wednesday, *right*?"

Sara said yes.

Maureen smiled and stretched out. "I'll keep the room for us."

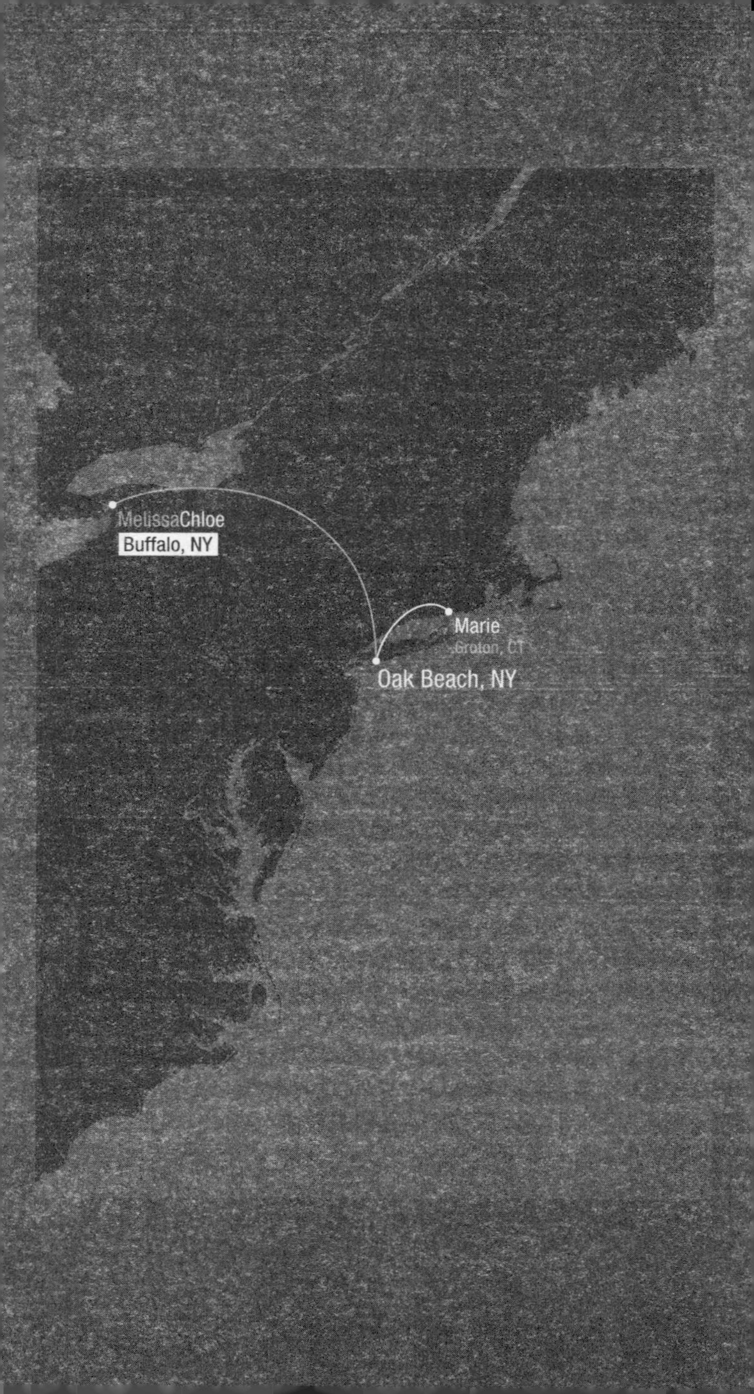
MelissaChloe
Buffalo, NY
Marie
Groton, CT
Oak Beach, NY

CHLOE

The girls grab at the arms or shoulders first. It's best to start by touching them. They've spent all night at a strip club, where the women can't go too far.

Hey, sweetie, what's your name? Where are you from?

They answer: *Oh, I'm just visiting : . . This is my vacation . . . I just came here on business.* They're almost always from out of town.

Really? Yeah? Would you like a nice massage—a nice back massage? Hot towels? Lotion?

Sometimes they're interested. Sometimes they're disgusted. Sometimes they smile. Some guys play along smugly: "Oh, but why do I have to *pay* when I can give you the best night of your life?" Melissa and Kritzia would look at them and be like, *Oh, please, fuck you.*

But some guys get excited. That's when you say you'll give them a blow job. Then you touch them again. Then you make the deal.

Kritzia Lugo was small and round, with lush lips and big eyes and a gift for gab. In Times Square, she was known as Mariah, a salute to her idol, Mariah Carey. Melissa Barthelemy was known as Chloe. Friday and Saturday nights were slow, too many families clogging up the sidewalks. But almost every other night, Melissa and Kritzia would hang outside Lace, the strip club on Seventh Avenue north of Forty-eighth Street—Melissa with a cigarette and Kritzia with some weed; their pimps, Blaze and Mel, standing a safe distance away, across the street or around the corner—waiting for men to come out.

Their workday began long after the Broadway theaters went dark, just as the few strip clubs left in Times Square were getting ready to close. In the new New York—after mayors Rudy Giuliani and Michael Bloomberg helped make over the porn palaces into a family-friendly tourist hub, as safe and secure, almost, as a theme park—the escorts and their pimps have to be discreet. The girls dress a little more modestly. They're a little quieter. They walk longer lengths up and down the block so that, technically, they can't be accused of loitering. The pimps are still there, but at a remove, able to watch the girls work and to bolt if need be.

Times Square at three A.M. is a complicated place: volatile and dangerous but also, in its way, like any other workplace, with protocols and procedures, a social hierarchy, and intra-staff dramas. The McDonald's on Broadway, south of Forty-seventh, was like the company commissary. Melissa knew that many of the drunkest guys stumbling out of the strip clubs ended up there. Even some of the homeless guys were part of the social hierarchy, rounding up guys and bringing them to the girls in exchange for a finder's fee. Melissa and Kritzia would throw them a big tip so they would come back. Around the corner, on Forty-seventh between Sixth and Seventh, was the break room: a tiny open-air public plaza with a few metal tables and chairs and some slate decor. The girls called it the Batcave. One time Melissa braided Kritzia's hair while they sat there talking, helping her tighten her extensions and curl them at the bottom with a curling iron. She often boasted about her beauty-school training, like a physician boasting about medical school, and then she'd laugh and threaten to cover Kritzia's head with bald spots, chasing her around the Batcave with the curling iron.

When she first saw Melissa in Times Square sometime in 2006, Kritzia didn't talk to her. This skinny white girl, always laughing at something. *What's so funny to you?* Kritzia thought. But when Kritzia stared her down, Melissa gave as well as she got. That broke the spell, and they became close friends, sharing the same irreverence and attitude. Then Kritzia saw the risks Melissa took—she'd go with anyone who would rent a room—and she thought that Melissa wasn't built to last, not even a year.

Melissa proved her wrong. She was in New York for three years, until 2009. When Kritzia heard about her family in Buffalo, ready and waiting to take her home, she would wonder why she was here at all. Melissa would say only, "I'm here because I want to be here." In those moments, Kritzia thought maybe she and Melissa weren't such kindred spirits. She figured Melissa had been this wild since she was a little girl, and when she got that taste of something else, she wanted more.

Where you worked in Manhattan depended on how you looked. The fast-track girls—the ones on Ninth Avenue or the West Side Highway, waiting for guys to pull over—were usually the hard-luck cases, strung out and ragged. The girls who ran around Times Square were average, like Melissa and Kritzia. Prettier ones—tall, skinny girls—had better luck on the East Side. Within each of those worlds, there was a pecking order: The girls with pimps hated the girls who worked for escort services; the girls who worked for escort services couldn't stand the girls who worked solo on Craigslist. If you had a pimp, your money wasn't your own, but you had protection. If you were with a service, you were often working harder than a lot of hos who had pimps, and you were making a lot less. Strippers were at the bottom, mere geishas, catering to the vanity of any man who walked through the door, and the men are not permitted to touch. The street-walkers like Melissa and Kritzia played such games for only the briefest of moments, as long as it took to get a client to say yes.

They had sex as soon as they could and as fast as they could, and they moved on. It always annoyed them that the strippers had the more dishonest job—they were the biggest teases—and yet were the ones on the right side of the law.

From Kritzia and some of the others, Melissa had learned the parameters of the stroll. You couldn't look at other pimps. You couldn't talk to other pimps. When there was a pimp on the side-walk, you had to walk in the street; if you stayed on the sidewalk, they could touch you. If they touched you, that meant you were out of pocket, and if you were out of pocket, the code dictated that they could take your money.

You weren't supposed to talk with other pimps' girls, which was obviously a rule they broke every day. It was insubordination, pure and simple, but Melissa had nerve. She had swag. The big entertainment of the evening sometimes was waiting to see what nasty things came out of that little white girl's mouth. She would make fun of strippers: *Dance, dance, dance, dance all night long, for next to no money; who would waste their time like that?* She would even make fun of her pimp. Like the time she said, "I don't give Blaze all my money, I keep my money," and pulled out her credit card to show them all. Blaze thought he controlled Melissa, but for as long as she could remember, Melissa answered to no one but herself.

When Melissa would come home to Buffalo for a visit—not of-ten, but never less than once a year—she and her mother, Lynn, Lynn's boyfriend, Jeff, and her aunt Dawn would all go out to a club or a corner bar where they could talk and drink. When the bar closed, they'd come back to Jeff's parents' house, where Me-lissa would sit up on the kitchen counter and keep talking. There was none of the old friction. Melissa was a grown woman, mak-ing her own decisions.

They would laugh about old times, and whenever her current situation came up, Melissa would be guarded about how things were in the city. Jeff thought that she wasn't making as much money as she wanted to—not enough to afford to start a business, not nearly. That didn't stop her from coming back with gifts: She sent Amanda five hundred dollars to shop for new clothes for school when all she needed was a hundred. Several months after moving, Melissa told Lynn and Jeff that the hair salon had closed. Now, she said, she was dancing in a nightclub. They struggled with how to react. No one they knew in Buffalo had ever done anything like that.

"Is it stripping?" Jeff asked.

Melissa was nonchalant. "Oh, yeah, we just take our tops off. There's no touching."

Lynn wasn't sure what to say. "You know, I'm not around the corner. It would take me eight hours to get to you."

Melissa reassured them that she never worked alone, and Lynn knew Melissa all too well to force the issue.

Melissa didn't talk much about men. She did say that her old childhood boyfriend, Jordan, was history—that she'd left him soon after arriving in New York, for Johnny Terry, the guy who had lined up the hairstylist job for her before she moved. On the phone with her mother, Melissa would laugh and say, "Oh, Johnny and Jordan, they can't stand each other."

The summer after Melissa moved, Amanda asked to visit her in New York. Despite everything that Melissa had told them, Lynn was all right with it. Amanda was so different from the teenager Melissa had been—docile, even-keeled. Rather than worry that Melissa would be a bad influence, Lynn hoped that Amanda would keep Melissa in their orbit and maybe even persuade her to come home.

Amanda visited for the first time in the summer of 2007. She saw where Melissa was living. The basement apartment in the Bronx wasn't exactly legal; there was no real division between Melissa's room and the upstairs level, where a quiet family lived. Amanda couldn't believe the number of Melissa's cats, too many to keep them straight. Melissa, it appeared, had grown a formidable soft spot for strays.

Amanda also met Johnny, though she quickly learned that no one called him that. Everyone called him Blaze.

Kritzia thought Melissa was lucky, in a way, to have fallen in with Blaze, because even if he wasn't enough of a fighter to protect her, everyone knew Blaze was close to Mel, Kritzia's pimp, and no one would ever make Mel angry. Kritzia and Melissa soon learned they could mess with practically anyone and not worry about reprisals. When rival girls went after them, their men would stop them, telling them there was nothing to be done. Thanks to Mel, they were bulletproof.

Mel and Blaze called each other brothers and operated like business partners. Mel was the muscle, solidly built, with a reputation throughout Times Square as not just a pimp but a drug dealer. After going through a few bad pimps, Kritzia had chosen Mel. She was as infatuated with Mel as any girl could be with a pimp, but it wasn't quite like that with Melissa and Blaze. Blaze was flashier and funnier, as well as less menacing. His whole persona—the flyboy, the pretty boy, the player—made him come off as a phony, trying too hard. There were rules for pimps, too, and Blaze ignored a lot of them. Pimps can't have sex for pleasure. The only girls you can sleep with are the girls who are paying you. But Blaze would go to a club and pick up girls—square girls, not working girls. Blaze might have thought he could do that because he never considered himself a real pimp—he was, he thought, above that kind of work.

Blaze and Mel shared a house on Watson Avenue in the Bronx. Kritzia and Mel had the master bedroom. Blaze had a smaller bedroom that he kept to himself. Melissa begged Blaze to let her live there, too, but he said they didn't have space. The real reason was clear, at least to Kritzia: Another girl, Em, was Blaze's bottom bitch—the girl with the most seniority. At times the situation got the better of Melissa. She'd lose her temper and scream at Blaze: "I'm tired of you using me up to take care of your *wife*." Em knew how to protect her position. She would sob and wail and accuse Blaze of not loving her. The situation never changed.

When talking with Melissa about the life, Kritzia often overflowed with conflicting emotions—sentimentality and self-pity, remorse and fury, repulsion and attraction. "Let me tell you, Manhattan is disgusting," she would say. "All these frickin' rich people with all this money who just want to blow it on coke and hookers. And then a whole bunch of homeless people, sleeping on all the corners, cold, hungry, smelling like urine. And then a whole bunch of prostitutes, trying to make cash. And then we all get to know each other." Melissa didn't see it like that at first. Everything about her had a conspiratorial quality: the smirks, the insolence, and the teasing, punctuated by her saying, "Right?" and laughing. When Melissa came to hang out at the house on Watson Avenue, she and Kritzia would spend the whole time in a bedroom, sealed away from Em and everyone else.

With Mel's muscle backing up their every move, Melissa and Kritzia were emboldened. All the other girls were too scared to speak up and do whatever it was they wanted to do. Kritzia and Melissa, they just did it. They would walk on a sidewalk occupied by pimps. When they saw the other pimps' girls with a trick, they would go up to him and try to steal the trick. "Honey, don't do black, do white," Melissa would coo. "You know it's the only way to go." They got tattoos together. Melissa's said *Blaze,* Kritzia's said *Mel.* Melissa had wanted Kritzia to choose the same spot she did, on her back, but Kritzia wanted hers on the back of her neck, where nobody would see it but Mel.

They worked together a lot. Guys liked the duo. Once a guy told Kritzia, "You're pretty, but I need something more." When he saw Melissa, he was like, "Oh, you two are perfect. Skinny and titties, titties and skinny! Ooh!" Kritzia shook her head at how stupid that sounded. For one john, they took a bath at the Marriott Residence Inn, earning four hundred dollars each. They met a guy who wanted human waste on him. Kritzia couldn't do it, but Melissa did. She wanted the extra money. He wasn't even masturbating while it happened. He just lay in the tub in his room at the Intercontinental Hotel.

They saw how worn out some of the other girls were—their eyes sunken, their faces saggy. "Wrinkled!" they would shriek. "How can you be wrinkled at twenty?" To ensure their own future viability, Melissa and Kritzia came up with a few methods of screening johns for safety. A guy with a briefcase probably just came from work, had a life, and was less likely to be trouble. A guy staying somewhere nice—at the Waldorf, the Sheraton, the Parker Meridien, the Westin, the W—wasn't likely to be in the mood for any drama, only a good time. And older men were always preferable to the young ones. Kritzia made that rule after one too many young guys tried to attack her, alone in a room. In hindsight, she realized how suspicious she should have been: Why would a young guy pay when he could get his mack on for free? A guy like that had to be messed up.

The guys who annoyed them the most were the young

white guys. They were stingy—they wanted to pay fifty for everything—and then they wanted to boast about it before, during, and after: "I don't have to do this, I'm doing it to help you out." Melissa and Kritzia would have to keep from scratching out their eyes. *You want to help me out, give me a little money and get lost! That's how you help me out.*

On the other end of the spectrum were the johns who bought them dinner, took them to the movies. One guy took Kritzia shopping for a dress and shoes and asked her to model them for him. They went back to his place on Eighty-sixth Street, and he took pictures and gave her three hundred dollars and said goodbye. Another guy played dominoes with her. Still another filled her iPod with music—Christina Aguilera, Britney Spears, whatever she wanted. Another guy, he just wanted company. When he fell asleep, she left.

Countless johns wanted to do coke, which was always welcome. Most of the time, after a line or two, their little friend wouldn't cooperate, so they'd be there for hours, racking up a sizable bill while waiting to get hard. Kritzia would wonder about these men—with too much time and too much money, men who just killed time with a hooker. Guys like that would want the girls to do coke, too. They knew ways to fake it—instead of sniffing it with the rolled-up bill, they'd lean down to block the john's view and pretend, sniffing nothing and sweeping the coke on the floor in one swift motion. The art of the swindle extended to sex. Sometimes a guy was too drunk or high to notice that he was having sex with the girl's hand. If someone complained, all she would have to say was "No, honey, we have to hold the condom in place."

At times it seemed almost like a game—how quickly they could turn around a call, how much money they could take. They ran scams together, running to the bank to pull money off of debit cards lifted from their johns. Some guys would foolishly send them to an ATM to get the cash to pay them, naively giving them cards and PINs. Why should they take out only a hundred dollars? They took everything the guy had and threw the card in the garbage.

They got busted together. Once, they were at the Hilton and stole a hundred dollars from a guy who ran after them in his underpants even though it was almost snowing outside, the little crystals that drift down right before it snows for real. The guy caught Kritzia, but Melissa kept running. Then Kritzia broke free, caught up to Melissa, and grabbed her by the hair as payback for having left her behind. Melissa fell and lost one of her heels, then started running off balance. That was when the police grabbed them both, and the john, too.

While Kritzia spent a fair amount of time in jail, Melissa seemed to get bothered by the police less. She had just one recorded arrest, on September 12, 2008, at Sixth Avenue and Forty-sixth Street. The following April, she pleaded guilty to attempted prostitution, a misdemeanor, and was sentenced to five days of community service. Melissa once told Kritzia that a cop tried to get a blow job before he let her go. Kritzia believed her; it had happened to her, too.

Kritzia really liked weed, but Melissa couldn't tolerate it. Two pulls and she'd run around thinking she could fly, and she'd still be high the next morning. Instead, Melissa would drink a lot. It wasn't that she drank for fun—she drank to be okay, to mellow out. They'd go to a deli in the fashion district, just south of Times Square, whenever Kritzia got the munchies; Melissa would order only a cup with ice. Then she'd pull a beer out of her purse and pour it into the cup. Kritzia never met a white girl who did anything like that. She told Melissa not to do it while she worked, but she would go on a date, and a guy would offer her a drink, and she'd take it. "You don't know who opened this bottle!" Kritzia said. But Melissa seemed to trust everybody, as if nobody would ever harm her. When Kritzia tried to call her on it, Melissa would say, "So what?"

Melissa had advice for Kritzia, too; usually about her hair. One night they got into Blaze's car together, and Melissa smiled. "Mariah, it's time for you to start cutting your hair—your ends are getting all burned."

Kritzia snorted. "What do you know about ends being burned?"

"Girl, I went to school for hair! Come over sometime. I'm gonna fix you up."

"Uh-uh."

"Come on, Mariah! Let me, let me!"

"No, I'm good."

"A long time ago, I dyed my hair red," said Melissa. She reached in her purse and pulled out a picture of her with her hair dyed red, in a ponytail. The picture had the posed quality of a school photo, Melissa facing forward, smiling like she was ready to show up for cheerleading practice. Kritzia would remember that picture later.

Melissa kept talking about Buffalo with Kritzia, if for no other reason than to mention her little sister, Amanda. When Kritzia told her she also had a sister, Melissa said, "We should all go hang out one day!"

Kritzia gave her a look. "Can you imagine, them and us?"

Melissa didn't skip a beat. "Yeah, we should just take them shopping, and they won't ask us any questions!"

Holy shit, Kritzia thought.

Lynn met Blaze only once over the years, a short hello in an Atlantic City casino. Lynn and Jeff had gone there on a trip with friends, and Melissa persuaded Blaze to drive her there to meet them. They stayed for a few hours, long enough to talk and play the slots. Lynn didn't like the way Johnny, as she knew him, was dressed, a giant baggy T-shirt and jeans tenuously attached to his waist. This was Jordan all over again. Melissa troubled her, too. She was wearing a cream-colored dress and spike heels. Lynn thought she looked sleazy. When she said as much, Melissa sat up a little straighter. "I look beautiful," she said.

Blaze snorted when he heard that. "*I* look better than you do," he said.

Amanda didn't like Blaze, either. She thought he was a pretty boy—vain and petulant. Every conversation had to be about him. Amanda's first visit to the Bronx was low-key but fun. Afternoons were for the sisters—shopping, the Bronx Zoo, the Statue of Liberty. The nights were Melissa's alone. She would throw on a dress, and a car would be waiting, and she would leave Amanda at the apartment by herself, telling her not to leave, calling to check in before Amanda went to sleep. Mornings, Amanda would hang out on the stoop, waiting for Melissa to wake up from her night out.

A year later, in the spring of 2008, Amanda visited Melissa again. This time things seemed much bleaker for Melissa. She had broken up with Blaze and didn't talk about him much anymore. Maybe it was that the surroundings weren't so new this time; in any case, Amanda saw through to the bare facts of what her sister was doing to herself. She understood that there might never have been a hair salon, at least not one run by Blaze. She saw Melissa on the computer, a laptop she'd bought secondhand, posting ads on Craigslist, and she saw the cars that picked her up—livery cabs, mostly. She saw it all.

But Amanda was nine years younger than her sister. She didn't know how to talk about something like this. Amanda and Melissa never discussed where she went in the black cars. And when she returned home, Amanda didn't tell a soul what she had discovered.

One day in Times Square, Melissa said to Kritzia, "Mariah, why don't you come with me?"

Kritzia squinted. "Go with you? Go with you where?"

"Go with me—we're just gonna go."

"Where?"

"Let's go to Buffalo."

"*Hell,* no!"

Melissa seemed so sad. Kritzia knew she had been fighting with Blaze. And she had mentioned that her mom was putting pressure on her to come home. The street was getting harder for her. Melissa didn't like walking all night. She told Kritzia, "This is not for me. I just can't be here." To Kritzia, that was the worst paradox of the life. You had to be strong enough to work hard and long in order to convince so many men to part with their money, but weak enough to be there in the first place.

Kritzia started to see Melissa doing calls without Blaze around. Melissa said, "*Shhh!* Don't tell."

"Bitch, what are you doing?"

Melissa waved her off. "Oh, Mariah, nobody can do nothing to me."

Melissa had more than enough reasons to leave Blaze. She lived on her own and, most of the time, paid her own rent. The two of them were touch and go, a pattern of breakup and reconciliation. Toward the end, Melissa wasn't giving Blaze anything close to all her money. Why should she, she thought, when she didn't have a reliable pimp like Mel to protect her? Thanks to Blaze, Melissa had slammed right into the system's great fallacy: Why should she sacrifice herself to a pimp who spent all her money when he didn't even look after her?

By 2008, Melissa had switched almost entirely to Craigslist. She wasn't the only one. Kritzia had another friend, Fabulous, who did it, too. In the few years since the website had caught on, Craigslist had done more to delegitimize the age-old system of pimps and escorts than a platoon of police officers could. Why sign on with a pimp when it was so easy to take a picture and let a guy call you—way easier than walking the streets and looking for a guy and then trying to convince him and then waiting forever at the ATM while he tried to sober up enough to remember his PIN? With Craigslist, johns came to you, and you didn't have to share the money with anybody.

Melissa asked Kritzia to join her. Kritzia refused. She was scared. The streets weren't easy, but you could see a guy first. You couldn't get to know him well, but at least you could make a snap judgment, look in his eyes, check out his clothes, see his cash, and assess his body language. As far as Kritzia was concerned, with Craigslist, you were completely in the dark. Every time you met a client was another roll of the dice, with only a few seconds on the phone to suggest if the person was for real—not a cop, not a crook, not a psycho.

As Chloe, Melissa advertised outcalls only: She'd only go out to a john's place. She charged $100 for fifteen minutes, $150 for a half hour, $250 for an hour, and $1,000 for overnight. She was openly breaking her arrangement with Blaze. She made enough money to come home to Buffalo at Christmastime and take Amanda and Lynn to a spa for massages. "You deserve to be pampered," she said. On Christmas morning, Amanda and all the cousins each unwrapped an iPod Touch.

There were consequences. A few weeks after she returned, Melissa got jumped by a group of women with one man nearby. Police later said she had her cell phone and that a witness picked it up off the ground and tried to give it back, but Melissa was curled up in a ball and wouldn't take it. The witness heard the man say something like "This is what you get for disrespecting me." He later identified that man as John Terry—Blaze—from a photo the police showed him.

On the last night of the Christmas visit, Jeff and Lynn got Melissa so drunk that she got down on the floor and started playing with Emily, his dog, barking at the top of her lungs. They'd been out at Neighbor's pub on Cleveland Drive, just down the street from Jeff's parents' place in Cheektowaga, and Melissa had been putting away 7 and 7's. When they came back, she had some beers. Now it was two A.M. Jeff tried to shush her, but she wouldn't stop: "Come here, Emily! *Woof! Woof! Woof!*"

Jeff's parents were asleep down the hall, but they were both going deaf, so it didn't really matter. Still, he was reminded of what a lightweight she was, so tiny that three drinks would put her over. She pounded them down, anyway.

That night at Neighbor's, Jeff had tried, as usual, to introduce the idea of Melissa coming back to Buffalo. There seemed to be a little more urgency, in Jeff's view: Melissa wasn't acting like herself. Something was bothering her. She just was not happy. After the barking fit ended, she lay down on the couch, resting her head against Jeff, and he tried again.

"Come home," he said. His sister-in-law ran a cosmetology school. He could get her a job there.

"Not yet," Melissa said. "I'm almost ready, though."

The Bronx. July 12, 2009.

On July 11, Melissa sent a late-night text message to Amanda to firm things up for another visit to New York. The next day, the security camera of her local bank recorded Melissa depositing a thousand dollars into her account—the proceeds, it is believed, from a date she'd had earlier that night. She withdrew a hundred dollars before heading out the door.

Melissa was seen alive that afternoon, July 12, sitting on the curb outside her building on Underhill Avenue in the Bronx. Her phone records show a call to Blaze that evening, under a minute long. It might have gone to voice mail. Blaze would later say that he knew Melissa had lined up another thousand-dollar date the next night, somewhere on Long Island. He even said he knew the place and knew of the john. But he said that Melissa was working on her own; he'd offered her a ride that she'd declined.

The next day, when Melissa stopped returning all calls and texts, Lynn and Jeff called off Amanda's trip and began calling local hospitals. Melissa's landlady got worried, too, when she heard the cats crying and scratching at the door. Lynn and Jeff tried to file a missing-persons report. But for three days, the police deflected them. They said Melissa was twenty-four years old with no history of mental illness and no psychiatric prescriptions; just because her family couldn't find her, they said, didn't necessarily mean she was missing. If Lynn wondered whether police weren't interested in searching because Melissa was an escort, she didn't have to wonder for long. The Buffalo police said as much to the family's attorney, Steven Cohen. She's a hooker, they told him. They weren't going to assign a detective to something like this.

Only ten days later would the police start a missing-persons investigation. Only then would they subpoena Melissa's phone records, canvass the neighborhood, and pull a DNA sample from her toothbrush. That was when they learned that her phone records showed access to her voice mail on the night of her disappearance, and that the calls were traced to a cell tower in Massapequa, Long Island. Only after that—nearly two weeks after she went missing—would the police visit two nearby motels, Budget Inn and Best Western, to speak to the staff and review security tapes, and find nothing.

The police might not have been stirred into action at all if, on the fourth day of Melissa's disappearance—July 16—Amanda's cell hadn't rung in Buffalo. When she saw her sister's number on the caller ID, Amanda rejoiced. "Melissa?"

Instead of her sister's voice, she heard another: controlled, comfortable, soft-spoken. Male.

"Oh, this isn't Melissa."

Chloe
Buffalo, NY

ShannanAngelina
Ellenville, NY

Marie
Groton, CT

Oak Beach, NY

ANGELINA

Alex had been driving for World Class Party Girls every day for months, and every day he'd meet someone new. Most of the girls, he forgot right away. But he remembered Shannan.

She stood out—the full lips, the wide eyes, the dark skin, the smile. She introduced herself as Sabrina. Later, she'd be Madison, and then Angelina. He was picking up Shannan and another girl outside the Journal Square PATH station. He assumed they were both coming in off the commuter line connecting Jersey City to Manhattan. In Alex's Cadillac, the other girl was quiet and forgettable, at least to him. Shannan chatted nonstop, at home with herself and what she was doing. She said she was working as a receptionist, and she picked up the newspaper one day and saw an ad for the agency, and she wanted to give it a try. She called them, and they called her back and said come on in. She was hired on the spot.

Alex could see why. The other girls looked hot, but once they spoke, he understood why they were in this line of work; he could see it in their blank stares, or the way some of them would grind their jaws. Shannan was not only pretty but well spoken, intelligent, charming. As he drove Shannan to her appointments that day, he struggled to understand why she was doing this at all.

Alex Diaz was born and raised in Jersey City, in a two-bedroom apartment not far from Journal Square. His father worked downtown in maintenance jobs. His mother was a housewife. An only child, Alex went to Dickinson, the enormous high school on a hill that drivers pass along the elevated highway connecting the New Jersey Turnpike to the Holland Tunnel. Alex didn't graduate. He was arrested at sixteen for fighting—aggravated assault—and then at seventeen for taking part in an armed robbery. He and his friends wore masks and held up the bodegas on Kennedy Boulevard. Getting a gun wasn't difficult in his part of Jersey City—there were a few older guys who sold them, $300 or $400 for a .22 or a .45. Alex hid his in his bedroom closet at his parents' place. One night he and his friends stole about five hundred dollars—a lot, for them—and ran right into the police.

Alex went away to a juvenile facility in Secaucus, then the New Jersey Training School for Boys in Jamesburg. He served two and a half years, most of it housed boot camp–style, in barracks with fifty other juvenile convicts. A few were friends he knew from the streets. His parents visited. They were upset, especially his mother. "When you come home," she said, "try to do a better job. Try to fix up your life." When he got out, Alex was almost twenty years old. He finished high school at night and enrolled in community college for a year and a half, then lost interest. He never had a major. He felt like he was wasting time.

He thought about studying criminal justice, but his previous gun charge meant he couldn't ever become a police officer. The next best thing was private security. He guarded factories and water facilities and the parking lot of the Prudential Center in Newark. He was making about twelve dollars an hour. All his friends from childhood had gone their own way, gotten older; some had kids. Alex had just one old friend, one of his partners in the bodega robbery. He was the one who told Alex about World Class Party Girls.

The agency was run by an entrepreneur named Joseph Ruis,

whom Alex knew as the owner of a kebab house he frequented in Journal Square. Alex had no idea that Ruis was also running an escort service with dozens of girls and almost as many drivers. But Alex's friend did, and through him, Alex learned quickly how it worked to be a driver. Simply put, the more girls he drove, the more money he'd make. But it was never that simple. Not every girl charged the same rate, and how much Alex made depended on how much each of them took home. To keep things straight, the agency gave all the drivers and girls a chart—a little like a tip calculator—with all the different possible hourly pay rates, broken down into separate shares for the agency, the driver, and the girls. The driver would always get the least, about a quarter, and the agency and the girl would get pretty much equal shares of the rest.

Drivers usually supplied their own cars. The service had a dispatcher in the main office who called Alex on his cell. At first the dispatcher wouldn't send Alex on the expensive calls. Even at the bottom of the pay scale, the hourly rate for a girl was never lower than $200. Of that, Alex would get $45 or $50, ending the night with $300 or $400. If he worked three or four nights a week, that would bring him $1,000: not bad for a twenty-one-year-old with no college degree.

The more expensive the call, the larger the driver's take—$400 an hour would earn him as much as $120 for that one hour. He'd go all over Manhattan, Rutherford, the Meadowlands, and North Jersey. The farthest south he'd go was central Jersey, like Middlesex County. Most of the calls came from the suburbs and Westchester County. In the city, he'd bring girls to the Marriott in Times Square as well as more expensive places, like the Carlyle on the Upper East Side. The rates were far higher than anything a girl on the street would charge, and the clientele was different, too: travelers with lots of money, willing to pay for the convenience of a girl arriving at their door. There was built-in pressure for all of these dates. The guys ordered an hour and often wanted to make the most of it, but the girls wanted to finish as fast as they could and get out. What the guys didn't know was that the escort service had an unspoken rule: During an hour's call, after forty-five minutes, they were supposed to be on to the next call.

Some of the girls, including Shannan, would bring coke to help extend calls past an hour or two. When they didn't have coke, the agency would be there to help. "You want some party material?" the dispatcher would ask the john. He would say, "Yeah," and the agency would send it over with Alex, charging it to the john's credit card. Sometimes Alex would buy the coke himself. He'd lived in Jersey City his whole life. He knew the right people.

The money was great, but the stress was terrible. Alex would work until four or five in the morning, and then he'd turn around and start his regular job at seven. For a while he told his parents that he was going out, and then he said he had a second job driving go-go girls to parties. Keeping the secret only added to the pressure. He started losing sleep, worried that the girls had drugs on them and the police would find drugs in his car, worried that the police would look at the girls in the back and decide that he was a pimp. Sure enough, two months into the job, he got pulled over along Route 3 in Little Falls, New Jersey, with a girl in the back. Alex tried giving the cop the runaround: "She's my friend." He got lucky.

That was too close a call. Alex walked away from the job for four years. He went back to being a security guard, making $13.50 an hour. He had a girlfriend, a normal girl with a normal job and a normal life. Then his expenses piled up. He was financing a new Cadillac CTS. After he paid off all his other bills, he never had any money for himself, for fun. The old friend who had first connected him with Joseph Ruis told him that World Class Party Girls had grown. It was big now—celebrities, lawyers, doctors. The minimum call was now $400 or $500. That got Alex's attention.

His first night back, he made almost $1,000. He didn't tell his girlfriend.

During his first tour of duty, Alex had never felt in control. But he was older now, more self-assured, not a kid anymore. He kept his security job until they fired him for dozing off. It hardly mattered. He went on unemployment, collecting a check from the government while getting paid handsomely by the escort service.

When his girlfriend asked why he was gone all night, she didn't take the answer well. Alex was a little surprised. In his mind, she should have respected him, maybe been proud of him for taking charge and making money. She didn't see things that way. "You might do something with one of them," she shrieked, "and get me a disease!"

Alex gave her some money to calm down. They stayed together. He told her it wasn't about the girls, and he meant it. Then he got to know Shannan.

About two months after their first meeting, Alex was assigned to drive Shannan again. He remembered her. He wanted to talk to her more this time. He was happy when she sat up front in the Cadillac, leaving another girl alone in the back.

She talked, and he listened. She was living upstate, taking a bus to Manhattan from Rockland County and the PATH out to New Jersey to work for the agency. Alex guessed she did that to be as far away from home as possible. Maybe she didn't want her boyfriend or family knowing. She told Alex that she had finished high school early, skipping a grade. She brought a thick textbook in the car, and he marveled at how fast she was reading it. She told him she liked writing, too. That was something Alex hated. But Shannan wrote poetry. She said she used to write crazy stuff— sometimes sweet and cute, sometimes ugly and aggressive. She enrolled in online college classes, and she was trying to sing professionally, heading into Manhattan during the day for cattle-call auditions.

She said she wanted to be famous. It seemed to Alex that the job with the escort service scratched the same itch in a different way, bringing her attention, adoration, and money. He wasn't interested in making that comparison directly. Instead, he told Shannan to go for it. "Maybe you can," he told her. "Nobody's stopping you. Nobody's holding you back. Go."

He was more convinced than ever that Shannan had chosen the wrong job, fallen into it accidentally. From there, it was a small step to thinking that he might be able to help her—and an even smaller one to entertaining fantasies of rescuing her.

Their third night working together—their third date, as he thought of it—they made sure to be together the whole time. It was a day shift, and there were not a lot of calls, just two or three. That night they grew even closer. The shift ended, and they kept talking. They found a place to park, and she pulled out a fifth of vodka, and they passed it back and forth. She said things to Alex about the work that he hadn't heard from the other girls. She said that sometimes the calls would be just about the sex, and sometimes they would be about keeping someone company—a john paying someone to hear him out. She told him she liked those calls best of all.

What happened next came naturally. They had the money for a hotel, but neither wanted to wait. They had sex in the car. Shannan told him she liked it. He believed her, but only to a point. When she left his car for the PATH station, he thought that would be the last time he'd see her.

He was wrong. The next day, she called him. "I'm coming back to Jersey—do you want to meet up?"

Alex ended it with his girlfriend. He had changed too much. He used to feel like a family man. Now he was an agency man, and Shannan was the perfect girl for his new life. That life had its own rhythm, to which he and Shannan adapted quickly. Sometimes Alex would drive her and sometimes he wouldn't, but it wouldn't matter. On rare nights when he drove her, they would sleep together between calls. When they worked separately, they would meet up every morning and check in to one of the hotels on Tonnelle Avenue. Their favorite was the Washington Motel. The staff knew Shannan and got to know them both. In the hotel rooms, they drank and watched movies and ordered in, like going on a little vacation. Alex liked coke. An eight ball, or three and a half grams, would go for as much as two hundred dollars, but Alex and Shannan were fine with something smaller, like five twenties, or two and a half grams. They had enough money to splurge.

Shannan moved to Jersey in early 2008, both to be with Alex and to work more. They found an apartment on Columbia Avenue in Jersey City. When he stopped to think about it, their apparent domesticity seemed strange. He'd be driving girls all over the place to have sex, and Shannan would have been having sex all night, and they would meet at the end of every shift as the sun came up, and they would stay in the whole day and then go back to work.

The more time they spent together, the more Alex got to see Shannan's mood swings—cheerful one minute, beside herself the next. She was at her saddest when she talked about her childhood. She told him that she was a foster-care child and her other sisters got to grow up at home. She said she felt like a nomad, always roaming around and never where she wanted to be. When he asked her why, she said she couldn't talk about it. "I don't know," she said. "Maybe because I was a wild kid, they couldn't take care of me." Alex didn't believe that, and he never learned another reason, but he did learn that there were triggers—she'd explode if she thought somebody had lied to her, or if she felt like she was running low on money, or if she was having a conflict with her mother or sisters. Sometimes all it took was for Mari or Sherre not to answer the phone for Shannan to feel rejected—the black sheep all over again. Arguments with her mother and sisters ended with her in tears. Alex would try to come to her aid: "Fuck your sisters!" To his surprise, that sometimes worked. In an instant, she'd brighten, as if the storm had never happened, and they would go watch a movie.

Alex never considered how hard it might have been on Mari and the sisters, dealing with someone so volatile. He was too busy fantasizing about helping Shannan. He started to think that their home together could be the first real home that Shannan ever had.

On her visits back to Ellenville, Shannan seemed different—less combative, more confident. Where once she would shriek at Mari about being abandoned, now she took her mother out to get her hair done. She showed up for birthdays and holidays, determined to cook for everyone and do her sisters' makeup. She brought magazines and ordered Chinese food and handed out bootleg

DVDs she had picked up in Jersey City. She'd think nothing of spending nine hundred or a thousand dollars in one weekend. "No one else could compete," Sherre said.

Her job wasn't a secret. Shannan made no effort to dash away from Mari when her cell buzzed. She would answer in a ridiculous code that made Mari laugh—"Hi, this is Julie Smith, is this the pizzeria?"—as the dispatcher gave Shannan the next job. She wouldn't go into much detail about the work—"That was her business," Sherre said—but she had no problem talking about the money. "You would not believe the clients I have," she once told Mari. "They're rich. I hardly have to do nothing, and I get thousands of dollars."

To her family, not just Mari, Shannan was leading such a removed, alien existence that questioning it seemed almost beside the point. Shannan had proved she was smart by graduating early. The money showed she could take care of herself. Her old friends from Ellenville were more scandalized. On the phone one night, her old friend Anthony almost didn't know what to say. "Does your family know?" he asked, and Shannan said, "Yeah. They're letting me live my life." This stopped him short. If his daughter told him she was an escort, he'd snatch her and lock her in a room until she came to her senses.

Shannan reassured him. "I'm only doing it until I'm done with school." He thought there had to be more to it than that, some other reason why Mari and the sisters never took the extra step to make sure Shannan stopped. To Anthony, that reason was clear: She was sending a lot of money home. "The only time I ever seen Shannan and her mom on good terms was when she started in this business," he said, "when she was bringing home money and gifts and stuff like that."

Mari saw how the money had changed Shannan's life and marveled at her taste. In Jersey City, Shannan filled the apartment with four-hundred-thread-count sheets, designer clothes, and a plasma TV. She would take her sisters shopping, to the mall, to the movies. Sherre's sons got Timberlands and Akademiks jackets. For one of the boys' first birthdays, Shannan wanted to bring over a cake from Carlo's Bake Shop in Hoboken, featured on the *Cake Boss* reality show. Sherre was offended: She wanted to bake for her own son, and here Shannan was, swooping in with her money again. Shannan had more success shopping for her mother. If Mari even mentioned something, it was hers. "'Oh, the new Stevie Nicks CD is coming out.' 'Okay, Mommy, I'll get it for you,'" Mari remembered.

As far as Shannan was concerned, her choice was a success. The money was washing away years of estrangement. Even Sherre came around to accepting her sister. "We got closer," she said. The plan was working. Shannan's success drew her family—especially her mother—closer to her at last.

On June 23, 2009, Shannan and a forty-two-year-old man named Elpidio Evangelista were arrested outside a bar along Sinatra Drive, a waterfront road in Hoboken. They both were charged with promoting prostitution; conspiracy; and manufacturing, distributing, or dispensing a controlled dangerous substance. They were both released on a summons. They weren't the ones the police were after.

Less than a week later, the police picked up the head of World Class Party Girls, Joseph Ruis. Acting on a tip, the police had spent a year tracing credit-card bills and placing undercover officers. They knew everything about the business—how they offered clients cocaine and charged up to $3,500 an hour. The prosecutor said that the escort service took in about $250,000 per month before it was shut down. The client list was never made public. The Hudson County, New Jersey, prosecutor appeared eager to exchange the johns' anonymity for their agreement to testify against Ruis if the case ever made it to trial. The case didn't get that far: Ruis pleaded guilty a year later to laundering over $3 million annually that he made off of prostitution and drugs.

World Class Party Girls was out of business. Overnight, Alex and Shannan lost the ability to make money. Weighing his options, Alex realized how good he'd had it. The owner had known him, and he was one of the favorites, one of their biggest money-makers. He felt like if he went to another agency, he'd come home with two hundred dollars a day, a waste of time. Shannan tried a normal waitressing job, but she wasn't making anything close to what she was used to. So she went looking for a new agency, which eventually brought her to Craigslist.

At home, she and Alex argued more. The arguments were never directly about money; they were about the future. But any talk of the future inevitably circled back to money. "What are you gonna do?" she'd say. "You're planning on doing nothing?" Alex, shouting now, would play the hooker card: "What about *you*? You gonna do *this* for the rest of your life?"

They both knew who was paying the bills. Alex was on un-employment, and his benefits ran out at the end of the year. Now he had no income at all. Shannan said she wanted to finish her online classes and get her degree before she quit. Meanwhile, she kept going on calls. Alex understood the life she was in—he used to be in it—but his life was changing. He wasn't always faithful to her, either.

It was early, close to six A.M. Alex was sleeping, and Shannan came home from work drunk. She started pushing him, testing him, trash-talking him. "You ain't trying to do nothing with your life. You're a loser."

"Stay quiet!" Alex said, glancing at the other bedroom. They had moved out of their apartment in downtown Jersey City and were living across town with Alex's father.

"Fuck that! Fuck you!"

"You don't have to stay here. Stay quiet, he's sleeping over there!"

"You're a daddy's boy!"

She hit him in the chest—not too hard but hard enough for Alex to notice.

"Let's leave," he said.

"I'm not going nowhere!"

"Stop!"

"Oh, fuck you!"

That was when he hit her. His left hand, clenched in a fist, caught Shannan on the chin.

Shannan cried out. Then she screamed. Alex's father woke up. Shannan wanted to call the police. Alex didn't know what to do. She wouldn't stop screaming. Finally, he threw up his hands. "Maybe I have to get arrested," he said.

Shannan quieted down a little. Calling the police was never a good idea. Alex knew that. He knew she knew that, too.

She stayed. His father lectured him: "You shouldn't have done that. You're a guy. You don't hit a girl." Two days went by. Alex bought her gifts, trying to make it up to her. But Shannan couldn't tolerate the pain. Her jaw throbbed so much that biting down sent her into hysterics.

Alex finally took her to a hospital in Newark. Her jaw was fractured. Shannan had two options: Get her jaw wired, or have a titanium plate grafted onto the bone. The plate was faster.

Shannan paid for it herself on an installment plan.

On a sunny day in September, two months after World Class Party Girls went under, Shannan was waiting on a corner in Astoria, Queens, to meet her new driver. She was starting up with an escort service out of the Bronx called Fallen Angelz. The business was changing. Shannan had learned the hard way that big agencies were easy targets for the police. Now she'd learn how hard it could be to start all over with a new one.

The driver she met that day was Michael Pak, a skinny, low-key Korean guy from Queens. Unlike Alex, who'd had one employer, Michael was a free agent, available at a moment's notice for any number of agencies. He never went to any of their offices; he would just send the agency its cut of what the girl earned. They gave him an account number, and he would go to a Rite Aid or any place that handled Green Dot transactions—a service not unlike PayPal on the Web, where you can securely drop off money for any account holder. Other times he sent the money by Western Union or MoneyGram.

When Michael first saw Shannan on the corner, his reaction was not unlike Alex's: *Whoa, is that her?* They had said to look for a blonde. She seemed part black, though her hair was light and straightened; it might have been a wig. Shannan got into the backseat of his black Ford Explorer, and soon they got a call from the dispatcher, who instructed them to drive to a spot near the Brooklyn and Queens border and await further instructions. They complied but heard nothing for hours. Michael kept calling the agency, and finally, they were sent to a Russian neighborhood in South Brooklyn, near Coney Island. It turned out to be a bogus call. No client.

They both felt strung along. They realized they were being treated this way because they didn't have seniority. The service trusted the older girls more, and Shannan was new. It was almost like a union rule—you needed enough hours with the company to be granted the first position. Michael thought this was especially dumb, since older girls had been in the business longer and may be more drugged up and erratic and less attractive. Right then and there, Shannan and Michael decided to go freelance. He would ferry her to calls in exchange for a third of the fee. Shannan would keep the rest. Finding johns wasn't a problem. They'd just use the Web.

With Alex still dithering at home, Shannan and Michael made a good team. He was quiet and shy, partial to wearing sunglasses even at night. She was tiny and curvy and always in motion, a dervish, antic and erratic and fun. Most of the time, his studied nonchalance meshed well with her free-flowing energy. Shannan liked to call him her brother from another mother. Between calls, motoring around Manhattan and the boroughs, she would tell him all her war stories, like the time she got in a fight with a girl who had come to work the same party she'd been called to, or the time a driver wanted her to pay him with sex, or the many, many times she got stiffed.

Shannan never gave Michael much of a chance to tell her about his own life. She never heard how he'd grown up in Jackson Heights, the middle child in a striving Korean-American family. He never told her how, when he was nine, his father died of a stroke, and his mother supported the family by opening a supermarket and gas station on Long Island. Or how, after college at a state university, he blew the LSAT, took a job at an insurance company, got laid off, and moved back in with his mother. Or of his big screwup. As Michael told the story, a friend let him know about what seemed like a good deal, getting paid to help a rich girl from China travel to America. The job paid three thousand dollars. Michael insisted he didn't sense at the time that it was a scam, and that the girl was coming to America illegally, and that Michael was being paid to act as a cover so she wouldn't attract attention at customs. He flew to Sri Lanka to meet the girl, then accompanied her back to America. On May 11, 2004, he was arrested at the Dallas/Fort Worth airport and charged with conspiracy to misuse a passport.

Michael served six months in federal prison, picking up a little Spanish from his fellow inmates and playing a lot of Risk. Inmates made their own dice out of little rocks. He shared a cell with a young black guy who had Mike Tyson's build and would kick Michael's bed to wake him up so he could sit in audience of the black guy's poems. His brother brought Michael back to New York after prison and found him a five-hundred-dollar-a-month SRO with a shared bathroom. He worked at a pool hall his brother owned. He'd run out of what little ambition he had, and prison had convinced him to drop any pretense of a straight life. After a year or so, he answered an ad to be a driver for an escort service. He had always thought that would be a sweet job.

Shannan went by the name Angelina now, to emphasize her lips, and charged two hundred an hour—less than what World Class Party Girls charged, though she got more of the cut. On a good night, she made as many as seven or eight calls. She'd take the PATH train into the city, Michael would pull up to some prearranged corner, and she'd pile into the SUV with all her stuff: a tall soda from McDonald's, often spiked with vodka; a bag with extra clothes; her purse; a book from one of her online college classes; and a netbook she'd use to post and refresh her Craigslist profile.

For Shannan, Craigslist was a slot machine that almost always paid out. Every time she posted an ad with a photo—usually one of her leaning over from behind—her cell would ring within seconds. She'd pitch the johns over the phone, work out a price, and get an address. If she managed to make it through the night without partying away any of her share of her fees, she could get home to Alex in the morning with over half of their twelve-hundred-dollar monthly rent in her pocket. All she needed was a driver to take her around and provide some semblance of security.

Sitting so close in the car for hours, she and Michael kept the conversation light. She didn't talk about her mother or sisters. Sometimes she would mention Alex. Once she even asked if Michael could find a customer for her on a night when Alex was going to drive her. But with Alex mostly retired, Shannan spent more nights with Michael. He knew she was argumentative—"fiery" was how he put it. She seemed ready to fight over any little thing, and she was murder on Michael's car. She burned a polka-dot pattern into his car seat with her cigarettes. Sometimes she'd be very happy. Other times, she made no sense at all. It wasn't really about drugs. She didn't like cocaine, though if the customer wanted to do a line, she would. She did like ecstasy—he'd drive her to meetings with dealers—and she really liked to drink.

When Shannan wanted to work and Michael didn't, she called another driver named Blake. Blake always posted the ads for the girls he drove, and Shannan was no different: *busty blue-eyed blonde ready for you,* he wrote. Her face was never in the photos, just her body. "Shannan was not photogenic," he said. "Her smile always came out crooked." When men called, he told them to picture

Julia Roberts—those big eyes, that oversize mouth. No one ever complained, at least in person.

By winter, Shannan was a steady enough presence that at least one person commented about her on Whojustcalledhere.net, a website that lists comments on phone numbers linked to a variety of businesses, including anonymous Craigslist ads. *Good body,* one commenter wrote in December 2009. *But her description of herself as refined and upscale is a joke. Nasty fake blonde hair.*

Blake had spent a few years working for large, established escort services until Craigslist started cutting into the bottom line. Shannan had called him out of the blue. She said she got his number from a woman he spoke with just once, someone with an agency he decided not to work for because it seemed too fly-by-night. Shannan's deal with Blake was similar to the one she had with Michael: She would come in from her place in Jersey City, and he'd pick her up at an agreed-upon corner in Manhattan.

In the car, Shannan would talk a little bit about Alex, blaming her boyfriend for how much she was working. It wasn't clear if she meant that she felt pressure to work more because Alex wasn't working, or if he was essentially pimping for her now, or if she was still furious about the way he had hit her. In any case, Blake came to believe that Shannan worked too much. He noticed her makeup fading over the course of a night, how she slumped in the car between calls, ragged, making no effort to freshen up. She would look better a week or two later, after she presumably took a break. When he remarked on how messed up she seemed the last time they worked together, Shannan would laugh. "Honey," she'd say, "I couldn't do half the things I'm supposed to do if I wasn't."

They didn't always get along. Like Michael, Blake found her unpredictable. In the spring, just a couple of weeks before she disappeared, he brought her to a call not far from the Caton Avenue exit on the Brooklyn-Queens Expressway. Hours went by, and Shannan wasn't calling in. Finally, at the four-hour mark, she called and said she would be out in twenty minutes. She came out, got in the car, and gave Blake money for just two hours.

Blake demanded to be paid for the other two. Shannan refused. It was eight A.M. now, rush hour, and they were sitting in the car under the BQE. Blake saw a bunch of cabs zipping by. "Shannan," he said, "either give me what you owe me, or you can take a cab home."

Shannan got out of the car. At the time, he figured she did the math and realized the $150 she owed Blake was more than the $40 it would take to cab back to Jersey. It was the last time he would see her.

Shannan never let Alex forget about her jaw. Her family knew about it, too. It colored everything about their relationship. He couldn't be her savior anymore.

They spent months in a holding pattern. They had stopped arguing, but she seemed to give up on the idea of college. It seemed unclear which direction she would go or how much longer she would stay with him.

But on the last night of April 2010, Alex and Shannan went out on a date, and they were actually having a good time. They went to the Hudson Mall on Route 440 together and sneaked some Taco Bell into the new Freddy Krueger movie. Alex thought it felt like a real relationship at last, and that maybe she was going to change very soon. Maybe she'd finish college and try to live a normal life. He knew at least part of her really wanted that.

She told Alex she had to meet up with Michael afterward. After the movie, she got on the PATH. She texted him later, around one A.M.: *I'm about to go in for a call, I'll call you right back.* Maybe it ended with *I love you.* Alex can't remember.

Oak Beach. May 1, 2010.

Just before five A.M., the john tapped on the window of Michael Pak's Explorer.

"Can you get her out?"

"What?"

"She won't leave."

The john, Joe Brewer, didn't seem angry or scared—just polite, if a little impatient.

Michael and Shannan had done a few Long Island calls, but not Oak Beach. The appointment was for two hours, which made it worth their while. Even if they missed calls while they were out there, it made sense to go to Long Island for three hundred dollars—or more, if she could extend the date.

And Shannan did. They were in their third hour when Brewer came out to get Michael. Until that moment, Michael hadn't ever spoken to a john. The protocol was for drivers to wait outside; usually, the men didn't want anything to do with anyone besides the girls. But Brewer seemed pretty relaxed about it. Michael guessed that he had done this a lot. A first-timer would be more nervous. Brewer was game. Michael had gotten a glimpse of him earlier, when he'd come out to open the gate, and about twenty minutes after that, when Brewer and Shannan left the house in his car to run an errand. Shannan had cleared it with Michael beforehand; he assumed it was to buy drugs.

Shannan called Michael after she and Brewer returned. She wanted him to go to a pharmacy for baby oil, K-Y jelly, and playing cards, all typical tools of the trade that helped an escort draw out the length of a date; when you're on coke, playing cards makes the time fly by. Michael didn't want to do it. The CVS was too far away, all the way across Great South Bay. Shannan snapped, "I'll find my own way home!" and hung up.

Now this. Michael got out of the Explorer and followed Brewer inside. The house was small, more like a cottage, raised on stilts to protect it from flooding. Michael followed him up the patio steps and through the door. It was the first time he had ever been in a client's house. Brewer seemed like a hoarder, or at least a slob. Michael couldn't see the floor, and he felt he had to watch his step. The front door opened into the dining area. The dining table was full of knickknacks and half-eaten food. Beyond the dining area was the living room. Shannan was standing near the doorway to the kitchen. She looked the same: chestnut-brown wig with blond streaks, a pair of dangly hoop earrings, a brown leather jacket, jeans.

"Shannan," he said, "let's go home."

"You guys are trying to kill me."

Michael wanted to laugh. But Shannan seemed so serious—scared, though not quite panicking. He thought maybe she was acting, or high, or both. He decided to treat her gently, to try to calm her down. "Come on, do you want to go home? Let's go home." He turned to Brewer. "How come she won't leave?"

But Brewer had lost his patience. He was approaching Shannan from behind, and when he got close enough, he put his arms around her. She shrieked, and Brewer let go. "Fuck this!" he said, and left the room.

The message was clear enough. Shannan was Michael's problem now.

"Shannan, do you wanna go?" Michael said.

"I'll find my own way home!"

She crawled behind the couch. Michael was still near the front door. He decided to take her at her word. He turned and opened the door.

"Mike, where are you going?" she said.

"Huh? You wanna go?"

She didn't answer. He didn't know what to do, so he sat down in a chair at the dining room table.

"Why are you sitting?" Shannan asked.

That really confused him. After watching what had happened when Brewer approached her, Michael didn't want to go anywhere near her. Then something weird came to him. Looking at her there behind the couch, he thought about a scene in the movie *Fear and Loathing in Las Vegas* that he and Shannan liked a lot—Johnny Depp, playing a drug-addled Hunter S. Thompson, had done the same thing, crouching behind a couch, fearing for his life.

Michael sighed. *She's faking.* "Oh my God, you're doing it just like in that movie."

Shannan didn't reply. She was talking into the phone. "Long Island," she said.

It sounded like she was on the phone with 911. Now he was even more confused and upset. The last thing an escort would ever do was call the police. His first impulse was to run. He felt set up, cornered. *First she says she'd find her own way home, and now she's calling 911?*

That's when Michael says he left. In the driveway, he sat in the car for a moment, collecting himself, furious. He'd dragged his ass to a strange place way the hell out on Long Island, and now he'd have nothing to show for it.

Michael looked out at the house and spotted Brewer, standing outside on a second-floor balcony. Michael shouted up to him. "She's still inside!"

Brewer looked surprised. He spun around and went back inside. He must have startled Shannan, because she burst toward him and out the front door, stumbling with a thud down the patio stairs.

She picked herself up and ran. Michael, still in the car, could barely make her out as she headed up the road. He called to her. "Shannan! Shannan!" Part of him was a little encouraged. *She wants to go home finally.*

He switched on the headlights, turned the car around, and went after her. The road was narrow and poorly lit, with high bushes on the left. He couldn't see where she'd gone. As he drove slowly, he dialed her cell, but she didn't answer. He texted her and started shouting her name again. "Shannan! Where are you?"

He drove through the gate at the entrance of Oak Beach and looked for her along the long access road, then doubled back through the gate, turning right on the Fairway. He got back in time to see Shannan running out of the house on the corner. He followed to where she crouched behind a boat parked not far from a neighbor's front door.

Michael was relieved. "Shannan, let's go!"

An older man, Gus Coletti, came out of the house and walked up to the SUV. "What's going on?" he asked.

"Nothing," Michael said. "We're just leaving a party."

"I'm calling the police," Gus said.

"No, don't do that, I'm driving her home," Michael said.

But Coletti had distracted him long enough for him to miss which way Shannan went when she took off again, running past the front of the SUV. Michael didn't even know there were more roads and houses beyond the drive that he'd taken to get to Brewer's house. So he went out the gate, searching for her all over again, up the access road. He couldn't believe he'd lost her a second time. Where else could she be?

As he drove, he called her phone over and over, driving slowly down that long road. Could she be in one of the tall bushes on the side? Finally, he just kept going, out the drive and onto Ocean Parkway, heading back west, toward home.

Forget it, he told himself. *She couldn't have run this far.*

The farther he got from Oak Beach, the harder he pressed the gas.

Chloe
Buffalo, NY

Angelina
Ellenville, NY

MeganLexi
Portland, ME

Marie
Groton, CT

Oak Beach, NY

LEXI

The police in Portland know a lot about the New York crew now—young black men from Brooklyn driving up Route 95 to Portland's new waterfront district, visiting the nightclubs, making some sales, then heading back home. Supply was so limited in Portland that the margin on cocaine was through the roof. Often the customers were so desperate that they didn't notice if they were being shorted—if the gram was mostly baking powder, or if the gram was really half a gram.

Thanks to her experience with Lili's father, Megan knew that there was a certain type of small-town white girl who was excited by a black guy from the big city. Some of those guys would collect girls from the nightclubs like trophies. Megan did not think she was one of those girls. If anything, she collected the men. In time, some of Megan's oldest and closest friends fell away. In their place were the New York guys. Lili's father had come from New England, but the guys who came after him were from New York. There was Justin, and there was Woody, and there was L.L., and there was Banks. After Banks came Akeem Cruz—or Vybe, as everyone in Portland knew him—whom Megan considered the love of her life and whom others would call her pimp and abuser.

Vybe was a year younger than Megan but tall and heavy— five-ten and over two hundred pounds. He'd grown up in Brooklyn, where his mother lived in a project near Coney Island. In June 2008, when he was eighteen and a half, he was arrested in

135

Brooklyn and charged with reckless driving, unlawful possession of marijuana, illegal signal, failure to stay in a single lane, and criminal possession of a weapon. Rather than face those charges, he came to Portland. Everyone knew that Vybe's crew sold cocaine, but it was hard to tell who among them was in charge and who was along for the ride, and Vybe seemed a little too chill to be a criminal mastermind. At a party, he hung to the side. He'd smoke weed and sip a 40 but never do anything harder. He was funny and talkative. Around women, he was a good listener, dispensed advice about relationships, and never demanded anything in return, the way some of his friends did. "You could ask him to do anything for you, and he would do it," said Shareena Howard, a childhood friend of Megan's.

Megan's half sister, Allie—one of the three children Lorraine gave up after losing Megan and Greg—got to know the New York crew when she reconnected with her mother's side of the family. She recalled that Megan's first escort gigs were arranged not by Vybe but by her previous boyfriend, Banks, who was also one of Vybe's friends. With the money from escorting, Megan was able to move out of the Crystal Springs trailer park and into an apartment at Brick Hill, an apartment complex in South Portland. She told her grandparents she'd gotten a job dancing at Platinum Plus, a strip club located away from the center of town, a minute or two from Happy Wheels. It wasn't true—an old friend of Megan's who did dance there said it was a cover story—but Muriel and Doug were too cowed by Megan to question anything she did.

Lili, then about six months old, was with Muriel and Doug most nights. Megan would come back to the trailer for a night or two of cuddling with her daughter. But at Brick Hill, Megan celebrated her independence. She threw parties, selling some of the drugs she came across, including Suboxone, a painkiller as addictive as OxyContin. With the New York guys, Megan had moved on from vodka to coke and ecstasy. "Her whole demeanor changed," said her old friend Rachel Porter, who admittedly was one of Megan's customers for the pills. "She turned lovey-dovey and sensitive, like an act, almost."

Vybe and Megan grew closer after Banks was abusive to Megan. Vybe was gentler than some of the other guys, disarming in his mellowness. At the time, it seemed that Vybe had rescued Megan from Banks, given her refuge and protection, though later on, some of Megan's relatives would believe that everything Banks and Vybe did, they'd planned ahead of time, a fiction designed to drive Megan into Vybe's orbit. In the well-worn narrative of the Romeo pimp, Banks was the abuser, Vybe the knight in shining armor, and Megan the easy mark: a poor single mother looking for a new life. If that was the case, even some of Megan's closest friends were convinced that she was going into the relationship with her eyes wide open. She had been so formidable for so long, who would believe that she'd get roped into anything she didn't want to do? Even Megan's friend Shareena, who had seen how the New York guys played other women, said, "He couldn't tell Megan what to do. She had her own voice, her own mind. She was strong." Many of Megan's friends agreed that nothing anyone said could have changed the way Megan felt about Vybe. When she fell in love, everything clicked in a way it never had before. With him, Megan saw the promise of a life without worry: security for Lili, the chance to make money, the ability to leave behind the trailer parks of the world, and most of all, what seemed like unconditional love.

Megan left the Sherman Street apartment and split her time between the trailer in Crystal Springs and hotels in downtown Portland where she and Vybe could be together for nights at a time. When Vybe visited Crystal Springs, he was deferential, polite to a fault. He'd talk about his mother a lot, saying that she kept her white carpets spotless and you always had to take your shoes off at her place. When Megan yelled at her grandparents, Vybe would shake his head and gently scold her, asking her to speak to them respectfully. He didn't exactly hide his money. He drove a silver Cadillac with custom TVs in the back of the headrests. He'd bought the car used, off of Craigslist. "He offered me a new truck," Doug said, "so I knew he was dealing. But of course I couldn't prove it. And Megan had a mind of her own."

In the hotel, Vybe would play Madden NFL on his PlayStation 3, and Megan would do her nails. They used those hotel rooms for calls, too. Online, she was mostly Lexi (*hi my name is lexi i have blond hair blue eyes great attitude . . . i love what i do ur time with me is never rushed . . .*) and sometimes Jasmine and Tiffany. Vybe would post ads for her. She assured her friend Nicci Haycock that the calls were safe—protection always; no kissing; no doing anything she didn't want to do. "Megan wanted to please him," Nicci said. "But she also liked the money." Megan charged as much as $300 an hour, $150 a half hour, and $100 for 15 minutes. On a busy night, she said, she could make $1,500.

By confiding in Nicci, whom she'd known since their days together in the Youth Center, Megan knew she was risking having her brother, Greg, find out. Greg and Nicci had been together for a while and had a child together. It was only a matter of time before Nicci let it slip. He exploded, as she expected. "I wanted to kill her myself," Greg said. But Megan didn't take him seriously. "To her, I was just her paranoid older brother talking shit." When he kept pressing, Megan responded confidently, in a way that stopped the debate in its tracks. "I enjoy having sex," she said. "Why not get paid for it?"

In the spring of 2009, Megan and Vybe made their first trip to Long Island. She told Muriel and Lorraine that she was visiting Vybe's family in Brooklyn. Lexi, with a photo of a recently bleached-blond Megan, posted an ad in the Suffolk County section of Craigslist on May 13:

NEW IN TOWN—MODEL TYPE

She posted again on June 16:

SWEET SEXY AND SEDUCTIVE

And again on June 23:

CHERRY BLOSSOM BEAUTY

this time offering to do outcalls for a little extra (*$300, depending on your location*). She moved back to incalls only on September 2, going by the name Tiffany:

I'M A HOTT NEW SUPER CUTE GIRL IN TOWN

Megan wasn't in Portland anymore, and her Craigslist ads were drawing from a broader population; she had no good way of vetting the clientele before meeting them face-to-face. Sure enough, on October 19, Megan got stung by a Nassau County undercover who had answered one of the ads. Megan had agreed to meet him at the Extended Stay Hotel in Bethpage. They settled on a price, and she was promptly arrested and charged with prostitution. Her family never knew about it, and she never served any time.

She got robbed twice on Long Island by two different johns. Only when they heard about the robberies did Nicci and Greg realize that Vybe, who was supposedly there to protect her, wasn't with her every minute. "All she said about it was 'Okay, I'm just gonna protect myself more,'" Nicci said. "He wouldn't be there for dates. She'd just call him and tell him what was going on."

Lorraine found out about Megan and Craigslist on the checkout line of a supermarket in a neighboring town. The cashier recognized Lorraine—she once dated Greg—and told Lorraine that she'd seen a Craigslist ad with Megan's picture. Lorraine didn't believe it. Then she rushed home and scoured the Web. She went through hundreds of photos until she found Megan's ad.

Muriel and Doug didn't believe her. Then they all convened at the home of Lorraine's sister Ella and looked at the computer screen together. They confronted Megan the next day. She told them she was just dancing, nothing more. "That's all I'm doing! I swear to God!"

Muriel had no power over Megan anymore, if she ever did. And Lorraine was the last person on earth who could tell Megan what to do. Megan did deign to discuss what was happening with her mother during one of Lorraine's rare visits to Crystal Springs. Megan said that she had been scared before the first few calls. She didn't know what was going to happen. But then nothing happened, so she kept going. She maintained that she was just dancing, not having sex, and that Vybe was with her the whole time.

She also told Lorraine that she and Vybe had plans for the money. They were going to get a place together. They were going to get married. Lorraine even took Megan around town to look at apartments a few times. But there were some obstacles. Megan had a criminal record, and Vybe still faced those pending drug and weapons charges in Brooklyn. They needed a place that didn't require a background check. That required a good amount of cash.

The two of them often stayed at a Howard Johnson that was a short walk from where Greg and Nicci lived in Westbrook. Megan brought Lili back and forth on days when Vybe was busy. Vybe didn't like leaving the hotel when he could help it, because the police were starting to follow him, so usually, Greg or Nicci picked up Megan and Lili from the hotel and brought them down the road. They went to the playground together with their kids, or to movies or shows, or back to Happy Wheels, for old times' sake. At the hotel, Greg got to see Vybe's business up close. He saw which guys came and got what. He saw some coke fiends trade their possessions when they were low on cash; DVD players and cameras were stacked up in the hotel room. Once, Vybe traded a $2,500 laptop for $100 worth of coke. "He didn't trade shit to get shit and trade it again," Greg said. "If he had no use for it, he didn't want it."

Greg and Nicci's understanding was that Megan's involvement in that side of Vybe's business was limited to hiding portions of his supply at Muriel's place in Scarborough. A trailer has any number of compartments and hiding places; Muriel and Doug never knew a thing about it. In fact, Megan did more than that. She helped Vybe deal, and she was also his customer. The irony was that Vybe was as angry as anyone that Megan was using. "I know there were times when there was a little bit missing and he wasn't happy," Allie said. "He wasn't happy she was using at all."

That winter, an old friend of Megan's was at her place on Boyd Street with her daughter, waiting for her boyfriend to come back from picking up some heroin. She heard a scream. She ran outside. Vybe was there, beating up a woman. Megan's friend watched as he grabbed the woman by the hair and smashed her face against the side of the house.

Megan's friend screamed. When Vybe was finished, she approached the woman and saw her face. "Megan?"

Megan was crying but then seemed shocked to see her friend.

"She just ripped me off," the boyfriend said.

"I bet she smoked it all herself," said Vybe.

Megan's friend called an ambulance and went with her to the hospital. Megan wouldn't talk about what had happened. When her friend tried to ask any questions, Megan snapped, "I know what I'm doing! You're not my mother!" She never saw Megan again.

At Christmas, Vybe got presents for Megan and Lili. They were starting to seem more like a family. But in April 2010, Nicci got a call from Megan. She'd messed up again. She was selling some of Vybe's coke to a neighbor in the trailer park—a guy named Wayne who was older than she was, someone who had watched her grow up—and they'd done the whole stash. Megan needed a cover story. She wanted to tell Vybe that she and Nicci had gone out drinking the night before. She needed Nicci to back her up. Nicci agreed.

Later that day, Megan called Nicci again. She sounded upset but resigned. "He didn't punch me, he didn't choke me." But he had hit her. He'd clotheslined her, she said, not clenching his fist.

"Do you have any bruises?" Nicci asked. "Are you bleeding?"

"No."

When Greg found out, he looked at Megan closely. There was no black eye, no bruises. She seemed contrite: *I know I messed up. I pretty much deserved what I got.* He thought about it. He understood. He thought maybe Megan would smarten up a little.

Vybe didn't see her for a time. He went to stay with an old girlfriend, Ashley Carroll, who heard his side of phone calls with Megan. He'd yell, and she would talk back, and he would threaten her: "I'm gonna set your stuff on fire!" Then Ashley would hear weeping from the other side of the line, and Vybe would soothe her. "I love you. I miss you. I'm sorry. I love you. We'll have a baby. We'll have a home. Everything's gonna be fine." Ashley would keep listening as he purred into the phone: "I want you to have my baby. I love you, no one else."

Vybe's hotel room had been the center of too much action—dealing, prostitution, maybe stolen goods—for the police not to take notice. In the middle of May, while Megan and Vybe were still apart, the police staged a raid. They arrested him and three others and found drugs and weapons in the room. Megan kept a vigil at her friend Shareena's house, crying and worrying. It happened that Vybe and the other three had the resources to make bail, set at fifty thousand each. The whole matter was thrown out because the police didn't have a warrant.

On the day of Vybe's release, Megan walked two miles from the top of Cumberland Avenue through the center of Portland to meet him at the jail. They embraced. On May 31, she posted an ad in Portland (*hey boys its lexy im back in town*). The next day, she and Vybe started packing for another trip to Long Island. Megan told practically everyone that it was going to be one of her last trips. All she needed was a little bit of money to get Liliana into day care, and a little more to get an apartment for her and Vybe.

Megan couldn't have been more thrilled that Vybe said he wanted a baby. Looking at Nicci's four children, she had always said she wanted only one child, that Lili was enough. Yet when Vybe said he wanted a boy, Megan decided that was what she wanted, too.

Hauppauge. June 5, 2010.

On a Friday afternoon, Megan took a bus from Portland to Long Island. Vybe had left a few days earlier on his own to see his family in Brooklyn. Megan checked in alone at a Holiday Inn Express in Hauppauge, on a bare stretch of the Long Island Expressway.

She had company soon after. At eight P.M., the security camera recorded Vybe and Megan leaving the hotel together. But at eight-thirty, Megan came back alone. In her room, she made some calls. She briefly talked with Lorraine at around ten. She called Nicci at about eleven, but Nicci was too tired to talk; she told Megan she'd call the next day. Just before midnight, Megan called Muriel and said that Vybe was out with some friends and she was tired and going to bed. She asked if Lili was up. Muriel scoffed. "Um, it's midnight," she said. "Are you kidding?" Megan told Muriel she would call in the morning.

Sometime after midnight, Lexi posted an ad on Craigslist:

Jump Into A World Like No Other—Please no blocked calls or text messages

Vybe spoke with Megan on the phone at around 1:20 A.M. Ten minutes later, at 1:30 A.M., the security camera in the lobby of the Holiday Inn Express recorded Megan walking out through the automatic sliding door. The hotel is isolated, on a narrow service road to the highway. One witness later said Megan seemed to be walking down the service road toward a nearby convenience store—a good meeting place, perhaps, for a john who didn't want to be seen.

Vybe called Shareena the next morning. "I've been to the hotel, she's not there, her phone's not there, nothing's there."

Shareena reassured him. "She's a wild thing," she said. "She may have just gone and got something to eat and didn't tell you." But Megan's phone was going to voicemail, and they both knew Megan never turned off her phone.

Vybe was concerned enough to call Megan's grandmother. He had a story ready: He said he and some buddies had gone out drinking, and Megan had called his phone and said she was getting something to eat and would call when she got back. When Megan never called, Vybe said, he figured she'd crashed. At six in the morning, he came by her room. The concierge wouldn't let him in but did open the door to see if Megan was sleeping. She wasn't there.

Vybe did call the police to say that Megan had been wearing silver hoop earrings, a silver garnet ring, and a silver necklace. What he wouldn't do, due to his criminal record, was risk seeing them in person. For the next week, he wouldn't tell anyone exactly where he was. Meanwhile, everyone Megan knew in Portland was talking about him: what he really knew, whether he was telling the truth. The police caught up with him as soon as he returned to Portland. A girl they all knew named Krystal Alexander—not a particularly good friend of Megan's—accused Vybe of slashing her tires and threatening her. She had been telling people that even her boyfriend, a friend of Vybe's named Piff, was suspicious of him.

Vybe was arrested and charged with criminal menacing with a dangerous weapon. Before he could leave on bail, the police issued a warrant for him on July 1 for failing to appear in court on an old charge of driving without a license. He got out again. The third time was the charm: On Tuesday, August 10, Vybe was arrested in a raid of his hotel room. The police were more careful than they'd been in the May raid. They had a warrant. They seized thirteen grams of crack with a reported street value of thirteen hundred dollars. There was no bail set this time. Vybe had become everyone's prime suspect. In the eyes of Megan's family, he was more than a dealer and a pimp. He was a human trafficker. Now that he was in jail, he wasn't saying anything to anyone.

Megan's disappearance didn't do much to resolve the family feuds. Muriel and Lorraine cooperated a little at first—on a vigil at Congress Square in Portland and a spaghetti dinner at the First Congregational Church on Congress Street. Then Lorraine learned that Muriel was angling to take custody of Lili. It was Megan and Greg all over again: Muriel had decided that Lorraine wasn't maternal enough to handle it. Instead, she wanted her oldest daughter, Liz Meserve, to share custody. Liz was happy to oblige.

Even as she was losing her granddaughter, Lorraine was being sought by the local media as the grieving mother. As long as Megan was missing, her case held attraction for cable news. In August, CNN's *Jane Velez-Mitchell* show called to put Lorraine on the air ("A twenty-two-year-old mother who may have advertised herself as an escort on Craigslist has vanished. Could Megan Waterman's disappearance be tied to her alleged online postings?"). Even as she was genuinely mourning, Lorraine was offered a chance to be something she never was in real life: a devoted mother who had a close relationship with her loving daughter. Muriel, watching from Crystal Springs, could hardly believe her eyes.

Chloe
Buffalo, NY

Lexi
Portland, ME

Angelina
Ellenville, NY

Marie
Groton, CT

Oak Beach, NY

Amber Carolina
Wilmington, NC

CAROLINA

Dave had a weakness for girls like Kim: the short hair, the glasses, the smile. When he first saw her behind the counter at the pizzeria in Northport, Long Island, part of him fell in love. When she spoke, he heard her Southern accent and saw his opening. "Oh, where are you from? Between your haircut, your glasses, and your accent, you're the perfect woman."

Kim laughed and gave him her phone number. "Why don't you call me?" she said.

Dave didn't, and he was too shy to come back. But a few days later, he was driving down Montauk Highway in his Acura and noticed her walking along the sidewalk. Dave summoned his nerve, flew around in a U-turn, and pulled over. "Hey, pizza girl!" He couldn't remember her name.

Kim peered through the window at Dave. "Hey!" She remembered him.

Dave smiled. "Want a ride?"

Pretty much everything Dave Schaller did, he picked up on the fly. He graduated from high school in East Meadow, Long Island, and went for a short time to Nassau Community College—where he was better at drinking than anything else—but he liked to cook, and in his twenties, he pretty much taught himself to be a chef. Next, he got work on fishing charters and earned his captain's license. Then Dave got into mixed martial arts and ultimate fighting. He had the build for it—six feet tall and 250 pounds, with a shock of red hair and tattoos up and down each arm. He made some money in underground fights in Manhattan basements and parking garages—$500 for a loss and as much as $4,000 for a win. He did it six times and stopped only after he broke his hands in his single loss.

He was thirty-two when he met Kim. It was the fall of 2009, and Dave had recently become a partner in a buddy's used-car dealership in the town of Babylon, Long Island. From his job there, he had as many as four cars at a time in his driveway—an Acura TL, a Nissan Sentra, a Ford Durango, and a black GMC Denali. He was living well, even as he was living with chronic pain, a steady aching in his legs that resulted from a nerve disorder called reflex sympathetic dystrophy syndrome, or RSD. Dave had been prescribed opiates, such as OxyContin, that he didn't like to use if he could help it. The pills that he didn't take, he'd sell every month, making thousands of dollars from a dealer who bought everything in one bundle, quick and easy. The money helped him invest in the dealership and pay the rent on a little cottage on America Avenue in West Babylon. The house was deeper than it looked from the street, with lots of storage space. The surrounding neighborhood was Italian, middle class, nice. Dave planted sea grass and perennials on the lawn. His last relationship had shattered him, but Dave was a born romantic, always harboring a crush or looking for someone new to protect, to take care of.

Those first few months, Kim was sweet as a peach—caring and comforting, a natural listener and an even more natural talker. In time, Dave would share all his pains and heartaches, and she'd sit and take it all in, putting her head on his shoulder, saying, "Don't worry about it." They would spend hours together, shopping at the Roosevelt Field mall, having lunch at the Post Office Café in Babylon, walking the boardwalk at Jones Beach, going to the movies, Dave tagging along to the nail salon for a few laughs.

Kim persuaded Dave to get his nails and toes done along with her, and even an eyebrow wax, and he eventually agreed, sitting there, all 250 pounds of him, next to all these fifty-year-old Long Island yentas, with all these Chinese ladies tending to him. The waxing was traumatic; he howled hilariously. He went back with Kim every two weeks.

Kim supplied Dave with a considerably sanitized version of her life story: the childhood in Wilmington and the kids—six of them now, three in North Carolina and three here on Long Island—but none of the drugs and none of the prostitution. She told him that she was living two towns away with her boyfriend, Mike Donato, and their kids. Dave learned later that Mike's parents were doing most, if not all, of the child care; Mike and Kim had even signed over custody. He didn't meet Mike right away; Kim said he was in jail for passing bad checks. So the coast was clear for them to get together.

Kim made a big show of having fun in bed with Dave. If, in hindsight, something about her seemed a little too rote, with no sense of discovery or surprise, it didn't matter to him. He was ready to do anything for her and to show her off to everyone. He brought Kim to a friend's wedding, shopping for the dress with her beforehand. He sent presents to her kids in North Carolina—clothes, gift certificates, roller skates. He bought Kim a cell phone and signed her on to his friends-and-family plan. He would talk to Kim's oldest daughter, Marissa, in North Carolina when Kim wouldn't return her calls. "I wish she'd marry you so she'd have a nice guy and be normal," Marissa would say.

But the one he got to know best on the phone was Kim's little sister. Amber was a drunk dialer. Calling constantly from Florida, she referred to Dave as her brother-in-law. "I want to meet you," she'd say. Kim seemed unhappy about the idea of Amber coming up to Long Island. She said her sister was persona non grata around her boyfriend's parents, that if they ever saw Amber in town, they would suspect Kim was up to no good.

Thanks to Dave, Kim didn't have a choice. He would listen as Amber rambled, picking up on the desperation in her voice. He heard her allude to drug deals gone bad, mounting debts, and dangerous men, and he wasn't good at doing nothing when something needed doing. No matter how antsy Kim was about the idea, he made it his business to get Amber up to Long Island and into rehab. He sent Amber money for a plane ticket. She cashed it in and got high. He sent another one, and in February 2010, Amber arrived at MacArthur Airport in Islip. Dave brought her home.

When Kim saw her, she started tearing up. She hadn't seen her sister in nearly three years. Amber weighed something like eighty pounds. Her arms had track marks everywhere. She smelled—her hygiene was horrible—and she was missing a lot of teeth. Dave could see past it all. He saw a mini-Kim standing there—every bit as beautiful, only more vulnerable, more in need, he thought, of his care.

Those first few weeks, while he hustled to find her a bed in a rehab, Dave didn't know whether she would sneak away or try to steal some of his things. Dave had some Oxys and Suboxones that helped take the sting out of her withdrawal. He had one bed, a king, and he wasn't going to make her sleep on the couch, so they all shared it. A few weeks later, after chasing down all of Amber's documents, Dave found Amber a spot in a detox at Nassau University Medical Center in East Meadow, then a bed in a thirty-six-day rehab at St. Charles Hospital in Port Jefferson.

Dave did all this out of love for Kim. He knew she was still with Mike, and when Mike got out of jail, he understood why she didn't come around quite as often. She'd never promised to run off with him, and he insisted that was fine with him, too. What he was less fine with was the way Kim avoided going to see her sister. Granted, she was juggling a lot: her boyfriend and her kids, her boyfriend's parents presumably looking over her shoulder. And while Dave didn't know the extent of it at the time, she had her own crack habit to manage. But he saw Amber every Saturday and Sunday in rehab, and Kim never visited once. Even as he made nice to Kim on the phone, Dave was fuming, screaming at her, but only to himself: What, did she think this was like having a cat?

Every new person Amber had met after her epiphany with Crystal back in Wilmington seemed like another chance to find the family she craved. Every time that chance slipped away, she was lost all over again. She had found her faith, then lost it, then found it and lost it again.

According to Amber's father, Al, pastor Charles West of the Open Door Church in the town of Leland, outside Wilmington, had taken her in for a short while. The pastor and his daughter treated Amber like one of their own. Amber later said her time with them was the only time when the withdrawal completely left her, when she was completely free. She called them "my family."

She was all right, Al said, as long as the pastor was alive. When he died suddenly, the church dissipated. Amber relapsed, then cleaned up long enough to be married briefly, to a man ten years her senior named Michael Wilhelm, only to divorce after another relapse. "She was a good girl, but she just had bad habits," Al said.

In 2005, Amber's mom, Margie, died after the ulcer that had laid her low years earlier had repeatedly ruptured. That was when Amber moved to Florida with Kim and Mike Donato, looking for a fresh start. Amber had soon drifted away from Kim and joined a Christian congregation in Dunedin, a town on the little peninsula west of Tampa on the gulf. Amber had worked her way into the church community with the same zeal she'd thrown into fitting in at Coed Confidential. She sang in the choir. She attended women's retreats. She found a job serving food at a diner near the church and the new house where she had moved close by. She joined Celebrate Recovery, a church-affiliated group that helped people deal openly with addiction. When she talked about the rape, one woman said, "Amber, I kind of knew. I was just waiting for you to tell me."

She married again in 2007, to a man named Don Costello. Amber told a friend that the marriage was like a promise from God—one of the rare promises that God actually kept. They had lived in Don's apartment, a condo in a desirable building, across the street from a top-rated public school. They had joined his church, and Amber worked in the nursery there. She and Don had even tried to start a family of their own and had endured some heartbreaking setbacks—a miscarriage and adoption plans that fell through. A year or so into the marriage, a family in the church had had a child they couldn't take care of, a baby named Gabriel. Child Protective Services got involved. While the church helped the couple sort out their problems, Amber and Don had stepped in and taken care of the boy, which made Amber de-liriously happy. She had taken Gabriel to Wilmington and intro-duced him to her father, whom she encouraged to become more religious, too. "She just told me I needed to get closer to God," Al said. "'Just believe—you got to believe.'" While she was there, she had taught the boy to call Al "Granddaddy."

The euphoria didn't last. Everything good in Amber's life couldn't paper over the wound that wouldn't heal. There was the person she longed to be and the person she was. Time and again, she'd come close to becoming that new person only to snap back.

Her marriage to Don ended in March 2009, fifteen months after it began. He didn't like talking about it; when he did, he suggested that he had been deceived. "She was not truthful throughout our marriage," Don said. He saw her one last time before Christmas, when she came by to pick up some holiday decorations. That same month, she was arrested at a Publix super-market for trying to shoplift toothpaste. Amber had told the cop she worked at the Clearwater Library. She'd been ordered to ap-pear in court in February, but by then she was long gone. She had moved to Long Island to clean herself up for good. Kim was waiting there with a new friend who promised to help Amber change her life for real.

When Amber came out of rehab, Dave learned that she'd made another new friend. Björn Brodsky—Bear to his friends—showed up at St. Charles a week after Amber. He was about as tall as Dave but rail-thin. Two of him would be as wide as Dave. Amber cracked Bear up, this itty-bitty thing, barely five feet tall, with eyes that always seemed on fire. When Bear got out a week after she did, Amber asked Dave to pick him up. Bear came home with them, and the three of them lived together in the house in West Babylon. That was when things started to change.

Like Dave, Bear spoke in a gruff Long Island accent, but he was more confident and smooth—a natural salesman, adept at making his life seem mythic and romantic and pure and righ-teous. Björn means *bear* in Swedish. He'd laugh about being called Bear. "Because no one could pronounce Björn, for some reason? There's two dots above the O, ya retard!" He told Amber and Dave that he'd grown up in Great Neck, part of a middle-class family in a fairly well-off section of Long Island's North Shore. His father was a construction foreman, working class and Jewish, and his mother was a Tennessee Baptist. Bear embraced his Southern background—poor white-trash moonshiners. While his Great Neck friends all got brand-new Mercedes drop-tops, Bear's first car was a 1979 Buick Skylark, $340 out of a junkyard in Tennessee.

Dave liked Bear. Having him around the house, he thought, was better than letting Amber go off somewhere on her own, unsupervised. For a while, Dave could make a pretty good case to himself that he was taking in a bunch of screwups and fixing them all. As they grew closer, Dave learned that in the year before, Bear had successfully torpedoed his entire life, spending eight months in jail for breaking and entering—roped in by an ex-friend, he insisted—and that his longtime girlfriend had a baby boy while he was away. The girlfriend was not into drugs. When Bear got out of jail, he saw the baby and then went right back to using. At the St. Charles rehab, Bear was hoping to straighten out so he could be part of his son's life. Then he met Amber.

Both Dave and Bear got to know Amber better, too. They saw how determined she was to be liked and how much she craved intimacy. Amber always needed to be held by Bear, to cuddle, to have some sort of physical contact. She was embarrassed by her teeth—it seemed to Dave that more than half were gone—but as brash and sexually open as she'd always been. When she coyly joked about what she called her "million-dollar pussy," Dave and Bear saw through the posturing. They saw how nearly everything about Amber could be traced back to a deep, unbridled need to be loved, including how territorial she became. She hated hearing that Bear had a baby son with another woman, and she hated it more when he would cut away for the day to see them. She didn't talk much about her spiritual life, but she did dwell on her failed marriages, weeping about her failed quest for a child of her own.

If all Amber had ever wanted was a family, that was what they became on America Avenue. Kim and Dave were the mom and dad, and Amber and Bear were the kids. Whenever Kim could pull away from her boyfriend, Mom and Dad would head off to lunch at the Post Office pub, where Dave would ogle the waitresses until Kim sneered at him; Amber and Bear would do their own thing at home. The neighborhood around Dave's cottage reminded Bear a little of Tennessee: a little laid-back, a little country. When Bear noticed that Dave headed out every day to Nassau University Hospital, for methadone to help with his chronic pain, then asked him about it, Dave was pissed off at first. But when Bear promised not to tell anyone, the secret drew them closer.

When Kim couldn't come by Dave's place, they formed a trio. Amber was Dave's little buddy, his comrade-in-arms, and Bear made for a happy third member of the crew. When Kim visited less and less often, Dave felt like a divorced stay-at-home dad. He felt played by Kim. For the first time, he thought she might only have let him sleep with her so she could get what she needed: money, a phone, and a babysitter for her sister.

They were going to the movies, Amber in the backseat, Kim up front next to Dave.

Amber nudged her sister. "Kim. *Ask* him."

Dave glanced at her. "What?"

Silence.

"Kim!" Amber said a second later. "Ask him!"

Dave was annoyed now. "What the fuck?"

Kim turned to Dave. "Do you know Craigslist?"

"Yeah."

"You know how they have the escorts on there?"

"Yeah," Dave said. "Whores."

"No, escorts," said Kim.

"Listen, I'm not an idiot," he said.

Kim didn't blink. "What would you think if I were to do that? Would you be mad?"

Dave wasn't about to let on that he would be. "Why would I be mad?" he said. "You're not my girlfriend. Of course not."

Later that night, Amber made it clear to Dave that Kim was asking for them both.

"Can you protect me?" Amber said. "If I do this, can you protect me?"

Dave saw the ad in his head. *Sisters*.

Amber had asked Bear, too. The guys were on the fence at first, but they came around. Dave told himself that Amber could save enough to find an apartment and restart her life. He told them he wanted nothing to do with the money. He didn't want to think of himself as a pimp. Better to be a bodyguard: Amber and Kim's guardian angel.

Hanging out of view in the kitchen, Dave and Bear would hear Amber—she used the name Carolina on Craigslist—recycling the same old Coed Confidential line to every john: "I'll get as funky as you want dancing, but you're not going to touch me." That boundary had always been easy for Amber to play with, and she knew that flouting the rules was one reason a lot of the men were there. Amber would do little things, such as play with herself, but there were always johns who wanted more for their $250.

Early on, Dave and Bear came up with a way of assuring that Amber wouldn't ever have to go further—an angry-husband scam that stopped her calls not long after she collected the johns' cash.

Bear or Dave would barge in just after the start of every date, as soon as the money was collected, screaming bloody murder— "HELL, no! Where's my shotgun!"—and the guys would run out, shitting themselves. "These men would go *flying* out," Bear said. "I'm talking naked, dick swinging, out the front door." The routine didn't always work. Once, Bear came through the front door and saw a huge black guy, built like a linebacker. The guy was stone-cold angry. "I'm not leaving without my money," he said.

Bear broke character. "Give the man his cash," he said to Amber.

The phone never stopped ringing. Dave and Bear were amazed by how easy Craigslist was; the money came straight to their door. They didn't know it at the time, but Carolina was starting to make a name for herself in chat rooms and on websites for johns, like the Erotic Review and UtopiaGuide and Longislanderotic .com. On July 11, 2010, a john complained about getting robbed by some men with baseball bats after paying a girl named Carolina two hundred dollars for sex. Another member of the group asked for the address. *No one from this board needs to be involved,* he wrote. *I have friends who can take care of this shit.* The angry john supplied the address and Amber's number. Three days later, someone named Morrie posted a message: *A friend of ours told me today that "You won't hear from those 2 girls anymore."* But nothing had happened to Amber—not at that point, at least—and the three of them kept on going.

Kim was posting ads, too, under the name Italia. Sometimes she worked with Amber, sometimes alone. Kim had the keys to Dave's house, but she came around only when she needed money or she knew that Amber had some. When she could upsell the johns for sex, Kim sometimes made five hundred dollars. Two calls like that and she had enough to call it a day. For long stretches,

Kim wouldn't work at all, perhaps because she felt Amber was making more than enough for them both. Whenever Kim was short on money, she would call Amber and tell her to post an ad. Amber would say no, and they would quarrel: "Are you kidding me? You go do it." "No, you do it." But most of the time, Amber would post the ad and make some money, and along would come Kim again, inviting her sister on a shopping trip.

Amber needed Kim in spite of it all. Dave and Bear came to believe that Kim looked at her sister as a burden—and this wasn't something that Kim ever really denied. Dave remembered her saying once, "If it wasn't for her pussy, I wouldn't have anything to do with her. Because her fucking pussy makes money."

Bear was the first to start using again. He hadn't stopped for long. Every day he took the train from West Babylon to get his methadone at the Greenwich House on Delancey Street on the Lower East Side. Greenwich House was a quick walk from Tompkins Square Park. Bear knew dealers on Crusty Row—"the asshole of New York," as he put it, the southwest corner of the park, near Avenue A and Seventh Street. So he would get a bundle first and then his methadone.

Amber sweet-talked Dave into driving Bear there once to pick up stuff for her. Then it turned into twice. Dave couldn't stand it. Amber was using now, too. Next came Kim, who would glare at Amber shooting heroin, and then cook up any coke that was lying around for herself.

One afternoon in June, Dave decided he'd try it, too. Amber wasn't around, and neither was Kim. Bear had some dope but tried to talk him out of it; Dave was the only grown-up left in the house, the sole voice of reason.

"Go fuck yourself," Dave said. He had never shot up before.

"How much should I do?" he asked. "If it's up to me, I'll just put a whole shitload of it together and fucking do it."

Bear told him he'd wind up killing himself that way. So Dave diluted two bags to start, then pulled up on the needle. He had been on methadone for so long that what came through the needle brought him finally home.

Each bundle held ten little parchment-paper bags of brown powder. They'd take the powder and dilute it with cold water from the tap, mixing it. The needles came from CVS. Bear needed ten bags, dumped into a cooker, just to feel normal. He'd shoot a whole bundle at once and be fine for the day, stopping long enough to inform his less seasoned comrades that today's heroin wasn't as strong as it was in 1970 or even 2005. "Nowadays it's all fucking garbage," Bear said.

Dave always shot in his right arm. A whole bundle, too. That would last him three or four hours. He'd shoot up three or four times in a twenty-four-hour period.

Amber shot up everywhere. She spent a lot of time hunting for a spot, adding needle marks up and down her arms right up against her old ones, like a child playing with crayons and tracing paper. Dave wouldn't help; he had an aversion to shooting other people up. Her tolerance was as strong as Dave's and Bear's, though she was basically a third the weight of Dave. She started off doing a bag or two a day and then stepped up quickly to three bags in one hour and two bags another two hours later. By the end of the summer, Amber was doing twenty or thirty bags a day, two or three bundles. Even Bear had never met anyone that tiny who did so much dope.

Each day Dave led an expedition from West Babylon to Tompkins Square Park. Most of the time, Amber felt sick in the morning and didn't want to wait three hours for Dave to come back, so she would go with him. Prone to road rage, Dave would grind and gnash his teeth the whole length of the LIE, screaming at other drivers. In the city, Dave would spend anywhere from $250 to $500 for six or seven bundles, a day's supply. On the way back, Bear would already be high, and he'd try to give Dave some, too, just to chill him out. He'd shoot Dave with a needle in the neck— the jugular vein that always bulged from all of his screaming and yelling. Bear used to say he could throw a needle across a room and hit it.

Sometimes they brought home enough to tide them over for the next day. Other times it wouldn't last, and at ten-thirty or eleven at night, Dave would drive back to get some more.

Amber was never sober. The half of her day when she wasn't making money on calls, she spent nodding off. Dave, paradoxically, was hyper—relieved to be feeling serene for once—and felt exhilarated, even euphoric, like he was floating. When Kim could steal away from Mike and the kids, she would come by to smoke crack, and she'd be hyper, too.

Dave lost forty pounds. Now and then he would look at Amber, all eighty pounds of her, doing hundreds of dollars' worth of heroin a day, and it would dawn on him that she was back where she'd started, maybe worse than ever. Dave came to realize that Amber and Kim had reverted to the way they'd lived for years before he came along. This was the way they were. This was their norm. Now it was his, too.

In July 2010, he had a moment of conscience. "Get in the car," Dave said, and Amber freaked out, screaming and crying. He said, "Well, then, you're living on the street. I'm throwing you out of my fucking house. See if Kim helps you." He took Amber to Beth

Israel in Manhattan and dropped her off at the detox. A few days later, Amber came back. Dave stopped pressing the point.

Any pretense about Amber not having sex with her clients had long since faded away. She was the main economic engine of the house, bringing in $1,000 or more some days, though most of the time she averaged about $4,500 a week. That was enough for about $3,500 of dope a week, or $14,000 a month. By August, Dave had sold every car in the dealership and closed it. Anything worth any money started to disappear, starting with the big-screen TV.

The cottage had holes in the walls where Dave had thrown tantrums. Bear started descending into deep paranoia, convinced that everyone was trying to kill him. This wasn't about having a family anymore; it wasn't even about a routine. Everything of value had been stripped until the house, Bear would say, wasn't even a house anymore. It was a spot.

The neighbors, all too aware of the whorehouse, crack house, and heroin den on their street, called the police constantly. Bear's paranoia was infectious: The housemates would cut the lights at night and use a pair of night-vision goggles of Dave's to look out the windows, checking for saboteurs.

Then one night Amber got hurt. She did an outcall by herself, without Dave or Bear, and Dave got a phone call from her, crying. Dave floored it five exits down the Southern State Parkway, and there was Amber on the side of the road, her mouth bleeding. The guy had beaten her and thrown her out, she said, because she wouldn't blow him.

In August 2010, Bear was walking out of a liquor store near Crusty Row in Manhattan when an undercover cop jumped out of a fake taxi. The cop searched him and found a pocketknife. A more thorough frisk yielded a bundle and a half of heroin in a wax packet in Bear's wallet and three plastic bags of coke stuffed in his butt crack. Bear knew he was done: a convicted felon, collared for felony possession and the possession of a weapon.

At Rikers Island, Bear doubled over in pain, shaking from withdrawal. He saw Amber in court, and she said, "I'm going to get you out." Three days later, Bear was released on a $3,800 bail bond paid by Amber. She'd raised it all herself.

Amber thought she had solved the problem. But Bear had more experience with the police, and he knew the house on America Avenue would be raided any minute. He was worried about himself, too. He was drinking so much liquor and popping so much Xanax, over and above the dope, that an overdose started to seem like a foregone conclusion. The guilt over the mother of his child taking care of his little boy without him was too much. He could ignore that guilt as long as he was enjoying himself. Now he said he had always planned on leaving.

Amber was destroyed by the news. Another abandonment, another betrayal, another family ripped away from her. Bear checked himself in to North Shore University Hospital. He was too sick for a detox. He needed a regular hospital bed, where he was placed in a medically induced coma for the first few weeks. After he came out of the coma, he stayed in the hospital for another three weeks before being transferred to a residential rehab, a condition of his release from jail.

Amber came by to drop off some of his belongings. She still felt scorned. Bear remembers the way she looked then, emaciated. He knew there was nothing he could do to make her happy. She looked him in the eye and handed him the suitcase. With the other hand, she gave him a fifty-dollar bill.

Maybe she was calling him a pimp. Maybe she was reminding him who had gotten him out of jail. Maybe she was inviting him to go somewhere with her and find a use for that money. Maybe it was all those things. But Bear wouldn't take the money. And Amber wouldn't take it back. They were at an impasse.

Finally, she threw it on the floor. "Let it fly off or pick it up," she said, and walked.

When Amber came down to Dave's car, she was all smiles. She told him that she'd met Bear's father and mother, and that Bear had proposed to her, and that the parents were going to pay for them to get an apartment, and that she was pregnant.

All lies, of course. Dave knew that much. He understood. He took Amber back to the house on America Avenue, where she went back to work.

West Babylon. September 2, 2010.

Amber had one call early in the morning, at about eight. She went with Dave into Manhattan to get dope, and they hung out at the house with some old friends of Dave's, getting high and watching movies.

At about four or five P.M., Amber placed an ad on Craigslist. She got some responses, but nothing solid. Amber was on and off the phone with the same guy for a while. He called her and chatted, then called again. She was working her Southern accent, describing her body, and by the end of the day, she thought she had him on the hook. On some calls, Amber would upsell the guys— "You only want a half hour? I got my rent to pay, my landlord is on my ass"—but this guy was different. Even before they met, he was telling Amber that she would walk out with a lot of money.

They arrived at a price: $1,500 for the night. He would pick her up around eleven and have her back by six or seven the next morning. She told Dave. Leaving the house for an outcall was unusual, but something made her trust this guy. Maybe she knew him. Or maybe it was the money. Or maybe with Bear gone, she had less of a reason to think twice.

At the agreed-upon time, she and Dave left the house to-gether. He walked her over to the corner of the lawn, right by the mailbox, and they hugged. She walked down the block. Before heading inside, Dave might have glanced down the street at the taillights of a car. If he did, he was too high to remember.

Kim was in North Carolina when Dave called. Amber had been gone for three days. "Don't worry," Kim said. "She'll come back."

A few more days passed. Dave called again. Kim was out of ideas. Bringing the police in seemed like a bad idea. So she did nothing, hoping Amber had found a new crowd someplace.

Bear was sitting in rehab, harassing his counselors to use the phone every three hours to call Dave. "Is Amber back yet? Is Amber back yet?" Bear just knew she was lying in a ditch some-where. "Dave," he said, "I'm telling you—this girl is dead."

Interlude:
Oak Beach,
2010

GREAT SOUTH

OAK ISLAND

Ocean Parkway

JONES BEACH ISLAND

Gilgo Beach

ATLANTIC

B A Y

Robert Moses Causeway

CAPTREE ISLAND

Ocean Beach Rd.

Oak Beach

FIRE ISLAND INLET

Robert Moses State Parkway

Robert Moses State Park

FIRE ISLAND

O C E A N

Somewhere in the marshes of Oak Beach, past the sumac and the sea grass, a tiny greenfly lands on a strand of salt hay, a wiry plant, slender but strong, that first thatched the rooftops and insulated the walls and padded the mattresses in the growing city to the west. All through the nineteenth century, while the Vanderbilts and the Astors built estates on Long Island from Great Neck to Huntington, the barrier islands remained wild with salt hay and rich in oysters, small mountains of which soon scored a regular place on the menus of Manhattan's finest restaurants. That lasted a few decades, until too many outboard motors of too many pleasure boats ruined the oystering, and the people of Oak Beach were taught their primal lesson: Be wary of those who might ruin your very good thing.

The seventy-two homes in Oak Beach today are a mix of winterized old beach bungalows and modern McMansion–like Capes. Even now, to live along the windy, fogged-in roads is to resign yourself to a particular set of challenges that the inlanders of Long Island don't face, and without some of the basic comforts enjoyed by your Hamptons neighbors out east. The people of Oak Beach are miles from the nearest supermarket, gas station, drugstore, hospital, or police precinct. Flooding is a constant threat. The marsh beside Oak Beach is a mosquito's paradise, and the poison ivy in the marsh grows higher than the salt hay ever did—as tall as two men and as thick as the branch of a tree. All along the beach are piles of crumbling tombstones brought from the town of Babylon and stacked into jetties to help combat erosion.

The reward is solitude. The people of Oak Beach are there because they want to be left alone. The gate, with its quaint little gatehouse and electronic keypad, is the perfect embodiment of the place's ethos. Walking past the gate is not against the law, but it sends a message. The houses are built on public land and collectively overseen by a homeowners' association that has operated like a miniature government for over a century, its small, clubby leadership screening new arrivals and making rules and generally promoting the idea that, as far as members of the Oak Island Beach Association are concerned, their quiet village would be perfect in every way if not for the intrusions of the outside world.

Long before the latest influx of newcomers—before a reckless party boy named Joe Brewer set up a bachelor pad along the Fairway and a boastful doctor named Peter Hackett moved with his family to Larboard Court—Oak Beach was governed peaceably by the association, and neighbors let one another be. The presidency of the board collegially transferred over the years from Ira Haspel, an architect, to Connie Plaissay, a florist, to Gus Coletti, an insurance man, and they still meet regularly in the building that marks the community's first organized effort to live beside something other than a boggy marsh. In 1894 a Presbyterian pastor named John Dietrich Long scored a fifty-year lease from the Long Island town of Babylon, which controlled Oak Beach, to build a religious retreat and cultural center on the public land. In a year's time, the pastor's flock constructed a building large enough to seat a thousand people. A year later, the town of Babylon sold a nine-year lease to the Oak Island Beach Association. The terms were a hundred dollars per year from each member of the association, whether a house was built there or not, plus five dollars a year for every house that was built. The town's only requirement was the construction of at least twenty houses.

This same lease, renewed several times, is in effect today, and the Oak Island Beach Association continues to manage and oversee life there, collecting assessments, policing landscaping projects and renovations, maintaining the gatehouse, regulating speed bumps, mediating squabbles between neighbors, and above all, negotiating the terms of the lease every few decades with the town of Babylon. The lease is another reason, beyond the storms and the insects, why the situation at Oak Beach has always been precarious—not just naturally but bureaucratically, politically. Residents there may own their homes, but they don't own the land. Every few decades, the lease comes close to expiring, the town makes noises about taking back the land, and the inhabitants grow anxious, as if they're under siege.

No family of real means would ever own a home on land that could be pulled out from under them, so it stands to reason that the first summer people at Oak Beach would be hardy, self-sufficient, and decidedly middle class. In those early years, families came over from the mainland by rowboat, and later on a sidewheeler called the *Oak Islander,* manned for a time by an ill-tempered, white-mustached sea captain who people said once worked for the Vanderbilts. They walked on wooden planks over soggy marshes to get to their cottages. They cooked with kerosene and pumped from a cistern that collected rain, and they stored meat in barrels buried in cool sand beneath the house. Bathrooms were holes in the ground, garbage cans were holes on the beach. Their days were spent crabbing, clamming, and fluke fishing. At night, the Jones Beach aquacade would host a production of Billy Rose's water ballet. The ride back to Oak Beach was along narrow, rutted roads with no means of illumination; headlights were useless in the mist. Instead, passengers stuck their heads out the windows, shouting out warnings to drivers when they feared an imminent collision.

It might have gone on this way forever—remote and romantic, intimate and a little precious—if not for Robert Moses. The master builder of New York, the ruthless visionary who brought parks, highways, and bridges to a bursting metropolis, also happened to be Oak Beach's most famous summer resident. Moses rented a bungalow on the beach with a bay window that afforded him a perfect view of the construction of the causeway and state park that would bear his name. Jones Beach had been Moses's first great triumph, fifteen miles west of Oak Beach. His second act, the construction of Ocean Parkway in 1933, changed the barrier islands forever. The corps of engineers dredged the ocean and filled in the islands and ran the new highway right through the middle.

Ocean Parkway brought the world to Oak Beach. Day-trippers, sightseers, Long Islanders, Manhattannites choking for fresh air, all drove across the bay on the Wantagh, the Meadowbrook, and the Robert Moses Causeway from Babylon, West Islip, Bellmore, Seaford, and Massapequa. They came with reels to fish from day boats at Captree Island for fluke, winter flounder, bluefish, mackerel, black sea bass, porgy, and weakfish. They came to plunder the bay for hard-shelled clams, steamers, quahogs, bay scallops, and blue-claw crabs and lobsters. They brought binoculars and hoped for sightings of the piping plover, the least tern, the roseate tern, the common tern, and the marsh hawk. They sunbathed on their pick of "locals only" beaches—Cedar Lookout, Cedar, West Gilgo, and the most popular, unsettled and raw, perfect for surfing: Gilgo Beach.

The people of Oak Beach might have slept peacefully behind their gate all through the tourism boom and Long Island's subsequent great postwar middle-class explosion—Levittown, the first modern suburb, was a half-hour drive to the north—and all the teen rebellion and kitsch and car culture that came after that, if an old hotel called the Oak Beach Inn hadn't been built right off the access road that led to their private community. In the seventies, a college dropout named Bob Matherson remade the Oak Beach Inn into the South Shore version of Studio 54. Matherson had grown up farther inland, in Rockville Centre, but he knew what the barrier beaches meant to Long Island's youth. Throngs of partiers came to Oak Beach at all hours, jammed into convertibles, horns blaring, music playing. Drunks stumbled onto the little roads of Oak Beach—Anchor Way, the Bayou, Hawser Drive, the Fairway—and parked cars spilled down both sides of the access road, passing headlights affording views of parked cars with steamy windows. When the police tried to crack down, Matherson turned the Oak Beach Inn into a cause célèbre. Through the better part of the eighties, a SAVE THE OAK BEACH INN bumper sticker seemed to come standard with every Long Island car. Years later, people are still telling stories of seaplanes landing in the middle of the night with deliveries of cocaine.

With the onslaught of nightlife, the gate became less of a gesture toward civility and more of a necessity. It took until 1992 to get rid of the Oak Beach Inn, and by then the people of Oak Beach had fallen into the habit of measuring their lives as a series of indignities and threats. The dredging projects. The motorcyclists. The ramp for Jet Skis. The plans for condos, a twenty-four-room hotel, and wind turbines. The traffic, pollution, and mosquitoes. And, not least, the government. Old-timers mourned the loss of the old Coast Guard station, and they raged against the town of Babylon for not maintaining the roads, and against the Suffolk County civil servants for encouraging development. "At times, it would almost seem that a callous Bureaucracy has been Oak Beach's principal enemy," native son Ed Meade, Sr.—whose father had manned the Coast Guard station during the early years, and whose own birth took place, unexpectedly, in an Oak Beach bungalow—wrote in a brief reminiscence of the community, completed shortly before his death in 1983. Meade spoke for all his neighbors when he said he treasured the "sense of grace and purpose" of Oak Beach living.

In the early nineties, the town of Babylon raised the fee to about $3,800 per house. The new leases are set to expire in 2050—long enough for buyers to get mortgages but no guarantee that their grandchildren will be able to keep the homes. Some in town still called it a sweetheart deal. No matter what the people of Oak Beach do, they know their hold on paradise is temporary. The end will come at the hand of a jealous town government that will raise the rates on their land leases, or a gradually rising shoreline that could sink and flood the cottages, or a storm that might simply wash it all away.

The quintessential Oak Beach tale, or the one that neighbors seem to like the most, is a Norman Rockwell moment that comes across as almost too heartwarming to be true. It was at least true enough to merit mention in a sentimental piece by Newsday columnist Ed Lowe. It's about Joey Scalise, a seven-year-old boy who spent all day fishing off a pier at his house on the water and didn't catch a thing. When his father, Joe Sr., a schoolteacher who in the summer managed the lifeguard stations at Jones Beach, came home and saw his son brought low by disappointment, he turned around and drove across the bay to Babylon and bought a fish, then raced back to Oak Beach, swam up under the pier, and placed it on his son's hook. It was too good a trick to do just once. Years later, Joey, all grown up, noticed the boy next door having the same trouble on that pier. He got in the car and headed for the same market and did the same thing for the boy that his father had done for him. A white lie, passed down through generations, to shore up the pretense of an orderly world.

Behind the gate, families remained devoted to their vision of the simple life. Children, when they weren't on the school bus to and from Babylon, spent whole days on the beach or at the association's basketball and handball courts. If they tired of that, there was the menagerie of dogs, chickens, pigeons, and parakeets at the home of Gus Coletti, the insurance man and antique-car enthusiast who kept an impressive collection of fireworks in his garage on the Fairway. They were joined in 1990 by the Hacketts. Peter, a doctor; his wife, Barbara; and their three young children came to Oak Beach, it seemed, for the same reasons the old-timers loved the place. The son of a former administrator at Hempstead General Hospital, Hackett grew up in Point Lookout, a barrier-island community just west of Jones Beach. When he and his family arrived, he was in his mid-thirties, robust and exuberant—well over six feet tall and burly—and working steadily as an emergency-services surgeon. Many neighbors didn't notice his left leg until summer, when he wore shorts. Even then they would look twice at the prosthesis's flat, washed-out shade of yellow, so different from the doctor's sunburned pink skin. While in medical school, Hackett told them, he was on the Northern State Parkway, helping a driver in trouble get off the road, when another car hit him, crushed his leg, and kept on going. He was in the hospital for a year, he said, and since then he'd used a prosthetic leg that never seemed to slow him down.

The Hacketts lived in a four-bedroom cottage on Larboard Court, a short walk from the Colettis and the Brennans. Peter and Barbara were lively and social, making friends with Michael Newman, who ran a large dairy business with his wife, Lisa, who joined a real estate brokerage run by another neighbor, Susie

Hendricks. All those families around the hub of Larboard Court and Anchor Way were active on the board of the association. Affable almost to a fault, Hackett became the closest thing Oak Beach had to a kindly country doctor who made house calls. He could also be a braggart, puffing out his chest and playing the big shot in a way that invited resentment, an attitude that ran him into trouble professionally. For two years in the nineties, Hackett had served as the head of EMS for Suffolk County, leading the response to the crash of TWA Flight 800 off the shore of Montauk in 1996. A year after the disaster, Hackett resigned over what he called policy differences with his superiors. *Newsday* reported on disputes swirling around him, citing critics who painted him as "an erratic would-be hero who embellished his achievements and meddled with the volunteers' work while neglecting his job as an administrator." Hackett had claimed that hours after Flight 800 exploded, the Coast Guard flew him out to the wreckage and lowered him onto the deck of a yacht, where he swam through the fuel-slicked water to examine a body. The Coast Guard later denied that such a thing happened or would have been possible. In another incident, Hackett told his colleagues he'd been searching for survivors in the wreckage of a roof collapse in Bay Shore when, witnesses said, he was nowhere near the scene. Months before leaving his job, Hackett was lambasted one last time for interfering with the rescue of three men when he lowered himself into a frigid water tank that had collapsed at MacArthur Airport. Hackett said he rappelled down, while other witnesses said he climbed down a ladder. His actions were said to have caused some of those men to be injured, an accusation he continued to deny on his way out the door.

Pressured out by his superiors, Hackett took a job in Riverhead, Long Island, as director of emergency services at Central

Suffolk Hospital. In 2000, in his mid-forties, Hackett had another health emergency: chest pains that turned out to be the effects of a congenital heart problem. To regulate his heartbeat, he had a pacemaker and cardioverter defibrillator implanted that effectively forced his retirement as an EMT.

Back at Oak Beach, with ample time on his hands, Hackett made it seem like he was always on call, driving around the neighborhood with a flashing red light affixed to his truck, monitoring the police scanner and rushing out whenever the speaker blurped out anything about a jumper on the Wantagh or a disabled vehicle on Ocean Parkway. As one of the only medical men in the neighborhood, he once was called upon to reattach a neighbor's finger and treated a few others with chest pains or heart trouble. But as he had in his career, Hackett earned a reputation in the neighborhood for telling stories. He declared that the enormous kitchen island in his cottage on Larboard Court doubled as an examination table. He'd say he had a background in law enforcement. According to one neighbor, when Hackett heard that a certain teenager had smoked pot, he took him aside and said he worked for the DEA. He seemed almost too eager to resolve any given crisis, no matter how small. According to another neighbor, he heard about a bad case of poison ivy and showed up to offer the afflicted boy a syringe with a steroid, provoking the fury of the boy's father.

In Oak Beach, Hackett seemed determined to be a very big fish in a very small pond. But as polarizing as he might have seemed to some, he fit in well among those in charge of the association. The Hacketts embraced the communal barrier-island life, celebrating every Fourth of July with a neighborhood picnic, and they used the Reverend Long's old community center for "heritage" meetings—a historical-appreciation club spearheaded by the doctor's wife. They mourned when Frank Brennan, a jovial six-foot-seven senior vice president at Cantor Fitzgerald, was killed in the World Trade Center attacks, leaving his wife, Barbara, a widow. They mourned again when old-timers Michael Newman and Don Hendricks died. Their homes all sat near one another off the Bayou, the road in the center of Oak Beach—near the Suffolk County cop, John Bunkhard; and Charlie Entenmann, the pastry king; and Connie Plaissay, the Park Avenue florist. At night, with the waves lapping the tombstone jetties along the beach, they all could go back in time—experiencing, however briefly, that sense of grace and purpose.

The gate could do only so much. The rest of Long Island was becoming a Gothic fun-house mirror of suburban living, an early adopter of the coming decade's reality-show excess. Right across the Great South Bay was Massapequa, home of Amy Fisher, whose shooting of the wife of her boyfriend, Joey Buttafuoco, served as the starting gun for Long Island's long, low hustle toward tabloid infamy. Twenty miles away from Oak Beach was Mineola, where the body of a twenty-two-year-old prostitute named Tiffany Bresciani was discovered in 1993 in the back of a pickup truck. She was one of sixteen women killed by Long Island's most notorious serial killer, Joel Rifkin. Thirty miles away, the body of a twenty-eight-year-old prostitute named Kelly Sue Bunting was found in a trash bin in Melville in 1995; she was one of the five confirmed victims of the area's other great serial killer, Robert Shulman. More recently, fifty miles away, four bodies were discovered in Manorville, including that of a twenty-year-old prostitute named Jessica Taylor, whose head and hands had been cut off. The Manorville killer was never found.

As the people of Oak Beach tried to preserve their way of life, changes were coming from within, where the money was.

As much as the rest of Long Island, Oak Beach benefited from the great real estate boom of the nineties. People whose parents paid six thousand dollars for a cottage thirty years earlier had become paper millionaires. The increased value of the land meant more turnovers, more development, more tear-downs, more renovations, more curb cuts, more bathrooms, more screened-in porches, more swimming pools—and potentially, fewer sand dunes. The only entity able to stop a leaseholder's plans to remake his old bungalow into a twenty-first-century dream home was the Oak Island Beach Association.

After a century, the board remained the center of the neighborhood's money and power, collecting dues from each household and setting rules. How people felt about the way that power was used often depended on how friendly they were with the members of the board. The most active board members were the Hacketts and their friends; Gus Coletti became board president in the nineties after Connie Plaissay. But in a village that was smaller than Mayberry, where everyone was supposed to take care of their neighbors, people now looked at each other with suspicion. Who on the board was building a garage without the right approval? Who was running a business out of their house when the bylaws strictly prohibited that? Which board members were being employed by that business on the side? Were any of those people being paid with association dues? Who was getting two thousand dollars a month from the association for landscaping work, then paying a landscaper five hundred to do it? Then it got more personal: Which board members were out late without their spouses and seen together in parked cars, doing more than talking about driveway permits and sand dunes?

The whispers escalated to open conflict in 2004, when the father from Oak Beach's charming fish story—Joe Scalise, Sr.—

and his family were almost driven out of Oak Beach by the association. The Scalises lived in a cul-de-sac on the west end of Oak Beach, down the road a quarter mile or so from the Hacketts and the Cannings and the Brennans, next door to Frank Solina, who wanted to put in a swimming pool without a permit. Frank's good friend was the president of the board at the time, Gus Coletti, who did not object. Neither did the Scalise family until Frank bulldozed a sand dune that Joe liked. When Joe contacted the New York State Department of Environmental Conservation, it was war.

Solina persuaded Coletti to initiate eviction proceedings against the elder Joe Scalise and his son. For the first time that anyone could remember, a special meeting was called of the entire voting population of Oak Beach. The Scalises stood accused—by Coletti and Solina—of trimming some trees on association property and putting a snow fence on the beach. The seventy-two homeowners were asked to participate in a simple up-down vote: Should the Scalise family stay, or should they go? To some, it seemed ridiculous. "I said to Frank, 'You know this is never gonna happen,'" remembers one neighbor, Bruce Anderson. "He said, 'Oh, no, Gus told me he's gonna get rid of them, and he's got a list of other people he'll evict next.' And I said to myself, 'Aw, geez, maybe I'll be on the list!'"

When the vote didn't go the way Solina liked—twenty-one to nineteen against evicting the Scalises—Gus counted three absentee ballots and declared victory anyway. The Scalises hired a lawyer, and tens of thousands of dollars in legal fees later, the courts stopped the eviction on the grounds that the bylaws stated that members had to be present to vote. The judge issued an order for the association to treat the Scalises as members in good standing. A year later, the association, still controlled by Coletti, sued the Scalises again for cutting down trees. That suit was also dismissed. Since then, the Scalise family harbored a grudge against those who ran the association and their friends. They despised Gus Coletti, Frank Solina, and everyone on the board, including Dr. Peter Hackett.

Nearly everyone agreed that the feud had polluted the culture of Oak Beach. The ugliness of the outside world had made it past the gate, so it seemed almost like an afterthought, or a foregone conclusion, when Joe Brewer arrived on the Fairway, taking up residence in his mother's aging two-story Cape three doors down from the Colettis. Brewer was no scrappy South Shore survivor. He was an inland "lawn guyland" guy, unctuous and cloying and classless. The Brewer family owned a lot of real estate in central Long Island—apartments, a strip mall, some homes—and Joe, neighbors said, was the family's Fredo. In his mid-forties, paunchy, and unemployed, Brewer once worked on Wall Street but hadn't seemed to work at all in years. His mother's place at Oak Beach became Brewer's to do with as he pleased. The inside was a wreck—piles of junk everywhere, not an inch of floor exposed, nothing ever thrown away, and a pervasive smell of cat. Brewer had a young daughter but wasn't married, and neither the girl nor her mother ever came to Oak Beach. On his way in and out of the house, he always waved to neighbors, smiling broadly and often chuckling at some private joke.

Brewer was not active in the association, but he was no misanthrope. He was the kind of guy who would recognize a neighbor at the supermarket in Babylon and come up and shake hands, animated and hyper, his long monologues punctuated with laughter. Like Hackett, he considered himself a *macher,* though Brewer could be cruder. To a few people, men he may have wanted to impress, he would confide that the house in Oak Beach was a party pit for him and his friends, "a place where you can do whatever you wanted to do." These weren't *Animal House* bacchanals; they were small affairs with a handful of guys and a woman hired for the occasion. Not that he ever needed to pay for sex, he'd say. As he cheerfully reassured one neighbor, laughing all the way, "I've had rock-star success with women."

■

Alex Diaz had kissed Shannan good night on Friday evening at about ten, after their movie in Jersey City. He spent the next day thinking she would be home soon. She never returned, and by Sunday, Alex was concerned enough to try calling. He didn't even get a ring; her phone was shut off.

He wasn't sure what to do. He knew her driver's name, Michael Pak, but didn't have a number for him—or anyone in Shannan's family, for that matter. Finally, he rifled through Shannan's drawers and found a torn piece of paper with some numbers.

He first called Michael, who seemed surprised. "She's not home with you?"

Alex was furious; he was her driver, how could he lose her? Michael told Alex what had happened: how she didn't want to come to the car, how she was irrational, how she said he and the client were trying to kill her, how she ran. Michael said he just couldn't find her.

Alex couldn't understand. Nothing Michael was saying sounded like Shannan. Even when she was high, she didn't act like that. Together, they Googled and found six nearby hospitals and four police stations. Using three-way calling, they dialed them all, supplying her name, her description, her alias. No one had seen her.

Alex asked Michael to connect him with the john. Michael called. A man answered. "What happened to her?" Michael asked.

Joe Brewer laughed. "Oh, man! That's *your* job. *You* should know where she's at."

Alex spoke up. "I'm the boyfriend. What happened?"

Brewer was defensive. "I tried to hold her. I tried to tell her to calm down. But she took off."

"Why didn't you try to bring her to the car?"

"She wouldn't," Brewer said. "And then she just took off, really scared."

It didn't sound right to Alex. Michael said she'd been there for three hours already. What would set her off after all that time?

That night, at about eleven-thirty, Alex drove to Oak Beach, the first of three trips he would make in the next week. He was so nervous, he brought a gun, a little .25 he'd had for years. As he passed under one bridge, he felt a weird vibe: Getting thrown out of a car along this road could kill somebody.

Brewer came out to meet him at the gate. He looked like he'd been home all day—pants unbuttoned, dirty white T-shirt, stubble. Brewer tried to level with him. "Look, man, she came to my house. We were having a conversation. All of a sudden, I felt uncomfortable with the conversation."

They talked for what felt like a half hour. Brewer kept wanting Alex to follow him through the gate—"Come to my house and search it," he said—but Alex didn't want to. He was worried about what might be waiting for him on the other side.

"You know, I'm gonna call the police," Alex said.

"Okay," Brewer said. "I got nothing to hide."

"I'm going to go to the police station," Alex said. "Do you know where it is? Can you take me there?"

"All right," Brewer said. "Follow me."

Together, Alex and Brewer tried to file a report. Alex remembers the Suffolk County police officers having a hard time concealing their laughter. "She ran away? She'll probably come back to your house. Check your house—maybe she's there now." When Alex said he was from Jersey City, they told him to file a report there.

When Alex got home, he could barely sleep. The next day, he drove back, a photo of Shannan in hand, ready to knock on doors. He made it to the Oak Beach gate at about noon; a neighbor stopped him and asked him to wait. A moment later, a truck pulled up the drive and came to a stop. Out stepped a portly middle-aged man with a pasty complexion. Alex noticed his limp and his prosthetic leg. He lumbered over with surprising speed. The man had an easy smile and bright eyes. He reached out his hand and introduced himself as Dr. Peter Hackett.

The doctor listened intently to Alex, even writing down some of what he said in a little notebook. He told Alex he knew nothing about what had happened to Shannan. But he said, "We're gonna help you out with the case. I used to work with the police. We're gonna call them. We'll have this whole place searched." Sure enough, later that day, helicopters were sighted above Oak Beach. They found nothing—hardly a surprise to Alex, since she had been gone for two days.

That night Alex filed a missing-persons report for Shannan in Jersey City, listing all her distinguishing marks: a tattoo of cherries on her left wrist, a scorpion tattooed on her back. He also told them Shannan was bipolar and was known to use cocaine, pot, and prescription drugs. A few days later—either the fifth or the sixth, he can't remember—Alex came back to Oak Beach a third time, this time with Michael. Shannan's sisters and Mari were supposed to meet them but backed out at the last minute, concerned that residents might call the police.

Alex and Michael walked through the neighborhood and saw Hackett, this time at the doctor's cottage on Larboard Court. Hackett took notes again, asking about Shannan's medical history, what drugs she took. Alex gave him Shannan's picture to put on a flyer. Hackett offered to give Alex and Michael a ride around the neighborhood, down roads Michael hadn't known about the night he was there. "I'm gonna keep an eye on it around here," Hackett said. "Don't worry."

Before they parted ways, Hackett told them a story. Long ago, he said, he was stranded on a boat in the water in the dark, all alone, thinking he'd die there. But then he saw a boat from far away. He shot a flare gun. The flare hit the boat, but all was well; he was rescued. Later, he said, he became a doctor who specialized in emergency medicine. His specialty was saving lives.

No question about it, Dr. Hackett liked to talk.

Mari Gilbert had trouble remembering the details. It had happened so long ago, before she understood that Shannan might be gone. The content of the phone call, as she remembered it, was very strange.

Mari heard the man say that his name was Dr. Peter Hackett, and that he lived in Oak Beach, Long Island, and that he ran a home for wayward girls. She remembered him saying that he had seen Shannan the night before—that she was incoherent, so he took her into his home rehab to help her, and the next day, a driver came and picked her up. He wanted to know if Mari had seen her since.

It was a quick call, no longer than a few minutes. In time,

Mari would be questioned on every aspect of the call—when it took place, what was said, who really might have been the person calling. Alex and Michael would quibble about the timing, whether Hackett called Mari before they met him, as Mari said, or right after, the way they think it must have happened.

Hackett would deny calling Mari at all, at least at first. But Shannan's sister Sherre was there for the call, right next to her mother. She would confirm what Mari heard. And in time, there would be others—including neighbors at Oak Beach—who would come to believe that Dr. Peter Hackett knew far more about what had happened to Shannan than he ever let on.

There was no public outcry, no crush of camera crews. No one called *Newsday* or Channel 12, Long Island's cable news channel, to say that a woman had gone around the neighborhood banging on doors and screaming bloody murder before disappearing into the night. The police didn't come back to search Oak Beach after that first morning, either. There had been no official missing-persons report, so there was no case, just a sheepish john and an angry boyfriend.

A few days after Michael and Alex's visit, Shannan's sisters made it to Oak Beach to knock on doors and pass out flyers. Mari went with them but waited outside the gate, afraid they'd be accused of trespassing. The neighbors who spoke with them had little to offer. It seemed to Sherre that most would have preferred if they hadn't come at all.

Gus Coletti said he didn't think about the girl again at all until the middle of August, when a Suffolk County police officer knocked on his door—the same officer who had responded to the 911 calls from neighbors on the morning of May 1. The officer told Gus that on the morning when Shannan vanished, he had searched the whole neighborhood and hadn't found her. He said he'd put his hand on the hood of every SUV in the neighborhood to see if it was warm. He never saw the black SUV with the Asian driver. The officer was back, he told Gus, because a missing-persons report had been filed for Shannan in New Jersey. All this time later, there was a case. The officer wanted to know more from Gus about that morning: what Shannan was wearing, what she said, where she went.

"You know, it's been months," Gus said. "Somebody here dropped the ball."

"Well, that would be New Jersey," came the reply. This was the official line from the police: Only when the report was finally forwarded to Suffolk County did the police connect a 911 call from an upset girl in the early hours of May 1, 2010, with the reports from that same morning of a woman pounding on the doors of Oak Beach. It took that long because even after twenty-three minutes on the phone, Shannan hadn't been specific enough about her location to get help, and she hadn't been on the line long enough with the Suffolk County police for the operator to perform a trace. About three minutes into the call, Shannan said she thought she might be "near Jones Beach" and got transferred to the New York State police, because Jones Beach is their juris-diction. No patrol car was dispatched. A police spokesperson later said the dispatcher couldn't figure out where Shannan was: "We spoke with her, the call was lost, and she never called back."

With no body, Shannan had become a run-of-the-mill missing-persons case, and the taint of prostitution didn't add any momentum to a nearly nonexistent investigation. A jacket found on the ground near where Shannan was last seen was misplaced by the authorities. According to Gus, the police didn't even show any interest in Oak Beach's security video. Several cameras record who comes through the front gate at all hours; those cameras should have provided a full view of Shannan running up the Fairway and in and out of Gus's house, maybe even which direction she ran after dashing past Michael Pak's car. The video is stored on a hard drive for a month. According to Gus, the police first asked about the security video eight months after Shannan disappeared. "I told them who would have it, who was in charge of it," he said, a neighbor named Charlie Serota, a member of the association. By the time the police came back, Gus said, the tape had already been erased.

The neighbors who acknowledged seeing Shannan—Gus, Joe Brewer, and Barbara Brennan—appeared to have let the matter drop. Maybe they assumed they'd done their part and the police would take it from there. Maybe they thought she made it home one way or another, that she was not their problem. Maybe, when they learned that she was an escort, they cared a little less. Or maybe of all the bad luck Shannan Gilbert had that night, the worst was coming to a community that, for the better part of a century, had wanted nothing more than to be left alone.

The Suffolk County Police Department is the twelfth-largest police department in the country, with some twenty-five hundred officers serving and protecting the people of eastern Long Island. Aiding those officers is a unit of twenty-two dogs. The canine unit is composed of purebred male German shepherds imported from Eastern Europe. It takes two full-time police officers to train the dogs. Each dog develops a specialty, like a major in college: drugs, explosives, cadavers. The dogs are trained on the real thing, and when they find what they've been trained to find, they bark, bite, and scratch to get the attention of their handlers.

The one thing that an open missing-persons case with a lack

of leads may be good for, as far as the police are concerned, is a training exercise for the canine unit. Officer John Mallia was a thirty-one-year veteran of the Suffolk police, a fifty-nine-year-old former private investigator who, since 2005, had called his German shepherd his partner. Blue was seven years old, and Mallia had trained him since he was a puppy. While the accepted wisdom is that most police matters are resolved within forty-eight hours, Mallia looked at Shannan's disappearance a different way. He assumed the girl was dead. Logic suggested it would be only a matter of time before someone found her. And Blue needed on-the-job training.

Over the summer, Mallia and Blue searched all of Oak Beach. Parts of the neighborhood had already grown too thick with bramble and poison ivy for a dog and his handler to walk. As summer turned to fall and the obstacles shrank, he and Blue fanned out along the southern edge of Ocean Parkway. When they found nothing, they moved across the highway to the north. Blue got scratched up, and Mallia broke out in a wicked rash.

Then, at about 2:45 P.M. on Saturday, December 11, 2010, along the parkway near Gilgo Beach, Blue's tail started wagging. He buried his snout and dug with his forepaws, and Mallia craned to have a look at what the dog had discovered.

That was when he noticed the burlap. And the skeleton.

BOOK TWO

I.

BODIES

They found three more just like it, two days after the first—four sets of bones in all. Each was a full skeleton, kept whole and shrouded in burlap. Each had been placed with an odd specificity, staggered at roughly one-tenth-of-a-mile intervals along the edge of Ocean Parkway near Gilgo Beach. Right away, both the array of the bodies and the care given them seemed deliberate, precise, and methodical.

Convinced that at least one of them was Shannan, the police searched Joe Brewer's house and seized his car. Almost as soon as the find came over the police scanner, the parking lot where the Oak Beach Inn used to be became a staging area for the media, filled with trucks from all the local New York TV and radio news stations—WCBS, WABC, FOX 5, WNBC, News 12 Long Island. The cable-news networks followed later, then *Dateline* and *48 Hours*. Surrounded by reporters, the man outed by the police as Shannan's john was defiant: "I'm innocent in this case," Brewer said, "so I have truth on my side."

Brewer claimed to have taken a polygraph, and while the police didn't describe the results or confirm right away that he had submitted to the test, they also didn't declare Brewer a suspect or person of interest. The police talked to Michael Pak, too, picking him up and driving him out to headquarters on Long Island and interrogating him for the better part of a day. Like Brewer, he would say that he passed his polygraph. Unlike Brewer's, his name didn't leak out to the papers. The police wouldn't charge him with anything, nor would they declare him a suspect.

The people of Oak Beach felt under siege. That much wasn't unusual. But this time, the threat came from inside the gate. Where they once waved on the road, now they eyed one another as potential coconspirators in a serial-murder case. Now it wasn't just a question of what had become of Shannan that night but of why no one in Oak Beach had cared enough to help her. Most neighbors stayed inside their homes. The one exception was Gus Coletti, who tried to distance his community from the remains found down the highway. "What guy would murder four people and dump them right outside the door here?" he said. "That would be a pretty stupid thing to do." Nothing he said made a difference. Even the most routine questions about Shannan's last night seemed to hint at some broader conspiracy. When reporters learned there was no security video for that night, they wondered why the police hadn't cared enough to recover the footage right away—and why, after a girl went screaming down the road and two neighbors dialed 911, anyone in the Oak Island Beach Association would allow the memory on that hard drive to be wiped clean.

The makings of a media sensation weren't difficult to recognize. Four bodies on a beach. A neighborhood with secrets. A serial killer on the loose. Shannan, for her part, was the subject of a few cursory reports, most picking up on the line from her missing-persons file that mentioned bipolar disorder and drugs. All the questions in those first few days concerned her night at Brewer's. With no video evidence, reporters requested Shannan's 911 recording. When police refused to release it, no one knew that she had been bounced from jurisdiction to jurisdiction for the better part of half an hour. Shannan's family filled the vacuum. Mari told reporters that she had heard about a moment in the recording when Shannan says, "You're trying to kill me!" Sherre said the tape showed that Shannan had been trying to get away from someone.

The police weren't in a hurry to confirm anything. Suffolk Deputy Inspector Gerard McCarthy acknowledged that Shannan "intimates that she's being threatened," but he also described Shannan on the tape as "drifting in and out, intoxicated," concluding that "there's nothing to indicate she's a victim of a crime on those calls." Sherre and Mari were appalled. At least three witnesses had seen Shannan screaming and running, and the police still weren't acknowledging that there had been a crime.

Now there were four bodies to contend with, none of them identified. Off the record, the police confirmed that they were working under the assumption that all were escorts. The police and the press scoured open missing-persons cases, and within a day, on December 14, another name surfaced: Megan Waterman of Portland, Maine, last seen in June at a hotel in Hauppauge, about fifteen miles from Oak Beach. That night on CNN, Nancy Grace conducted a live remote interview with Megan's mother. In her clipped New England accent, Lorraine Waterman said the police had contacted her about the case that day and she expected they'd be coming to her for a DNA sample. Megan's mother answered barely three more questions before Grace cut her off, rhapsodizing about what Lorraine must be going through. "This is going to be one of the greatest Christmases of my life," Grace said. "And when I think about what these mothers are going through, like the mom that is joining us tonight, this could possibly be her daughter that she has loved and nurtured for all of these years, and now she's waiting to find out whether one of these skeletal remains is going to be her daughter."

Lorraine's interview was crowded out by speculation from a psychologist, Mark Hillman, author of *My Therapist Is Making Me Nuts!*; a former deputy medical examiner from Los Angeles, Howard Oliver, opining about the limitations of analyzing old bones found on a beach; legal correspondent Juan Casarez, stating, obviously, that "crime scene investigators are launching what I believe is going to be a massive, massive homicide investigation"; and CNN reporter Rupa Mikkilineni, live from Long Island, reporting that "all four of the bodies have very different levels of decomposition." When, in a segment from Ocean Parkway, one police officer said that Long Island might be home to a serial killer, Grace broke in.

"*Hello?*" she said. "It's a serial killer! The same man killed all four women! And there's probably more!"

It's been over fifty years since Richard Dormer came to America, and his voice still hasn't lost its Irish lilt: *these* and *there* and *this* come out as *deez* and *derr* and *diss*. The Suffolk County police commissioner was born outside of Dublin and grew up in the small town of Newtown Crettyard, County Louth. Small but tough, he wanted to be a cop ever since he was eleven years old. When he was fifteen, his father died, and his only future in Ireland seemed to be working in the same coal mine that had employed his dad. He came to New York three years later, in 1958, and worked in the kitchen of a state hospital for five years, playing Gaelic football in the Bronx on the weekends, before finishing nineteenth out of more than a thousand applicants in the Suffolk County detective's exam.

Dormer moved to Long Island, married, raised a family, and walked a beat. Over the next three decades, he earned an MBA, took classes at the FBI National Academy in Quantico, Virginia, and at Harvard's Kennedy School of Government, and saw himself promoted all the way to chief of the Suffolk County police. When a new county executive pushed out the commissioner and all the chiefs with him in 1993, Dormer bided his time managing a private security company. In 2004, another new county executive, Steve Levy, brought Dormer back as commissioner. He was sixty-three, with white hair and thick glasses. Most of his peers were retired or about to be. But Dormer was thrilled, telling *Newsday,* "I get the chance to get back into the police department that I love." In charge at last, Dormer alienated the rank and file with budget cuts, replacing Suffolk officers with redeployed state police, insisting all the while that he was a cop's cop. He remarked on how surprised his officers seemed when he'd lumber into their patrol cars, an old coot asking to come along on their shifts. If anyone ever questioned his decisions or priorities, all he had to do was point to Suffolk County's 20 percent drop in violent crime during his tenure as the man in charge.

By the close of 2010, the end was in sight. Dormer's boss was on his way out. Steve Levy had switched parties, from Democrat to Republican, in an ultimately unsuccessful run for the governor's office, and now the district attorney, a Democrat, was investigating Levy for misuse of campaign funds. A third term as county executive didn't seem to be in the cards for Levy. His replacement was likely to bring in his or her own police commissioner. Dormer, who was turning seventy, expected to serve one final, quiet year and cap off his long career with dignity.

Which might have explained the pained look on his face when, on Thursday, December 16—three days after the second, third, and fourth bodies were found, and two days after Nancy Grace joined in the national chorus of speculation about a serial killer in his jurisdiction—he stood in front of a phalanx of news cameras on the scene at Ocean Parkway, the wind from the Atlantic Ocean tousling his short shock of white hair, and made his first statements about the case that had already hijacked his legacy, overshadowing every other memory of his career in law enforcement.

"I don't think it's a coincidence that four bodies ended up in this area," he said. In the same breath, he almost tried to wish it away: "I don't want anyone to think we have a Jack the Ripper running around Suffolk County with blood dripping from a knife." Dormer blinked. "Which might be the impression that some people would get . . . " He trailed off.

"This is an anomaly," he said. "Don't worry."

Dormer and his team avoided all talk of a serial killer in the days that followed—"Anything is possible at this point," said Deputy Inspector William Neubauer, "because there's so many unanswered questions"—even as they kept searching for more bodies. They shut down ten miles of Ocean Parkway, between Tobay Beach and the Robert Moses Causeway, as teams of officers and dogs combed the bramble. The police from neighboring Nassau County were reviewing their open cases, too, searching for possible identities for the skeletons. On Friday, they joined the search effort along with the New York State Police, moving west toward Jones Beach, shutting down the highway most of the day. Snowfall was expected that weekend, adding to the pressure. "We want to make sure we don't miss anything," Dormer said.

What he wasn't saying was how unprepared his people were. Four sets of remains found along a beach would be more than enough for any police jurisdiction to deal with. Suffolk County medical examiner Yvonne Milewski guessed the skeletons had been left there for a year or longer, though it was possible that the wind, rain, and salt air along the beach had accelerated their decomposition. It wouldn't be long before, on TV and in print, criminologists and self-styled serial-killer experts would start speculating whether the killer ritualistically cleaned the bones of flesh before shrouding them in burlap and placing them at careful intervals along the highway. Many of the bones were so fully decomposed that it wasn't clear at first whether all four sets of remains had been female. Milewski sent the four skeletons to the New York City medical examiner's office, where a team led by a nationally recognized forensic anthropologist named Bradley Adams set about analyzing them for DNA and signs of trauma. As soon as his DNA analysis was complete, he would upload the information into the Combined DNA Index System, or CODIS, the FBI's national DNA database, to search for identity matches.

The one thing Milewski's team didn't need New York City's expertise for was a ruling on whether any of the four bodies was Shannan. Alex Diaz's punch had left Shannan with a unique distinguishing characteristic. There was no titanium plate in any of the four jaws. On December 16, the same day as Dormer's first press conference at Oak Beach, the police announced that none of the bodies was a match for Shannan.

Joe Brewer, having decamped to his mother's house in Islip, seemed only marginally relieved. Even if he really had no idea why Shannan had gone running that night, he knew he'd never be entirely free of scrutiny, and no matter where Shannan was, the four bodies on the beach would be linked to her case. "My life is ruined. I will still be judged forever. I'll have to move. I feel for my daughter," he said. "This has been a rough time for me, but I'm not the victim here. Those four girls are the real victims. I just hope there is some sort of ending that will give these families some peace."

For the second time in under a week, Mari Gilbert was brought low. "I'm confused," she told reporters. "Where is she?" Then she got angry, complaining that the police had ignored the case for months, taking it seriously only after four more bodies had turned up. "They were acting like it didn't happen," she said. A sister of Mari's back in Pennsylvania, Lori Grove, brought up that the police hadn't made it to Oak Beach until over an hour after the start of Shannan's 911 call. "If somebody had gotten there within ten or fifteen minutes, my niece, most likely, would be alive," she said. "She was on the phone with police for more than twenty minutes. Why did no one get there?"

Neighbors maintained their standoff with the news trucks in the parking lot, resenting the attention, wondering when life would go back to normal, and while the police awaited word from New York City on DNA matches, the search for Shannan went on. From the Robert Moses Causeway to the Nassau County line, the police charted out a search area, breaking it down into eight four-foot sections of maps they kept in a mobile command center. The highway was marked with bright orange arrows, pointing north to each spot where the remains had been found. Fluorescent orange flags were planted in the earth on each of the four sites. Officers started to weed through the bramble, fanning outward from the flags. Only when the first heavy snows came, just after Christmas, did the police bring the search to a halt. The plan was to come back after the first spring thaw, before new foliage had a chance to grow.

The people of Oak Beach had a reprieve, albeit a temporary one. The investigation entered a quiet period: no arrests, no confirmed identities for the bodies, and no more daily police updates from Oak Beach. Dormer created a task force with three supervisors and a dozen detectives, including specialists in cell-phone technology and computer forensics. The task force sought advice from the FBI's Behavioral Analysis Unit in Quantico, and in February, a team of federal investigators spent a few days touring the sites, looking at the evidence, and sitting at a round table to brainstorm. Through most of January, they refused to speak publicly about the case. If they found a clue or a suspect, they weren't saying.

Producers for cable TV news have a stable of pundits they turn to during hot crime stories—medical examiners, criminologists, forensic scientists, former prosecutors—and the serial-killer category has its own roster of subspecialists, ready to chime in on what could be learned from bones exposed to weather for eighteen months or longer, and what the burlap and the location might say about the killer's signature. They could fill the airtime talking about how Gary Ridgway was called the Green River Killer because he buried his victims in shallow graves near the river of that name in the state of Washington, and how Denis Rader became B.T.K. when it came out that he bound, tortured, and killed his victims. "It's a calling card," explained Vernon Geberth, a retired commander from Bronx homicide who has become something of a scholar of serial killers. Based on the placement and reported condition of the bodies, Geberth told *The New York Times* that he was convinced the killer was a local, familiar with the area. "He has a reason to be there," he said. "The biggest thing on his mind now is whether or not he's going to be linked to this."

Geberth wasn't alone in that opinion. As early as the first week, CNN was airing speculation that this killer was a clam fisherman who could come to the barrier island undetected from the Great South Bay. Geberth went deeper with the idea on his media rounds, suggesting to the *Daily News* that the killer had placed the bodies so that he could find them again, returning to the burial ground "to relive the murders for sexual gratification." Others concurred that the killer was every bit as systematic and intentional as Joel Rifkin—that his need for intimacy announced itself in the care he took; that he shrouded them in burlap, protecting them from the elements; that he seemed to want to control every aspect of their lives through their deaths, and to continue his relationship with them past death. Now that the bodies had been discovered, Geberth suggested that the killer was "in a panic state," but that was no reason to believe he wouldn't kill again.

For the ultimate expert opinion, the *Daily News* approached Joel Rifkin himself. Living out his days in an upstate prison, Long Island's most famous and prolific murderer couldn't resist critiquing this new killer for leaving all the bodies in one place; Rifkin, at least, had been savvy enough to sprinkle his victims' remains across the tristate area. Yet he suspected that they had a lot in common: growing up lonely, mocked, and bullied; grappling with anger. "America breeds serial killers," Rifkin said. "You don't see any from Europe." As for the victims, Rifkin said that prostitutes were obvious targets for any serial killer. "No family," he explained, occasionally breaking into laughter. "They can be gone six or eight months, and no one is looking." This was not a novel insight about serial killers and their choice of victims: The Green River Killer, during his admission of guilt at his 2003 sentencing, had said essentially the same thing.

There was one important and obvious difference between this killer and his predecessors. In Rifkin's day, Craigslist and Backpage didn't exist. Neither did cell phones with GPS. Common sense dictated that technology would help find this killer. The original Craigslist killer, Philip Haynes Markoff, left a digital trail traceable through the Erotic Services page of Craigslist in Boston. He wasn't even a serial killer: He had just one victim, and he'd been found in a matter of days. How hard could it be to find a killer of four?

When, in late January, the DNA samples from all four sets of remains were positively identified, the idea of a signature became impossible to ignore. Maureen Brainard-Barnes, Melissa Barthelemy, Megan Waterman, and Amber Lynn Costello were all about the same age. They all did the same thing for a living. And they all came from other towns, some settling nearby to work. Shannan's disappearance had taken place in the middle of the time line of the other four: Maureen went missing in 2007 and Melissa in 2009, but Megan disappeared just a month after Shannan, and Amber vanished that September. If all five were linked, it meant the killer continued to abduct and murder women even after Shannan's disappearance.

On January 25, Dormer and the Suffolk County district attorney, Thomas Spota, formally acknowledged that the police were looking for a serial killer. Spota took the extra step of appealing to other women to come forward with any information about missing friends or suspicious johns. "I find it very hard to believe that people engaged in the same business as them [don't] know something," he said. But Spota didn't seem to understand how dramatically the business was changing, or had already changed. In the Craigslist era, no one knew anyone. Pimps and madams were becoming a thing of the past. Escorts can work from a hotel with a laptop, or in a car on a smartphone. Alone. A missing girl is missing only to the people who notice.

■

Are you fuckin' kidding me, Maureen?

Sara Karnes had been gone barely an hour from the Super 8 in Times Square, and Maureen was already calling. It was 12:27 P.M., and Sara was in Matt's car, stuck in traffic on the West Side Highway. All Sara wanted was to get some sleep. She didn't answer.

Back in Connecticut that night, Sara got a call from Al, the big Italian guy she'd met at Tony's porn office on her first weekend in the city. "You hear from Maureen?" he asked.

"No."

"She called me."

"Why?"

"'Cause she couldn't get ahold of you. She got robbed. She said that guy you guys met last night—the guy with the dreads—robbed her for five grand."

Right away, something seemed out of place. "How the fuck did he rob her for five grand? She didn't have that much when I left."

"Well, she obviously must've pulled something out of her ass," Al said.

Sara hung up and called Maureen's phone. No answer. She left a voice mail: "I heard what happened. You need to call me back."

That same night, Maureen had called her sister Missy, at home in Groton with her husband, Chris Cann, and their three children. On the phone, Maureen kept things light. She didn't say anything about getting robbed or being in trouble, or how she had to be in court the next day, or that she needed cash or she'd be out on the street. She said she was calling from Penn Station. "Can Chris come pick me up?" she asked calmly.

"Maureen, it's eleven-thirty," Missy said. "Chris has to work in the morning."

"I'll call Will."

A moment later, Missy's phone rang again. Will had to work, too. Maureen said she had enough money to take the train and would take the next one.

On Tuesday, Missy called Maureen, but she wasn't answering. Maybe she was sleeping, she thought, or maybe her phone was out of minutes.

Will called Missy on Wednesday. He hadn't heard from Maureen, either. Her phone was going straight to voicemail.

On Thursday, Missy and Will called the Norwich police. As soon as they learned what Maureen was doing in Manhattan, the officers stopped taking them seriously. She was an escort in financial trouble; maybe she'd dropped off the grid until she made enough money to set things right. Missy knew that couldn't be true. Maureen would never be willingly out of touch with Caitlin and Aidan for that long.

Missy learned from Sara Karnes where they had been staying. Will and Chris got on their motorcycles for Manhattan. The clerks at the Super 8 blithely claimed to have no memory of the dark-haired woman who had just spent days on end in room 406. The hotel records showed Maureen checking out not on Monday but on Tuesday, the day she was supposed to be back in court. They learned later that she had not kept the appointment to look at the sublet. She didn't get back in touch with Al, either.

Missy rushed to her sister's apartment in Norwich. The entire place had been cleared out. All her sister's things were in a dump truck out front or gone—all of her composition books and all the books she loved to read aloud to her children. Her clothes were gone, too. A friend of Maureen's had taken them all, telling Missy that Maureen had said she could. A short time later, the police told Missy that Maureen's food-stamp EBT card had been used in Norwich. Missy and Will started searching all over Norwich until they discovered that the same friend was using it.

Missy logged in to her sister's e-mail—Maureen had shared her password—searching for clues but also for anything left of the sister she knew. She moved on to the Web, looking for photos of Maureen on adult websites, stories of unidentified bodies, or even women with amnesia. Weeks turned into months, and Missy never stopped calling the police in Groton and New York, pushing for word on any progress. When an internal-affairs detective took pity on her, Missy learned that one of the last people known to have responded to Maureen's Craigslist ad had been a New York police officer, a Staten Island resident ultimately cleared of any involvement in her disappearance. Then came more silence, more waiting, until Missy learned that the police had picked up a ping from her sister's cell phone—someone trying to access her voice mail, perhaps. The signal registered at a water tower on Fire Island. Police with cadaver dogs and helicopters searched the area but didn't find anything. At the time, Missy was confused; as far as she knew, Maureen never did outcalls on Long Island.

Missy didn't know what to do with her frustration. Once, when she thought of Maureen, it had been about what book she was reading, or who would do the shopping for the kids' birthday parties. Now it was about Craigslist, and incalls and outcalls. She began neglecting her kids, her husband, her job. She forced herself to think of any scenario in which Maureen might be alive. She ran into Maureen's friend Jay DuBrule and started talking about how Maureen might have gotten drugged up and abducted by a sex slaver and forced to work for a human-trafficking ring. Jay found himself hoping right along with her. Better, at least, to think she was alive.

While Missy became obsessed, her brother cast about, adrift, enraged, and morose. And then, he, too, was gone. On August 14, 2009, Will—the baby of the family, a muscular, square-jawed, hard-partying football star from Fitch High School, whose anguish over the loss of Maureen was so intense that he had his sister's name tattooed on his chest—was on his Harley before sunrise near Exit 78 on Route 95, a tricky merge that has since been marked by a traffic sign. Will had been at a party that night with other members of his motorcycle club. A few of his friends were with him on the road. He was out in front, as usual. There was a truck in front of him; the police said its lights were either off or dim. Will seemed to notice the truck only when he was a few feet from the back of its trailer. He slammed his brakes, but it was too late. The bike broke in half, and Will died on impact.

When Missy was seventeen, she'd almost died in a car crash. Maureen, nineteen and already a mother, had sat with her at the hospital, coaxing her back into consciousness. Maureen, Missy, and Will had always taken care of one another. Now there was just Missy, left with nothing but an inkling that it was never supposed to work out this way.

As horrible as Will's death was, even that presented Missy with a strange sense of possibility—a new scenario. She couldn't help playing it out like a movie trailer in her mind: Maureen running away and reinventing her life somewhere; Maureen walking through the door, embracing her, ready to grieve for their brother as a family, ready to come home.

When Maureen didn't show up at the funeral, that put an end to it. Missy knew she was gone for good.

Amanda received seven calls in all. Whoever it was always phoned in the evenings, speaking briefly and calmly, taunting Amanda in a low voice. "Is this Melissa's little sister? I hear you're a half-breed."

Amanda's father was black. The caller knew what Amanda looked like.

Her mind flooded. Had this man captured Melissa? Was he

holding her prisoner? Was she dead already? Or was this some sort of joke? Amanda seemed to be the only one he would talk to. The time Lynn answered, he hung up.

Steve Cohen, the Barthelemy family's lawyer, told the police about the calls. Only then did they seem to take Melissa's disappearance seriously. Starting with the third call, police traced the signal to cell towers in Times Square and Madison Square Garden. Detectives showed Melissa's picture around at strip clubs. They wondered if the caller worked in midtown and commuted from Long Island. The calls were too short to narrow down the location.

After the third call, Amanda, just fifteen years old, was being asked to function as bait. If he called, she was supposed to draw him out, keep the conversation going. She and her mother spent the next several weeks waiting for another call. Every time the phone would ring, she'd wonder, *Is this him, is there another clue?* Once, the caller seemed to toy with Amanda, asking if she knew what Melissa did for a living. Another time he said, "Are you gonna be a whore like your sister?" Little by little, he dropped more hints. He said he knew where she lived, and he suggested he might come after her. Amanda thought he knew exactly what he was doing; that he was enjoying it, controlling every second, revealing himself with steady precision.

The last call came on August 26, 2009: "I'm watching your sister's body rot."

Amanda was driven almost hysterical by the calls, not just because Melissa might be dead but because she had been keeping her sister's secret. She had been the only one in the family who traveled to New York and spent time with Melissa, the only one with anything close to an authentic glimpse of what her life was like.

Lynn had heard about how they went for mani-pedis and visited the Statue of Liberty. Now Amanda told her the rest: how she would hear Melissa on the phone making dates, and see her on the computer posting photos of herself. She told her mother that Melissa had a car service ferry her back and forth while Amanda waited in the house for her to call and say she was okay.

Lynn had always considered her older daughter a force of nature, independent and self-reliant. Now all she could do was wonder what more she and Jeff could have done to persuade her to come home.

Amanda had a hard time in school, missing classes and staying home, depressed. A full year passed with no word. Lynn and Jeff threw themselves into their work. Lynn had retired from making meals at Manhattan Manor to help out at the latest incarnation of Jeff's diner. Jeff had pulled up stakes at his inner-city location in Lovejoy, where Melissa had worked some shifts after beauty school classes, and found a new spot in Cheektowaga, a suburb to the east of Buffalo. The new diner, called JJ's Texas Hots, was on a four-lane commercial strip lined with dollar stores and Goodwill and Chick-N-Pizza and the Polish Villa and 7-Eleven. Across the street was Resurrection Church, dominating the intersection with an electronic bell that played on the hour. JJ's new building used to be a Dunkin' Donuts, and it showed: the floor-to-ceiling windows around the perimeter, the Formica tables. The doors had handwritten signs on whiteboard in different-colored markers, reading SORRY WE CANNOT TAKE CREDIT CARDS OR DEBIT CARDS and RESTROOM FOR CUSTOMERS ONLY. Nobody paid attention to either of them. After a while, Lynn and Jeff knew most of the patrons and what they were going to order. The term *Texas Hots* referred to the sauce as much as the dog—a mild meat sauce with a nice bite; hot enough but not super-hot. It was a family recipe. The connection to Texas was tenuous at best. Jeff's father, a Buffalo native, had opened the original JJ's thirty years earlier.

If the loss of Melissa hung over their emotional lives, JJ's had become the center of their financial anxieties. On bad days, it resembled a house of cards. It had cost Jeff and Lynn about twelve thousand dollars to open the location. It would have cost more, but he brought in some equipment from the old place in Lovejoy. They borrowed the money from relatives of Jeff's, and they felt horrible about the timing. A few months after they opened, the market crashed and the relatives lost their life savings. Not once did they ask for any money back. And when they came in to eat, they got angry if Jeff gave them free food. Both Jeff and Lynn spent nearly every waking hour there, each working seventy-two hours a week or more. Lynn's little sister, Dawn, came by to work a shift after her full-time job as a bank teller. Lynn's father, Elmer, washed dishes after pulling a full shift as a maintenance worker at Canterbury Woods, a well-heeled assisted living community that opened after Manhattan Manor. Lynn's mother, Linda, had helped get the place ready, scrubbing the floors and walls and painting.

The older generation was overextended. Linda had taken advantage of the loose standards for credit and signed a home-equity loan to buy a new in-ground swimming pool. When she died of heart failure just weeks after Melissa disappeared, the debt was on her estate. Elmer got a lawyer to tell the pool company that if he declared bankruptcy, everything he had would go toward the mortgage. They gave up trying to collect. He never declared bankruptcy, and he kept the pool.

Melissa's grandmother had lived just long enough to learn the truth about what her granddaughter had been doing in New York. Elmer, Lynn, and Dawn were convinced that the loss broke her heart. Elmer put on a brave face for a few months but soon sank into a deep depression. When he wasn't helping out behind the counter, he'd be sitting in the restaurant, telling strangers about his wife and his granddaughter, telling old stories about them both, treading lightly on the reasons for Melissa's disappearance. Elmer had failed a stress test but refused to do anything about it. If his time was up, he said, he was ready to join his wife. Lynn worried about him. So did Dawn, who from time to time tried to snap her dad out of his funk. "I know how you feel," she'd say. "I don't have it as deep as you, but you really have to snap out of it. You have to see the light. There *is* light . . . No child can do anything wrong."

Then came the day in December when Lynn, craning her neck up from the cash register at JJ's Texas Hots, saw the reports on television: four bodies on a Long Island beach, all presumed to be prostitutes. She burst into tears. It took until the end of January for her to learn that Melissa was the one John Mallia and Blue had discovered on December 11—the first of the four to be found.

Lorraine Waterman was never really rid of any of her history. She carried it with her in the form of guilt or anger: She was the real victim; the children, Megan and Greg, were stolen from her. No one understood her. She wore her story on her body now, for all to see. The initials of her boyfriend, Bill, were tattooed on her right shoulder. On her left arm, after the DNA match came back, she got a tattoo that read MEGAN RIP.

Lorraine's hard drinking was far behind her. Sober ten years, she was working on getting a medical-assistant degree from Kaplan University, around the corner from her home in South Portland.

The program was supposed to last two years, but she was taking an extra class each semester so she could finish early. At night, she worked at the Domino's managed by her boyfriend. Like Buffalo, Portland had lost most of its blue-collar jobs, but it had become a booming health-care town, with hospitals expanding all over and state laws facilitating the funding of assisted-living facilities. Even so, Lorraine thought that getting a medical-assistant job would be difficult, with so many younger people competing. It took two or three interviews to even be in the running for a job, and Lorraine wasn't exactly spry. Her mother, Muriel, and big sister Liz called her a hypochondriac—"Every time somebody has an ailment, Lorraine has it, too," Liz said—but Lorraine maintained that she suffered from bad kidneys, diabetes, and arthritis of the spine.

Lorraine's two-story detached house on a quiet wooded street smelled of cigarettes, with deep red curtains blocking the light in the living room. There was a fifty-five-gallon aquarium, two torn-up beige Barcaloungers, a large TV, and an inscription on the wall from the children's book *Guess How Much I Love You*: *I love you right up to the moon and back*. She shared the house with Bill, one of Bill's daughters, and Bill's three-year-old grandson, David, just a little younger than Megan's daughter, Lili. On any given day, Lili's toys would be strewn about the floor, and David often played with them. But Lili did not live here. She lived with Lorraine's mother, Muriel, just as Megan had for most of her childhood.

In the official version of Megan's life story—the one generally accepted by everyone in the family other than Lorraine—Megan and her brother were rescued as babies from a neglectful and sometimes abusive situation. For decades, Lorraine held on to her dissenting view: that Muriel took Megan and Greg away from her. Once the worst had befallen Megan—once she had become a murder victim—Lorraine was ready to lay that at Muriel's feet, too. She blamed Muriel's overprotectiveness for everything. "My mom defended Megan, protected Megan, lied about Megan," she said. "She got kicked out of school. She beat up the teachers. And my mom always protected her. Megan knew that, 'Hey, Nana and Grandpa are going to come bail me out.' If they had not covered for her, I think Megan would've smartened up."

When Megan disappeared, her estranged family wasn't in much of a condition to rally a search. Still, they tried. They held a vigil nineteen days after she was last seen—on June 25, 2010—in the bandstand area of Congress Square in Portland. Volunteers gathered at the Scarborough Walmart parking lot on Gallery Boulevard the next morning to hang Missing posters. Others, including Megan's brother, Greg, and her friend Nicci Haycock, had done the same in Hauppauge, Long Island, a few weeks later in July. Local newspaper and TV news shows took notice. By August, when CNN's Jane Velez-Mitchell put Lorraine on for a few minutes to talk about Craigslist, the short version of Megan's story wasn't exactly flattering. "I've got to ask you, Lorraine, did you try to stop your daughter from getting involved in this escort business?" Lorraine answered as honestly as she could: "Yes. Me and my whole family have. We have told Megan how dangerous it is for her to be doing that. And she did it anyways. She didn't listen."

Muriel and others were horrified. Some of Megan's friends were astonished to see Lorraine acting as the family spokesperson. "I was working with Lorraine and didn't even know she was Megan's mom until Lorraine was on TV," said Rachel Brown. "That's how involved Megan's mother was."

Lorraine saw only after the fact how terrible it looked to say such a thing in public. From then on, she and others in the family made sure to cast Megan as a victim. In September, Lorraine told one reporter that Akeem Cruz, now in jail, had been "her boyfriend-slash-pimp," who "told her how she could make easy, quick money, and he got her hooked on Craigslist. Her attitude, her personality—all of it changed when she met him." This wasn't exactly true—she'd been an escort before Vybe came along—but all the momentum was shifting against him. The family would call Akeem Cruz what anti-sex-trafficking activists call a Romeo pimp. He'd romanced Megan only to control her, they said; then he brought her to Hauppauge and abandoned her. Maybe he even had something to do with what happened.

That fall, the family planned another benefit to raise money for a reward: a spaghetti supper and silent auction with door prizes, a raffle, and a DJ. It was during the planning that Lorraine discovered that Muriel was taking steps to share custody of Lili not with Lorraine but with Lorraine's oldest sister, Liz Meserve. Lorraine lashed out at Liz; Liz unfriended Lorraine on Facebook; and the fund-raiser fell apart. If the feud had started with a struggle for control over Megan's memory, then Lili had become another front in the same war.

By December, when Lorraine got the call from Suffolk County that four skeletons had been found on Ocean Parkway, no two members of the family seemed to be on speaking terms. When Lorraine went on *Nancy Grace,* the others watched from home, amazed yet again by the performance. She wasn't a mother in real life, but there she was, playing one on TV.

The police came to Portland to tell Lorraine about the DNA match on January 20, the day after what would have been Megan's

The second Missy saw the news about Gilgo Beach, she knew that Maureen had to be one of them. That cell signal from Maureen's phone registering on Fire Island in 2008 finally made sense.

While waiting for a DNA match, Missy became desperate for something to do. Prowling the Web, she read a news story about Megan and found her mother, Lorraine, on Facebook. Weeks before either Maureen or Megan were confirmed as victims, Missy and Lorraine were talking on the phone every day—Missy, the younger of the two yet three years ahead in dealing with the loss. Missy wanted to tell Lorraine that the pain would go away. "But it doesn't," she said. "It gets harder as time goes by. And you've just got to know that it's coming and be strong."

By the time all the victims had been identified in late January, Missy and Lorraine's circle had widened to include Sherre and Mari; then Dawn, Melissa's aunt; and Kim. The Web, which once facilitated their lost loved ones' careers, now brought them all together. They convened on a memorial Facebook page that Mari had started for Shannan, where she posted several times a day with complaints about the press coverage and an occasional poem she'd written about her daughter (*I hold onto nothing but my nightmares / That one day I can finally leave this place / I hold onto nothing but my dreams / That one day both of us will meet again*). Missy started a similar page for Maureen and the other three Ocean Parkway victims. Lorraine dutifully went on Facebook every night after coming home from classes, posting throughout the day about everything she felt and thought (*Lorraine just discovered who loves her today*; *Lorraine just discovered who missed her today*; *On this day, God wants you to know . . .*).

On the phone and on Facebook, they searched for connections that might help the investigation: Were their daughters and sisters linked in some way? Did they know one another or have the same drivers? They pinged one another with daily affirmations, memorial videos, text message prayers, and curses at the press and the police. They stood by one another during the funerals. They held out hope that the visibility of the case meant it might be solved, the killer found.

And they called one another in shock when the police found more victims.

The police started up again on March 29, staking out a seven-and-a-half-mile stretch of bramble and poison ivy along Ocean Parkway, from Oak Beach to the Nassau County line. The first day they found nothing. But the next day, a cop driving slowly down the parkway, scanning dunes flanking Cedar Beach, noticed something on the side of the road and stopped the car. Cadaver dogs had searched many times already, but there it was: a fifth.

Again they thought it was Shannan, and again they were wrong. There was no titanium plate. Moreover, this set of remains was different from the first four—located a full mile from where the other bodies were found, and not on the edge of the bramble like the others but some thirty feet in from the highway. Dormer knew the search had to continue, but the method had to change. They needed to search the entire swath of bramble, even the parts too thick for a dog to penetrate. Where before the goal had been to search for clues around the grave sites, now they had to clear the brush entirely: If there was even one more body part in the fifteen-mile stretch of Ocean Parkway and beyond, they needed to find it.

More police came—150 officers on loan from the state police, the state park police, the police from neighboring Nassau County, and a busload of police recruits. They brought fire trucks with long ladders extended out and over the brush. Some sat in the elevated buckets and peered down; others scratched themselves up in the bramble below, wearing gardening gloves and high boots, using shovels and tree clippers and chain saws to slice through the brush and poison ivy. Still others donned diving gear and searched underwater, back off the dunes to the south and along Oak Beach, taking turns in pairs in Hemlock Bay. The FBI sent a Black Hawk helicopter and a fixed-wing aircraft to conduct flyovers with high-resolution cameras said to be able to clearly depict any object bigger than an inch—burlap, bones, signs of digging. Workers from the city medical examiner's office were on standby to look over all findings, distinguishing the animal bones from the human.

Five days later, on April 4, they found three more bodies. None of these was Shannan, either, and the new bodies also didn't fit the initial pattern. They were deeper in the underbrush, weren't wrapped in burlap, and had been left for a longer period of time. One was connected to a torso found a few years earlier farther out east in Manorville, Long Island. (The remains discovered on March 29 would also be linked to a torso found in Manorville, a twenty-year-old prostitute named Jessica Taylor killed in 2003.) Another wasn't a woman at all but a man, small and Asian, with what appeared to be women's clothes. Still another was a child, no bigger than a toddler, wrapped in a blanket. All the new finds were sent to New York City. This time the DNA analysis was complicated by the body parts having been found strewn about. Rather than taking one sample from each find, they had to take multiple samples, extracting DNA from any number of loose bones. Once that work was complete, they could make comparisons among the sets, then cross-check any matches against the FBI's DNA database.

That sort of work can take months. Dormer struggled to manage expectations. "Please keep in mind this is not an episode of *CSI*," he fumed at a press conference. But reports circulated that Steve Levy, the Suffolk County executive, had given Dormer a month to clean out his desk and leave, supposedly for sharing too many details about the bodies: "the burlap bags, that the victims were all on Craigslist, that they were prostitutes," a source told the *Post*. Levy was forced to issue a statement of support.

Daily rotations of camera crews descended on Oak Beach again. The neighbors couldn't believe it wasn't over. Oak Beach became the site of vigils, press conferences, and impromptu searches. Even Brewer said he thought that Shannan would be found soon. "I really do believe she's alive. What did she do? Just drop dead walking down the road?"

Few people following the case chose to believe that the killer's trail couldn't be traced in some way. A photograph from a traffic-light camera, say, outside Amber's place on America Avenue or where Maureen might have been picked up at Penn Station. A commuter on the Long Island Rail Road caught on video calling Melissa's sister from midtown. A voice recording of any person of interest—Brewer, Pak, even Coletti—that Melissa's sister could listen to and say whether it sounded like the man who had called her almost two years earlier.

Online, in print, and on TV, no rumor went unaired. *The killer knows the area like the back of his hand . . . He's a local clammer, with lots of access to burlap . . . He's a cop, or a retired cop, or a disgraced cop . . . He's my husband* (the last of which came from two different women). For a time, four victims of a killing spree in Atlantic City several years before seemed linked; one victim had even spent a few weeks on Long Island before she vanished. Dormer denied any connection. Then two NYPD officers, one active and one retired, were said to be under suspicion. Police denied those reports, too. It wasn't clear whether one of them had been the john of Maureen's that Missy had been told about. When the FBI filed an application seeking access to Akeem Cruz's laptop, reporters speculated on what Vybe might know about Megan's last night at the Holiday Inn Express in Hauppauge and whether he could have killed them all; that theory fizzled when the police didn't bite. Amber, too, seemed to have some potential suspects in her orbit: angry, ripped-off johns who had posted on Longisland erotic.com, lambasting her and her sister. Could the killer have been out for revenge?

The phone calls to Amanda had been well covered in Buffalo in 2009, and the media circled back to Melissa's family for more details. One reporter even reached Blaze, who, quoted by his given name, Johnny Terry, claimed he'd also received strange calls—about thirty, he said, over eight months—from someone he described as a "white guy." "He was threatening me," he said. "He said, 'You liked to do some crazy stuff with Melissa. I know where you be at.'" The police traced the caller's number not to Melissa's cell but to a disposable phone registered in the name of Mickey Mouse.

The search continued for weeks along the parkway, fanning westward toward Fire Island, the case warping into something beyond anyone's capacity to understand. Mari Gilbert started to dread the ring of her phone, expecting each time to hear news of another body. When the police stopped calling altogether, she felt shunted aside. She lost her patience when a lead detective in the case, Richard Higgins, asked her not to talk to the press. "Channel 7 calls me before the police," she said. "If you're not going to do anything, I'm going to talk." On April 6, on her front porch in Ellenville with Channel 2, she claimed that her persistence was the only reason the police kept searching for Shannan months after she was gone—and, she implied, the only thing that had brought the officer and his dog to Ocean Parkway. The next day she told the *Times* that Shannan, so complicated in life, was in death simply a hero: "If it wasn't for my daughter, these bodies never would have been found. Everyone has their destiny. Maybe this was hers." Soon Mari was fielding questions she wasn't ready for. Asked if she thought police would find Shannan with the other bodies, Mari paused before answering, "She's not there." Asked where she thought Shannan might be, Mari couldn't answer at all.

Like Lorraine, Mari was straining to recast her relationship with her daughter; to make amends. Kim was doing the same for her sister. Without fanfare, the same day Mari was opining from her front porch, Kim drove into the Oak Beach parking lot, hoping to see all the sites she'd been seeing on TV—Joe Brewer's house, Gus Coletti's house, the water, the beach, the highway. It happened that Kim had turned up on a day when the police were ferrying photographers on a bus to take photos of the ongoing search along the parkway. Kim boarded the bus and was quickly recognized. The reporters welcomed her; the day's story got that much better. When the bus stopped along the highway, Kim was disappointed by what she saw. To her, the whole thing seemed staged—two dozen cops walking through the bramble, as if on cue, just as the photographers arrived. The real search seemed to be happening somewhere else, farther down the road. Kim was frustrated, and when the police learned she was on the bus and got angry that she had been allowed on, that sent her over the edge. The video from Ocean Parkway that ran on the news that night was the sister of a Gilgo Beach victim leaving the scene in tears. "It's sad," Kim said on the air, "and I just wanted to get a chance to see where my sister was, but now I can't. And that's all I have to say."

Nothing about the family members held the media's attention for long. Soon enough, reporters went back to monitoring the search for new bodies. When some tried widening the lens of the story—discussing the dangers faced every night by escorts, hearing from a litany of advocates and activists who wanted to decriminalize prostitution, lock up johns, or shut down Craigslist and its competitor, Backpage—that only angered Mari more. Shannan hadn't even been found and was being held up as a poster child for the dangers of prostitution. Some of the frustration seeped out when Mari commented on an online story about Shannan:

> Shannan Maria Gilbert did NOT use any heavy drugs. She was a wonderful daughter, a best friend, a great sister, a special aunt, a good friend, and a nice cousin. What she chose to do takes NOTHING away from who she is to the people who love her . . .

Reporters waiting for word from the police in the Oak Beach parking lot kept knocking on doors, trolling for rumors behind the gate. On April 9, the *Post* published a story about an unnamed "forty-eight-year-old drifter with a penchant for strippers" said to have been at Brewer's house the night Shannan came out. The story ran a quote from the mother of the drifter, saying she thought her son had gone to Georgia. The police would continue to insist that Brewer was not a suspect.

Brewer offered more details of his evening with Shannan, all of which conveniently absolved him of any wrongdoing. Not only did he have nothing to do with Shannan's disappearance, now he was saying he hadn't even wanted to sleep with her. He told the Newark *Star-Ledger* that he'd been turned off by Shannan when she asked if he'd ever "come across any transvestites" when hiring escorts. Brewer said the comment made him wonder if she had something to hide—if she was really a man, or used to be. "I wanted her out," he said. That, he said, was when Shannan's behavior turned "erratic." "She saw things weren't going as she had hoped," he said. Of all the theories, only this one seemed too implausible for any other media outlet to pick up.

On April 11, the body count jumped to ten. The police made two more discoveries along the parkway to the west in Nassau County. Just a mile and a half from Jones Beach, they found human bones in a plastic bag. Four hours later, a Suffolk cop and cadaver dog found a human skull—most likely a woman's—in a wildlife sanctuary a mile away, west of Tobay Beach. Like Jessica Taylor's, these bodies would eventually demonstrate links to other unsolved cases farther out on Long Island. The head, hands, and right foot of a Jane Doe found along Ocean Parkway would be linked to a female torso discovered in Manorville in 2000. The head of another woman was discovered to be from the same victim as a pair of severed legs discovered in a black plastic bag in April 1996, along Blue Point Beach on the bay side of Fire Island, about a mile west of Davis Park.

The signature of these new finds didn't seem the same. Unlike the women in burlap, these remains had been scattered. The district attorney, Thomas Spota, suggested for the first time that while the four bodies in burlap were linked, the others might have been murdered by someone else, or even several killers. "It is clear that the area in and around Gilgo Beach has been used to discard human remains for some period of time," he said. "As distasteful and disturbing as that is, there is no evidence that all of these remains are the work of a single killer." The police's theory seemed to be changing. Gilgo Beach and its environs were, it seemed, a dumping ground, and more than one murderer was on the loose. Maureen, Melissa, Megan, and Amber were one small part of a continuum of murder that stretched for miles and miles along the South Shore of Long Island, from Jones Beach out east to Manorville.

Shannan was still missing, and the search continued. Nassau and state police officers with protective gear were using chain saws to cut through the bramble around Tobay and Jones Beach, clearing the land for helicopter flyovers. Suffolk was sending more divers around the docks and jetties on the bay and south sides of Oak Beach. If any casual observer still seemed fixated on a killer or killers, the victims seemed all but overlooked. "I think they look at them like they're throwaway," Mari told the *Times*. "They don't care." Her cause wasn't helped when, at a public-safety hearing in Suffolk County in early May, Dormer's chief of detectives, Dominick Varrone, called it a "consolation" that the killer didn't appear to be "selecting citizens at large—he's select-ing from a pool." The girls who used Craigslist, he said, "are very available, they're very vulnerable, they're willing to get into a car with a stranger."

The chief's message was clear: If they had been successful and well educated, like the Son of Sam's victims, all of Long Island might have been in a panic. But these were prostitutes. Of course they'd been killed.

Mari was losing hope. She had been patient—or patient enough— with the police, with the neighbors, and with the media, and her daughter's disappearance was being subsumed by a murder case that threatened to overlook her altogether. She decided to go public with information that, until then, had been kept strictly between her family and the police.

On April 12—just after the ninth and tenth sets of remains were found—WCBS 880, a twenty-four-hour local news radio station in New York, introduced a new angle on what might have happened to Shannan. In a segment picked up right away by her competitors, Sophia Hall became the first to report that just a few days after Shannan went missing, Mari had received a call at her home from someone identifying himself as Dr. Peter Hackett. "The doctor told them that Shannan was incoherent," Hall said. "So he took her into his home rehab to help her, and the next day, a driver came and picked her up."

Asked to comment, Hackett—speaking publicly for the first time about the Gilbert case—didn't confirm that he'd seen Shannan. But he didn't deny it, either. Instead, he said he had spoken to the police about Shannan. Then he made an anodyne speech about the case: "This is important that this is done, because these people need closure. And we need to find this girl if she's alive." The word *we* seemed to suggest that Hackett, as much as anyone else, was playing an active role in the search effort.

The same day, ABC News went to Hackett and ran his denial about seeing Shannan: "Of course not," he said. "That's ridiculous." It was too late. The next day, the local CBS News website recycled Hall's radio story from the day before, reporting that Hackett "said he saw Gilbert running at night near Oak Beach, looking both sick and distressed."

Hackett was not quoted directly in either report. There was no audio or video of him saying it. It was possible that the echo chamber of competing news reports had reprocessed Mari's claim into a reported fact, something that happens all too often in the scrum of a competitive news story. But for anyone looking to point fingers at Oak Beach neighbors—or wondering why more of them weren't speaking out—the Hackett subplot was a gift. The very possibility that he'd seen her that night shot new energy into the story. After months of reporters going back to Brewer and Coletti for new insights, the locked-room mystery of Oak Beach had an intriguing new character.

Reporters rushed to the doctor's cottage. A TV segment captured him walking outside, tall with slumping shoulders, wearing a baggy untucked oxford with an errantly knotted necktie flopped over a boulder-sized potbelly. Hackett had a round and boyish face with a double chin, sandy-gray hair, and deep-set eyes with dark circles beneath them. The limp from his false leg came off as more of a robust lurch. He glared at the camera with what seemed like a sneer.

For two days, all any reporter at Oak Beach wanted to know about was Peter Hackett. Mari couldn't help but be pleased, even if the doctor was still denying ever having spoken to her. On April 14, Hackett, wearing a tan windbreaker, a pink polo, and dark aviator sunglasses, was cornered by a camera crew from the CBS *Early Show*. "This has been a tough couple of days," he said, with his wife at his side.

"Did you see Shannan Gilbert that night?" asked the reporter, Seth Doane.

"Never," Hackett said.

"How could we?" said Barbara. "She was missing."

"She was missing," Hackett said.

The same day, Barbara came out of the cottage alone to talk with *Good Morning America*. "We've never met her," Barbara said. "We've never treated her. We don't treat rehab patients here."

The reporter, Andrea Canning, mentioned that Hackett had been interviewed by police three different times: news to the Gilberts, who were watching. "Ma'am," she asked Barbara, "why do you think that this woman had your husband's name, the mother of this potential victim?"

"They went door-to-door here. They talked to everybody here. And that's all."

"So you think maybe the mother remembered your name?"

"That's all I could figure," Barbara said.

"She said your husband told her he was a police officer."

"Do your research and you'll know all about Peter," Barbara said. "He's worked for the police. He was the Suffolk County EMS director for a few years. He was a police surgeon, yes."

"Would he ever hurt anyone?"

"No way. He's a great guy. The only thing he's guilty of is being late to dinner."

The police seemed surprised that Hackett was getting this much attention, or at least unsure how to react. "I think that was pretty much debunked," Dormer said during a news conference. "We spoke to that individual very early on, and he has been very cooperative."

As soon as this made the news, Sherre lashed out at the police. She and her family had told detectives half a dozen times in the past year about the phone call. How, she asked, could they be surprised to hear about him now? And why would they be so quick to exonerate him?

For the first time in months, Mari felt a sense of momentum. The doctor was calling her a liar. So were the police. The first of May was approaching: the first anniversary of Shannan's disappearance. Mari decided it was time to make her first trip beyond the Oak Beach gate.

■

They gathered in the parking lot at noon. About a dozen friends were there with Mari, including Sherre and Sarra; Mari's best friend, Johanna Gonzalez; and Johanna's daughter, Osheanna, who was close to Shannan. The plan was to retrace Shannan's steps, knock on doors, and raise hell.

Reporters and photographers trailed the group as they walked down the narrow access road and into the gated community. The residents were appalled. On the way in, a neighbor in a car slowed down enough to ask, "Do you need all these people?"

Another neighbor shouted across the street when she saw Mari at someone's door: "Just to let you people know, I am calling 911 now!"

Mari shouted back: "It's gonna take forty-five minutes for 911 to get here!" Her friends all laughed.

They spent two hours walking the streets. They knocked on the door of Hackett's cottage on Larboard Court, but there was no answer. Mari peered through his windows, searching for signs of burlap, TV cameras following her every move. She was energized, darting back and forth on the street, spoiling for a fight. At the end, they held hands in the parking lot while Shannan's aunt Lori said a prayer. "This candle is for Shannan," Sherre said. "May she come home alive and safe."

Though nothing she did changed the fact that Shannan was still missing, Mari had made some noise, and the visit steeled her resolve. "A lot of people want to contact me anonymously, because they're afraid," she said. "They're really afraid." Walking those roads past the bramble for the first time also fueled her suspicions. The police weren't talking. Either they were keeping secrets, or even they didn't know what else was hidden at Oak Beach.

FAMILIES

I first met Missy Cann on the Monday after Easter, a little over four months after the body of her sister, Maureen, had been discovered along Ocean Parkway. We agreed to have lunch at a well-known lobster shack on a pier in New London, Connecticut, with a tranquil view of the Long Island Sound. That day, our goals had intersected. I was a writer, looking to learn more about the victims of a tragedy who seemed overlooked. She was there to make sure her sister's case didn't grow cold all over again.

Missy is more or less a twin of her older sister, though her eyes are brown, not green. As her children weaved around Missy's legs beneath the picnic table, she went through the litany of tragedy that had followed her since Maureen disappeared. While the world was at Missy's doorstep, she would not forget the four years when getting anyone to take the case seriously had seemed almost impossible. She would not forget the police in Norwich who had brushed off the first missing-persons claims because Maureen was working as an escort. She would not forget the two years it took even to get Maureen's name onto the NamUs, the national registry of missing persons. In her soft, light voice, she talked about the two children Maureen left behind: the eleven-year-old girl, Caitlin, whom Missy saw on weekends; and the five-year-old boy, Aidan, whose father has kept out of contact with Maureen's family. Aidan is the same age as one of Missy's children and one of her brother's, too. The fact that all the cousins can't be together is yet another loss.

As she spoke, Missy seemed determined to list every misery afflicting her just to exorcise them all. She was building up to her family's second great tragedy—Will's death, two years after Maureen disappeared. Missy took to Facebook to post tribute videos of her sister and her brother as she found herself becoming obsessed with her sister's case. She lost her job as a hostess at Mohegan Sun. She didn't care. "I was like, 'I can find another job, but I can't find another sister.' Going on with my life felt guilty."

While, given the chance, she would shout from every rooftop to remind the world that they existed, there were others in Maureen's family who didn't appreciate the very public role she played, including her mother. Marie Ducharme's position was clear: Her daughter's life had been her own business, and nothing anyone said could change the fact that Maureen was gone, or correct the course of her life now that it was over. Missy and her mother didn't talk much anymore. Missy had once worried that the world would forget her sister. But now her greatest fear, apart from the absence of justice, was that Maureen would be misunderstood. Missy was struggling to reclaim the narrative of Maureen's life—to protect the best memories of her and perhaps soften the darker aspects of a woman who lived dangerously.

"I don't like how they're talking about her," Missy said. "I understand they only know what she was down there doing, and that's what they look at her as. But it doesn't *matter* what she did. She was still a mother. She still meant the world to her daughter, she meant the world to me." She was tearful now. "We needed her in our lives. The world lost such an imaginative, creative person. You don't know—she was in her mid-twenties. She had her whole life ahead of her. Who's to say that she was going to be doing this her whole life?"

Toward the end of lunch, Missy revealed another reason why

she had agreed to come that day. She and members of the other four families had been in close touch since January. With the new bodies bringing more visibility to the case, they'd come together to plan a vigil at Oak Beach in June. Missy was excited by the idea, as much as she could be. She and Lorraine had been the only family members to meet face-to-face, and now there was a chance to meet some of the few people who had shared the same awful experience.

I suggested they come together in New York for a group interview to help publicize the vigil and put a human face on their daughters and sisters. Missy agreed and set off to convince the others.

Two weeks later—May 2, 2011, a year and a day after Shannan disappeared—Lorraine took a flight to New York City from Portland, Maine, her arms folded around her laptop like she was embracing her daughter. Kim left her father's hospital bed in Wilmington, North Carolina. Lynn and Jeff shut down JJ's Texas Hots in Buffalo for a few days and brought along Melissa's teenage sister, Amanda. Mari, having just spent a full day knocking on doors at Oak Beach for her daughter's first anniversary, took a car back to New York from Ellenville, grateful for a driver who let her smoke the whole way down. Missy, too afraid to make the trip on her own, begged her husband to drive her after he worked the night shift at the navy base in Groton. "I have the best husband ever!" Missy posted on Facebook the night before, and several of her new friends agreed by clicking the "like" button.

We met in the lobby of a hotel in Tribeca. As they trickled in, we filled a long rectangular table at the hotel's restaurant. My task was to moderate the conversation. I wanted to talk about the case: those phone calls to Amanda, Amber's relationship with Kim, the circumstances of Shannan's last night at Oak Beach. I said very little and just listened while they started talking—tentatively at first, then warm and even raucous. Together, they made up a kind of grim sorority. Missy vented her anger at people who judged the victims because they were escorts. "I'll always love my sister, and I'm proud of her no matter what anyone says," she said. Mari agreed. "Some TV station said they were women whose families just didn't keep in touch," she said. Missy was glad to be with people who understood her. "It's amazing. I feel like I've known all these people my whole life." Mari added that "it's hard to talk to family. It's easier to talk to a stranger."

Only Mari seemed ill at ease. She knew that the rest of the women at the table at least knew where their loved ones were. They had a closure that she lacked, and she felt alone. On top of everything else, she knew it was her daughter's disappearance that had helped find them all. Mari wasn't sure whether to be jealous or grateful that she still had hope of finding Shannan alive. Either way, being there felt like a betrayal, a quiet acknowledgment that Shannan really was gone. "In retrospect, I shouldn't be here," she said stiffly. "Because my daughter has not passed."

Before they even ordered, they were speaking in a special short-hand.

"Melissa had Nextel," said Amanda. "Nextel, you can't do anything to trace it. It's prepaid."

"Well, my daughter had Sprint, she had five cell phones," Mari said. "She just turned on her fifth cell phone two weeks before this happened to her."

"What I did is, I called Boost directly," Missy said. "I called the customer service and I was like, 'Listen, my sister's missing, I need these phone records right now.' I said, 'I can give you my social security number, if anything happens, you can file charges against me, I just need her phone records now.' And he e-mailed me her phone records and the password to her Boost mobile phone line."

"One time he turned Melissa's cell phone on," said Lynn, "and they picked up the tower. It was Massapequa, and that's, like, right there."

"Oh, okay," said Mari. "And my daughter's cell phone and purse have never been found."

"Megan's hasn't been found, neither," said Lorraine.

"My sister had her phone," said Kim, "but four people worked off of that phone, too. After my sister went missing, there were still phone calls with girls using her ad. You just can't go off the phone records, at least not my sister's. And computer trails aren't as easy as you think, because the guys don't get you on the e-mail. You post a number, a cell-phone number, and they call a number. How do you track that? There wasn't any text at the time she went missing. And I spoke to her that day."

That got everyone's attention. What did she and her sister talk about?

Kim smiled. Then she looked down, shook her head, and laughed. "We were in a fight."

The others laughed softly.

Lorraine indulged herself with an uncomplicated version of her daughter. "Megan was fun, caring, a loving mom," she said. "If you ever met Megan, you would fall right in love with her." But her descriptions of Megan were fuzzy at best. Soon she owned up to being a drunk for most of Megan's life, and she said that since Megan disappeared, her own mother had been looking after Megan's daughter, Lili. "I have more bad days than I have good ones."

Missy nodded. "We got into arguments about things that I

thought that she was doing," she said, "but no one could keep Maureen from doing something she wanted to do."

"Melissa wanted to make money for a salon of her own," said Lynn. "And originally, when she moved to New York, she was working in a salon. We think the salon was a cover for her pimp here."

The women were too polite to zero in on Amanda right away, but it was lost on none of them that Melissa's sister was the one person who may have spoken with the killer. "The media pounded the shit out of us to get the content of the calls," Lynn said. "And we're like, 'We can't let you know anything more than what's already out there, because the only other person who knows what was said besides the police is the killer.'"

The others couldn't resist a question or two. "Can I just ask you," said Kim, "did he sound husky, or brusquey, or what?"

"No, he didn't have an accent," Amanda said. "He was white."

"Did he sound like a New Yorker?" said Kim.

Amanda struggled to answer. "Not really. It was just kinda plain. You know, he was white, probably in his thirties, forties, maybe."

"So he's not from New York?" Missy asked.

Amanda shrugged. "Maybe," she said. "He could have been."

The questions came faster: Was he angry, happy, nasty, mocking?

"He was calm, in control," Amanda said. "He knew what he was doing."

We left the hotel at lunchtime. Missy gasped the second she stepped through the hotel's revolving door. It was a bright spring day in New York, warm and breezy. But it was as if, at that moment, the fact sank in that this was the city where her sister was last seen. A few of the others also seemed anxious, unfamiliar with the city and suddenly wishing they were somewhere else. Back inside, a crowded, creaky elevator triggered screams. Every chance they got, everyone but Kim rushed back down the stairs and outside to smoke.

Kim had a little leverage in the gathering. An escort herself, she knew all about the money, how calls were arranged, the risks, the drugs. "The money is just as addictive as drugs," Kim said. "I've done this, and it isn't really about being naive. In the beginning you make the money, and you're making it without the drugs and without the bullshit. And then you get addicted to the money."

I asked Kim if she had a drug problem, too, like her sister.

"I've had my own, I'm not gonna lie to you. It's not exactly affiliated, you know, but eight out of ten calls nowadays are affiliated with drugs. Because drugs and this go together hand in hand. I was telling Lorraine that it's not uncommon for a girl to meet someone who sells crack or coke and team up with him and go on a call because both of you are gonna make money. I've had guys go, 'Look, if you can't bring coke, don't even come.'"

I opened the floor to others. Was anyone else at the table surprised by details like these?

"I hate to be so vivid about it," Kim boasted.

The others saw it almost as a trick question. To say they were surprised made them seem naive. To say they weren't made them seem complicit.

"Basically, my sister explained it almost exactly like that," Missy said.

"You know, it's so interesting," said Jeff Martina, sitting next to Lynn and Amanda. "Melissa wasn't into drugs."

"Yeah, Maureen wasn't into drugs, either," Missy said.

"But I know there are girls that she's talking about," Jeff said.

Kim seemed a little baffled. "I mean, I *lived* it."

"I mean, she drank to the point where she blacked out," Lynn said.

"The drinking is better than the coke because it's legal," Kim said. "Methadone? There's no difference. They call it hillbilly heroin."

Jeff tried to change the subject. "This is a dangerous profession," he said.

"I think they all knew him," Missy said, gently changing the subject back to the killer.

"I don't know whether they knew him or not," said Jeff.

"I think so," said Lynn.

Missy winced. "My sister would have never gone with someone—"

"My sister and I talked about that," Kim said. "The precautions you take. Like, the worst thing that ever happened to me was the guy's wife came home."

To one degree or another, all of the women had taken on the role of amateur homicide investigator. "It's like a little detective crew," Kim said. So little was known about the nights the other girls disappeared that the women tended to focus on the night Shannan went missing, replaying the details of what happened again and again, searching for clues to who the killer might be. No one engaged in that exercise more than Mari.

Everything about the day she'd just spent at Oak Beach made her feel like the people there were trying to wish her daughter away. "It's not even about the prostitution," Mari said. "It's about how all their clients were wealthy. Look where she was. They don't want the attention. There's doctors there, lawyers there, cops there. They don't want to be associated with that kind of behavior. That's why they don't care. Money can take care of anything."

For the first time, Mari talked publicly about her suspicions of the driver, Michael Pak. "During the twenty-three-minute 911 tape, she's screaming, pounding on doors. We were given an excerpt of it: 'Help me help me he's gonna kill me help me help me.' It was the driver she's getting away from. My daughter says his name. And in the background is this person, 'What are you talking about, I'm trying to help you, you're lying,' and the tape went dead."

Shannan's coat was found on the road, she said, but then the police misplaced it. "Come on, a big huge coat? How could they have lost it?" The errors didn't rile her as much as the apathy—and what she thought was a whitewashing. Mari didn't believe that John Mallia and his dog had been searching for the bodies when they came across them. She thought the police were just trying to look good, that the recent discoveries were more of a coincidence than a piece of crack police work. "The cop stopped along the side of the road to let the dog do his business," Mari said with a wave of her hand. "The dog *accidentally* found the remains."

She remained fixated on Hackett. She told the others about her attempt to talk to him a day earlier, during her visit to Oak Beach. ("Is that whose door you were banging on?" Lynn asked, and Mari laughed, answering, "Was that on TV?") After no one answered the bell, Mari said she peered through a window, noticing what she thought was burlap. "I was about ready to flip out," she said. "One of the news crews filmed it. I think they're going to keep that. They're going to give it to my lawyer."

No one could be sure that Mari really saw what she thought

she'd seen. If anything, Mari was more than a little out on a limb: After Mari and the Hacketts' go-round in the press a few weeks earlier, the police had said repeatedly that Hackett, like Brewer and Pak, was not a suspect. Still, the others fell silent as Mari explained what she believed had happened to her daughter, unfurling a theory that, for the time being, implicated Joe Brewer, Michael Pak, and Peter Hackett and linked her daughter's disappearance to the other murders. She said she thought that Brewer frequently brought girls to Oak Beach for parties, and that Hackett knew. She said she thought that Pak drove girls to other parties there. She blamed Hackett for what had happened to the security video; she said she'd learned that as a board member of the Oak Island Beach Association, he was listed as playing a security role. "They have no record of her screaming and yelling and running, they have no videotape of the truck that was chasing her! And Hackett has medical experience."

If Brewer, Hackett, and Pak were involved, I asked, why would they leave the bodies so close to home? That's the point, she replied. "Who would ever think?"

Missy nodded. "Maybe because they thought if they travel, they knew they'd get caught," she said. "And they knew that area."

Mari nodded along with her. "Yeah, she was probably *forced* to get stoned, drunk, high, whatever."

"Not forced," said Kim. "She probably did it. Because I've done it on calls, too."

That annoyed Mari. Who was Kim, of all people, to say what her daughter might or might not have done? Shannan was in line to become the next victim, Mari said. But Shannan, she insisted, wasn't like the other girls. She would not go quietly. "I think they underestimated her," Mari said. "She knew, 'This is not what I want to do.' And without her running and screaming, none of these other bodies would have been found."

The appeal of the theory was obvious. Any mother would want to think her daughter stood up for herself. Of course, it was all conjecture, and it also happened to be demeaning of the other girls, whom Mari was implying didn't try to fight back. Kim, for one, didn't think it happened that way. Drawing from her own experience as an escort, her theory was slightly less flattering to Shannan. She said that she thought Shannan got high with Brewer that night, even though he later denied it. "He got this girl probably so blown out of her mind, because that's how they are. They've got the drugs and they've got the money, and you're there for the hour. Then, for whatever reason, he did something to spook this girl. That girl was scared for her life. Something made her think that somebody's going to kill her."

"She was hiding behind his couch, right?" Missy asked.

"She wouldn't leave," Kim said. "She's scared. So Brewer calls the driver and says, 'Shannan won't leave.'"

One detail still confused Kim. "Why didn't she run to the driver?" she asked. "The driver's my safety. I don't give a damn how fucked up I was, my ass is going to the driver, because that's my way out, whether it's the police coming or somebody trying to kill me."

Mari offered an explanation. "Because when she was done with Brewer, she went back to the car to go home, and the driver's like, 'Where's my money?' And she said, 'I don't have any money.' So he brought her back to Brewer's, and Brewer said, 'What are you talking about? I paid her.' She said she's tired of the driver taking all her money. 'I've given you money every time, I want this money now.' And that's when they started arguing, and she hid in Brewer's house." Maybe Shannan ran off to safety, Mari believed, or maybe that was when the killer got her.

The others wanted to know why Mari thought Shannan wouldn't share her fee with the driver. "I was the last one Shannan talked to that night, six hours before she was missing," Mari said. "We had planned for her to come home for my birthday and for Mother's Day." Mari thought Shannan didn't want to give the driver his cut that night so she could have enough money to buy her mother a present. "She said, 'I have to work tonight, Mommy.'"

Everyone was quiet for a moment. The guilt permeating that theory was so overpowering that no one wanted to acknowledge it. Finally, Kim said, "Okay. So you don't know that conversation went on between her and that driver at that point? You're just guessing?"

"I'm assuming," Mari said tensely, "that when she went back to the driver and the driver said, 'Give me the money,' she said, 'No, I need the money for my mom's birthday.'" She paused and locked eyes with Kim. "Because she told me, 'I'm doing a job so I'll have some money to buy you something for your birthday.'"

Mari was incensed now. But to all the other women at the table, Kim was presenting an alternative image of all the girls—a less innocent one than some would care to picture. Unlike any of the others, Kim saw in all these murders an alternate ending to her own life, one she'd long imagined and yet somehow escaped. "I was thinking, *God, did I run across this person?*" she told me later. "And maybe I wasn't his type?"

Kim almost said something else to Mari but then stopped herself. "I'm telling you, I feel for you more than I feel for myself or any other lady here," she said. "Because Shannan is still missing, you know? At least I know where my sister is. And if I don't know nothing else, I have that closure."

Jeff Martina seemed to want to break the tension and bring everyone back together. "I just think all these girls, all our daughters, our sisters, whoever they are, I think they all met the same nut."

"To me, Joe Brewer is guilty even if he didn't kill her," Kim said. "Because he got Shannan in there. He got high with her. There was drugs. It was obvious." But later, she pressed her view again. "The connection between these four women is cocaine," she said when we were alone. "That wasn't my sister's drug of choice, but she had access to it. And if it was gonna make her money, she would do it. Shannan had a history of coke. Even though people won't admit it in public, just do your research and you'll see. So I think the killer likes to get high."

At dinner, after some drinks, Lynn and Jeff passed around family photos of Melissa as a teenager, looking a little like Amanda and exactly like her mother. Lynn showed the group the silver cross she wore around her neck with Melissa's ashes installed inside.

They dropped their guard a little. "It's tough enough to see my daughter go through this," Lynn said, "and a month later my mother dies and I've got to keep my whole family together. I've got to be strong for her, for my dad. Everything is dumped on me."

"I lost my mom, and my dad is dying," said Kim.

"It's made me a stronger person," said Lynn. She laughed. "I'm strong as hell, but I break down all the time."

"I do, too," Lorraine said.

They talked about the case again, its logistics and forensics. There was a robust discussion about whether the salt air from the

ocean corrodes human flesh more quickly or acts as a preserva-
tive.

"So Shannan had a metal jaw?" Kim said.

"I can't say," said Mari coolly before Kim asked her why the
police weren't searching the bramble with metal detectors. "It's
titanium. That can't be detected by a metal detector."

Missy and Kim glanced across the table at Amanda's cara-
mel skin. They both wondered if one common bond among the
girls was that they dated black men. "Everybody's assuming he's
white," Kim said. "Maybe that was the connection—they would
see black guys. The profile says white, but you never know."

The women talked about the vigil they were planning. They
hoped to march down Ocean Parkway, near where the bodies
were found, but the police were pushing back. "They don't want
us walking down that road," said Missy, who was serving as the
group's liaison to the Suffolk County police. Missy wanted the
people of Oak Beach to be as upset as she was—or, failing that,
at least to understand. "I may never get closure. But that's still a
place where she was. And I just feel like that community has to
see the families. All they care about is the values of their houses
and how their community looks. Because they're just stuck-up
rich people that don't care."

"Look at Natalee Holloway," Kim said—the white blond Ala-
bama girl whose disappearance in Aruba five years earlier had
become a cable-news staple. "People should have been elbow to
elbow out there, walking for this girl, Shannan Gilbert. Why not?
What makes her disappearance any different?"

Missy had taken it upon herself to police anyone seeking to
exploit the case. One target was Longislandserialkiller.com, a site
that reprinted every news story about the case and invited anony-

mous comments. "They were selling freaking T-shirts!" she said. She told the others that she had asked the police to shut down a posting of a rap video called "Ocean Parkway" that used photos of the dead girls without permission (sample lyric: *The white girl had to get it because she could snitch on me / They killed you because you were a menace to society*). Searching the Web, Missy had discovered the message board on Longislanderotic.com where anonymous johns had threatened to take revenge on Amber months before the media found it.

In the middle of dinner, two NYPD detectives who worked on Melissa's disappearance dropped by the restaurant to say hello to Lynn and Jeff. Jeff said the two detectives had been assigned to the NYPD's terrorist task force, but after being turned on to the case by Lynn and Jeff's lawyer, they went out of their way to help. "They went above and beyond. They were bangin' on strip club doors." As soon as they showed up, Mari scurried away for a cigarette. "I hate cops. I'm outta here."

When she came back, Mari was distant again. "What I'm going through is different," she said. "Shannan is still missing. She's not a body."

Kim reached out, trying to take the sting out of their conflict earlier. "We're all here together because of Shannan," she told Mari. "I don't care if they *ever* find her. As long as I live, she will always be dear to me."

After dinner, we returned to the hotel lobby to say goodbye. The women seemed to have wilted. The hugs started. "We'll be friends till the end," Lorraine said. "Even after they find him. We'll all be friends till we all go upstairs."

Lorraine handed the others identical trinkets she'd picked up at a shop in Maine. They were little pink hearts with angel wings.

"It's because the girls are all in our hearts," Lorraine said, "and they're all in heaven." The other women loved them. They were a new family, for now.

Mari liked the trinket, too. "I always worked for, like, normal-class people, like fourteen dollars an hour," she said. "But Shannan just liked really expensive things. I don't know who she picked it up from." She remembered the night Shannan disappeared and their last phone call. "I said, 'Look, Shannan, you coming is my gift. You don't have to bring me a present, just come home.'" After hanging up, she said she texted Shannan: *Be safe.*

Right away, she said, her daughter answered: *I always am.*

Everyone showed up at the June 11 vigil except Kim, who wasn't answering her phone or returning calls or e-mails. The others were concerned that she'd gone back to work.

The media was there, paying attention to the girls, and that counted for something. The TV outlets were stumbling over one another now. A News 12 camera crew was joined by crews from *Dateline, 48 Hours,* and a British crew preparing a documentary for A&E. Lorraine rolled in a little late with Greg and Nicci. In front of the cameras, Lorraine was transformed, so different from the woman who sat so quietly a month ago with the others. "I have to keep her name out there until this person is caught," she said. "She can't speak for herself."

Lynn and Jeff brought Lynn's sister, Dawn, and her father, Elmer. They all were wearing T-shirts in honor of Melissa. "We're celebrating the lives of the girls," Lynn said at a short press conference in the Oak Beach parking lot, "and just want everybody to know that you know these girls, they were mothers, daughters, sisters, aunts, cousins. You know, it doesn't matter what they did for their profession that they were victims."

Missy didn't speak directly to reporters—she was too self-conscious for that—but off-camera, she arranged a balloon release in honor of the dead and missing. She also got the police to arrange for the families to spend five minutes along the highway where the bodies had been found. The shoulder was narrow and the roadway dangerous. Everyone came away with ticks. When they spent a little longer there than they'd planned, the police urged them to finish. Mari cursed them out: "Fuck you, you fucking cops!"

Missy was appalled. So was Lynn. In time, Mari would do other things that puzzled them. When Missy planned another visit to Oak Beach for early August, to do some recon work of her own about Shannan's disappearance, Mari caught wind of it and got angry at Missy for not including her. "Shannan's *my* daughter," Mari said. "Not *her* daughter."

Missy didn't understand what had set Mari off. This was the first time that Mari's combativeness had come in her direction, though it wouldn't be the last. Missy decided to be diplomatic. She canceled her trip. "Mari is a peculiar person," Missy said.

That night they all jammed into a few rooms of a local hotel, playing with Missy's kids and bonding some more before heading off to bed. The next day, Lorraine returned home to Portland, Lynn to Buffalo, Missy to Groton. They resumed their Facebook relationships. Now and then, a few would be brought into the city again for on-camera interviews with networks and cable channels that had picked up on the story. In August, Lynn hosted a get-together for a few days, and she and Lorraine and Missy all got a chance to bond without reporters and camera crews. Mari was not invited. Kim didn't come, either. No one had heard a word from her since May. As she had before, she'd dropped out of sight.

CONSPIRACIES

Joe Scalise, Jr., lives with his wife in a house at the far end of the Bayou, the long east-west road in Oak Beach that connects to the Hacketts' street, Larboard Court. His father, Joe Sr., lives next door to Joe, and his sister, Dawn, is nearby, too, in a house with her husband. Together, they've assembled a little compound. Still stinging from the association's attempt to oust the whole family in the nineties, the Scalises do their best not to mingle with most of their neighbors.

Joe's father first bought a bungalow in Oak Beach in 1971, when the taxes, including association fees, were under a thousand a year. Services like sanitation and power were spotty at best in the winter, and most people flew the coop in the colder months. Today each house in the neighborhood pays about twenty thousand dollars a year in taxes, and the association fees are close to $3,800. What hasn't changed, according to Joe Sr., is the way the people of Oak Beach feel entitled to more than their share of privacy. "The interesting thing about Oak Beach," he told me, "is within that gate, it's like its own little country. You can do anything you want behind that gate."

Since Shannan's disappearance the previous May, Joe and his father have stood in disgust at the behavior of their neighbors, at the indignation over the investigation, as if they were only being threatened by the backflow of traffic clogging the quiet streets. Both the elder and younger Scalise were accustomed to feeling disgusted with Oak Beach. They would be the first to admit harboring a grudge against many of their neighbors for years—at least those who voted to have them drummed out. Come April, they watched as Hackett denied Mari's claim that he'd called her, and they watched Barbara Hackett deny it, too. For the Scalises, who had been listening carefully to every rumor floating around the neighborhood for the past year, their neighbors' paranoia made more sense: The killer, the Scalises said, was one of their own.

Neither Joe nor his father had ever liked Peter Hackett. He was friendly with Gus Coletti, who had led the charge against them. Beyond that, Joe and his father thought the doctor was a strange guy. "He's a wannabe cop," Joe Sr. said. Father and son heard a rumor that Hackett would offer neighbors a deal to be their doctor for life for twenty thousand dollars. Joe Jr. remembered the way Hackett used to tell people about a supposedly surefire way to ace a lie-detector test—by pressing a tack into your hand or foot each time you answer truthfully, giving the machine a faulty baseline to work off of when you lie. Joe Sr. remembered one night when there was a jumper on one of the bridges over the Great South Bay. "I get there, and there's Peter Hackett saying, 'I got this, Joe.' He must have been listening to the scanner."

Once they heard the reports on the news that Hackett might have called Mari Gilbert and said he'd helped Shannan, a light-bulb went off. Joe Scalise and his father became convinced that their neighbors had been covering up for a friend. They had no proof, of course. And Hackett repeatedly denied having ever seen Shannan. But Joe Jr. was offering Mari and the victims' families something every bit as powerful as proof: unfettered testimony from an Oak Beach insider. In late June, two months after Mari started pointing her finger at Hackett, Joe Jr. made his debut as the self-appointed Deep Throat of the Long Island serial-killer case. Using the pseudonym Flukeyou, Joe posted close to a hundred times on Longislandserialkiller.com over the next several months.

> The Dr. is a true psychopath!!!!!! He's been flying under the radar for years and has a whole pack of loyal followers inside the community. These are really sick people! There are only 72 houses in the association . . . everyone knows everyone's business and there is definitely something going on with the Dr!!!

One morning after a volley of e-mails and phone calls, I drove out to Oak Beach to visit with Joe and his father and hear them make their case against Hackett in person. The younger Joe is tall, handsome, and broad-shouldered, with dark hair and dark eyes. In his thirties, he works from home mostly as a financial consultant. His father has the tanned, leathered skin of a year-round beach resident; he still supervises the Jones Beach lifeguards every summer. "There are seventy-two houses here," the younger Joe told me over coffee in his airy kitchen. "There's about twenty-five people that are totally uninvolved, twenty-five that are in bed with Hackett, and about twenty-five that are, you know, free-thinking normal people that will go, 'What's going on here?'"

The Scalises are used to gossip. In their view, everyone is suspect. Joe Brewer is a slob, a party animal, out of control. Gus Coletti is a toady for the association, forever tainted in their eyes. And Peter Hackett? Over coffee, Joe Jr. unspooled his suspicions and theories, all as vividly and elaborately worked out as they were colored by his hatred for the man. He noted how Shannan and Joe Brewer had left the house briefly toward the start of their date, and that while no one knows where they went, he assumes, like a lot of people following the case, that they went to get drugs. Hackett, as a doctor already well known for treating his neighbors, would be—according to Joe Jr.—an ideal resource for anyone in the neighborhood who wanted a prescription. Hackett didn't seem to have a job at all, hadn't for years. Maybe he could use the money. What if Hackett sold drugs to all the teenagers, too? What if Hackett was Brewer's connection that night? And what if it wasn't the first time?

All through the summer after Shannan disappeared, Joe Jr. said he'd been hearing scuttlebutt from the neighborhood that when Shannan pounded on Barbara Brennan's door, Barbara didn't just call the police. She called a neighbor named Tom Canning, another active member of the association, and then Canning called Hackett, which would have put Hackett in a position to help Shannan, just as Mari said he professed. It made sense that neighbors would have called Hackett because of the role he'd always played at Oak Beach. He was even listed in the Oak Beach phone directory as the "medical director" of the defibrillator the community kept on-site. For anyone looking for evidence that Tom Canning had been involved that morning, they needed only to look in the *Post* a few days after police found the bodies in burlap, to see his son, Justin Canning, talking about the scene with a lot of familiarity. "She was in a panic," Justin said. "We thought she was on drugs."

In the Scalises' theory of that night, Hackett wasn't merely a Good Samaritan who tried to help Shannan and then was left with a body on his hands. Joe Jr. believed Shannan wasn't the first girl to get caught up in a party gone bad at Oak Beach, and he believed Hackett was one of the hosts that no one knew about. "Shannan was hunted down that night," he said. "These games have been going on at Oak Beach for years." He said he believed Hackett had killed the other four girls, and that Shannan was the one who'd almost tripped him up. He said Hackett's neighbors were in on it, and as proof, he mentioned a recent report about a black escort whom police found running down a highway on Long Island, saying she was part of a drug- and sex-trafficking ring and that people were trying to kill her. According to the *Long Island Press,* the woman spent some time in Nassau University Medical Center's psych ward before being released. "I've lived there my whole life, and for a girl to disappear, something happened," Joe Jr. said. "It's not a satanic cult. But there's a lot of shit that's not kosher about Oak Beach."

There was barely enough time to digest everything before Joe and his dad offered to show me where they thought the doctor got rid of the bodies. We got into Joe Jr.'s car and slipped up the Bayou to Larboard Court, stopping outside the Hackett cottage. Joe noted how close the doctor's place was to Barbara Brennan's house; then he noted that Hackett's house was right up against the edge of an enormous marsh. This marsh, Joe and his father said, was where they thought Shannan was now. The police hadn't searched there yet, despite how close the marsh was to where Shannan was last seen. The Scalises thought her body might be there because of the way they said Hackett reacted when he'd heard that the marsh would be drained as part of a mosquito-abatement project. "They wanted to dredge all back in the wetlands," Joe Jr. said. "If you Google Map it, it looks like a giant bathtub with one major artery that runs through it and a bunch of off-sprits. And one of those runs right to the back of Hackett's house."

Joe Jr.'s sister had led the movement to dig out and restore the marsh. The board didn't know about the project, Joe said, until his sister told them. "Peter Hackett starts calling my sister, asking, 'When are they gonna be digging?'" This, he said, was just a few weeks before—"lo and behold," Joe Sr. said—the four bodies were discovered on the side of Ocean Parkway.

They had more to show me. Joe drove down Anchor's Way—the street Shannan is believed to have run down from Coletti's house to Brennan's—and stopped at a pair of storage sheds about a hundred yards from Hackett's house, near what used to be a tennis court. From the car, Joe pointed toward the marsh again, then the sheds. "If the bodies weren't behind Hackett's house," he said, "then he was storing them right back here." Both sheds were empty now. But the Scalises believed that as soon as Hackett learned the marsh would be drained, risking the discovery of Shannan's body, he had to take action and dispose of the four girls in burlap he had hidden in the shed near his house.

Why just four bodies? I wondered. As long as Joe Jr. was saying Hackett killed them all, why wouldn't Shannan have been in the shed, too? Because, Joe explained, the attack on Shannan hadn't gone as planned. There wasn't enough time. She'd gone running, and people had seen her, and the police had come. After the chaos that early morning, she'd ended up in the marsh. Joe imagined that Hackett probably thought no one could possibly find her there—until the mosquito project was announced.

Ever since the morning Shannan had vanished, Joe and his father assumed that Hackett had been working to cover his tracks. They believed that Hackett had erased the security video. They thought that he was tipped to the search by his next-door neighbor, a Suffolk County cop. And they thought the doctor started acting especially guilty afterward. "Peter's a showboater," said Joe Jr. "He can't help himself. Which is why, if he *wasn't* involved in this, this would be his great moment. His big chance to catch a serial killer." In other words, the fact that Hackett had shied away from the limelight was, to the Scalises, at least, only further proof that he was hiding something.

We drove out of the gate, down the access road, and over to the far side of the parking lot to the old community center built by the Reverend John Dietrich Long, the building where the association holds its meetings. Next to the community center was a driveway, a direct egress to Ocean Parkway. The Scalises said that anyone in Oak Beach could have driven four bodies out via the driveway without ever being caught on the gatehouse security video. Only a few people had a key to the lock on the metal chain securing the driveway. The Scalises said that Hackett—the self-appointed emergency-preparedness expert of Oak Beach— was one of those people.

"Once you pop out through this thing," said Joe Sr., "you can actually make a left across the parkway, and you'll be almost to the dump sites."

The problem with conspiracy theories is what they don't say. Mull over any theory long enough, and suddenly, everything you see around you is proof. Aside from the fact that an astonishing number of neighbors would have had to be in on it, one of the biggest problems with the Scalises' theory is the simple lack of corroboration. Aside from Mari and Sherre, no one, except one CBS radio reporter, who didn't have a direct quote, had stepped forward to confirm hearing Hackett say he saw Shannan that night or tried to help her.

It would have been no exaggeration to say that ever since the first reports surfaced, every reporter working on the serial-killer story had been trying to find someone who had heard Hackett say he saw her. No one had found a thing. The closest I came myself was hearing from a private investigator, working briefly on behalf of a supporter of the families, who said that "everyone was calling Hackett" the morning Shannan disappeared. This investigator had gleaned this not by looking at phone records, which only the police possessed, but through interviews. Maybe everyone really was calling Hackett that morning. Or maybe everyone was repeating the same gossip that the Scalises had heard.

During my visit, the Scalises said they'd finally found the corroboration everyone was looking for. Joe Jr. said that one morning not long after Shannan vanished, an Oak Beach neighbor named Bruce Anderson had been standing near the front gate, talking with Coletti and Hackett, when Hackett said, "I was the last one to see her alive." The doctor then apparently told Bruce and Gus that he'd sedated Shannan and she'd stayed inside his house for a short time. When she was conscious, around seven in the morning, he said, he put her in Michael Pak's car.

If Bruce really had heard Hackett say this—and if it all really happened that way—then Hackett had harbored Shannan inside his home on Larboard Court, sedated, at the same time when the police responded to the 911 call. Hackett, the theory goes, must have known from his neighbors that the police were on their way.

After my visit with the Scalises, I reached Bruce Anderson at his second home in Florida to ask him directly. "Doc Hackett is a very strange individual," he said. Without my prompting, he told me what he'd heard—or thought he'd heard. "Hackett was telling everybody, including Gilbert's mother, that he found her that morning, gave her that sedative, he has a home for wayward girls in his house, and that she left the next day."

At the very least, Bruce had been hearing a lot of the same things that the Scalises had heard. What wasn't clear was whether he'd heard them straight from Hackett's mouth. I asked Bruce: Did he ever personally hear Hackett say anything about seeing or treating Shannan that morning?

"No, not personally heard him," he said, "but I heard through other people that he said it. And then I got talking with a couple of the detectives, and they said that he told the mother that."

Once again, an echo chamber: First Mari says Hackett called her, then the police tell neighbors about her claim, and then neighbors come away believing it.

As Bruce kept talking, he suggested that the police had more of an interest in Hackett than Dormer had ever let on. "The cops caught wind of this," he said, "and brought him in for questioning, and after a few hours he said, 'Well, I just said that.'"

Why would he just say it?

"He makes up a lot of stories," Bruce replied. "All kinds of crazy stuff, he makes up. So people say, 'Oh, that's just Peter, he wants to be a big shot.'"

And how did Bruce know that the police were looking into Hackett?

"Because they came door-to-door, saying, 'How well do you know this guy Peter Hackett?'" Bruce said. "And I said to them, 'You know, I wave to the guy, he waves back. I really don't socialize with the guy.' I heard through the grapevine he's a wacko. There's enough wackos in Oak Beach. I don't know if it's the salt air or the water. One of the locals told me it was the water."

Bruce had revealed something about the doctor and the police's suspicions. But he hadn't confirmed hearing anything directly from Hackett about seeing Shannan. When I circled back to Joe Jr., he said he wasn't surprised that Bruce had denied hearing anything firsthand. Like everyone else in Oak Beach, he said, Bruce didn't want publicity. He was careful. His wife had panicked when the police came to talk to him. He didn't want to be known as the neighbor responsible for fingering Hackett.

All that really mattered, Joe said, was that Bruce had told Mari everything. Joe had arranged the phone call himself, sometime after my visit. Thanks to Joe and Bruce, Mari felt she had confirmation that the doctor had said what he said, even if the police didn't seem to care. If nothing else, Mari was relieved. Before speaking with Bruce, she said, she had begun to wonder if she had dreamed up the whole thing.

Gus Coletti spent much of his time sitting on the porch of his two-story house on the Fairway, down the road and around the corner from the Scalise family, watching for strange cars coming through the Oak Beach gate. He and his wife, Laura, have lived in Oak Beach for thirty years. They bought their bungalow for twenty-two thousand dollars, and they used it as a summer home while Gus spent eight years building it up. He hired an engineering company to put in a foundation. Then he rewired the house and had the plumbing done. He replaced the windows and doors, added a room, redid the bathroom, and insulated the whole thing. By the time he added siding and replaced the roof, he'd spent more renovating the place than he would have if he'd knocked it down and built a new one.

The longer he stayed, the richer he and Laura got, at least on paper. A few years ago, they were offered $850,000 for their house. Gus wasn't ready to sell. It might have been the wrong decision. Now he didn't think he could get $500,000 for it. He got slammed twice: first by the economy, then by Shannan Gilbert and the bodies on Gilgo Beach. Two houses that were already sold, the buyers had backed out. Now they were both in court.

One of the sellers refused to return the deposit: Where in the contract did it say that dead bodies nullified the deal?

In his golden years, Gus had indulged his two great loves: restoring old cars and caring for pigeons. On the wall of his little living room, amid photos of his five grandchildren, was a plaque in his honor, bestowed by the Nassau Suffolk Pigeon Fanciers Club: *For your untiring efforts throughout the years.* (Gus is the president of the club.) Now that Oak Beach has become a possible crime scene, Gus remains the only neighbor who saw anything and is willing to talk. He's old. His story changes, the details shift: exactly when Shannan came to his door, whether he called 911 while she was there or after, whether he went to the front gate as soon as she ran away or waited a bit. What didn't change, in every telling, was that Gus behaved nobly. He talked to Shannan. He tried to help her. He even let her into his house—something Mari didn't believe was true, based on the excerpts of the 911 call that the police shared with her. Gus pointed to where she stood: a swath of carpet in front of a woodburning fireplace. There hadn't been much room for her to go beyond that. Gus said that when Shannan was there, Laura had been sleeping on the lower level, to recover from a knee replacement.

Gus headed over to his porch, reliving that morning yet again. He remembered her hair, the blond streaks, and her clothes, a white halter top covered by a sweater or jacket. He didn't remember a cell phone, though she apparently had it later when she knocked on Barbara Brennan's door. As Gus recalled, Shannan did nothing but scream, and then she ran away.

Gus said he believed Shannan was under the influence. "I had four kids. I'm sure one or two of them could probably tell you more about drugs than I could. But that girl was pretty well drugged up. She couldn't hardly stand. She almost fell over twice while I was talking to her. And she wasn't making any sense. Even though she was in the house and I was talking to her, she still was screaming, 'Help me, help me!' "

He said he picked up the phone in full view of her and even started talking to the dispatcher as she watched: "This girl here is screaming for help . . . " He said he finished the call and turned to her and said, "Sit down in that chair over there. Relax. I called the police, they're on the way here." As soon as he said that, out the door she went.

He pointed to the porch stairs. Gus said he saw Shannan stagger halfway down and fall the rest of the way. She got up and started running around to the right, back to the Fairway toward Joe Brewer's house, against the weeds on the far side of the street. Gus watched as she pounded on a neighbor's door, one she'd skipped on the way to Gus's because he'd had his light on. Then she ran back out to the road and stopped, looking down the road toward Brewer's house.

"It was obvious she was looking at something," Gus said, "and she started to run again and she fell a couple of times and she ran around here."

Gus was pointing to his front yard, where he'd parked a small boat. A car had been next to the boat that morning. Gus said Shannan got in between the car and the boat. "She knelt down there, like she was hiding."

Gus saw a car coming down the road, a black Ford Explorer, rolling a few feet and stopping, then rolling a few more feet. This was Michael Pak. "I stopped him right here," Gus said.

"You stopped him?" I asked. It seemed like a big step to take, to walk down the porch to the road and flag down a strange car.

Gus nodded. "I said, 'Where are you going?' And he said to

me, 'I came from Brewer's house. We were having a party and the girl got upset, and she's running around here. I'm trying to find her.'"

What did Gus say to Michael Pak?

Gus assumed his best John Wayne posture. "I said, 'Well, I've called the police, and they're on their way, so you stay right here.'"

And Pak's reaction?

"He said, 'Oh, you shouldn't have called the police. She's going to be in big trouble.' I said, 'So are you, if you leave. I already got your plate number, and I can identify you.'"

That was when Shannan got up and ran off again. Gus returned to his house and told his wife to stay by the phone in case the police called back. Then he went back out, walking over to the gate, where he stood waiting, he said, for over a half hour.

"I stood by the gate till the police came," Gus said. He said he never saw Shannan or Michael Pak again. "Nobody left here with a body in their car, because I would've seen it."

Nobody left here with a body in their car. That was exactly what the Scalises said did happen. They also said Gus was supplying a front, a cover story—"He would've at least seen Michael Pak drive out," Joe Jr. said. "Where did Michael Pak go that morning?"—and that all of Gus's accounts in the media were part of a community effort to stay silent about what really happened to Shannan.

What did Gus think of Peter Hackett? "He's one of the best neighbors you can have," Gus said as soon as the doctor's name was mentioned. "He's always ready to help everybody. He's always, if he hears you're sick, he's over here in minutes. He's helped more people on this beach than anybody else around has. He's a doctor. And he's a great guy. He's got the one weakness. He tells stories."

"He overelaborates," Laura said.

"Yeah," said Gus. "You tell him a little story, and he stands up making it a big one. But do I think he had anything to do with her disappearing? No."

Did he ever hear the doctor say that he helped Shannan out?

"No," he said. "I never heard that. As a matter of fact, we never even had any discussions about it, and I see him regularly."

This was strange, too. Shannan's disappearance was easily the biggest thing ever to happen at Oak Beach. If he and Hackett were so close—and if Hackett was such a big storyteller—how could they never have discussed it?

I asked Gus what he thought happened to Shannan.

"She died in the water," he said.

How?

"She was scared. She was drugged up pretty good. I think she slipped and fell. Have you looked at any of the jetties? They're as slick as glass when they're damp in the morning. If she ran out on one of them, she's gone."

Into the fall, the Scalises kept beating the drum about a conspiracy. They had company now. The first TV reports about Hackett had made the doctor a regular subject of scrutiny on Websleuths, a well-established Internet chat group devoted to dozens of open murder cases around the country. The armchair detectives pored over TV news reports, searching for snippets of the doctor warding off reporters, analyzing his repeated use of "No comment." *I've been watching that interview of the Dr. and observing his body language,* one commenter wrote. *He is blocking the doorway like he is afraid the reporter will try and go inside. He also averts his eyes down and to the left a few times while he is speaking. Isn't it a sign of deception when someone averts their eyes down and to the left? . . . Something about him seems, well, off!*

A commenter calling himself Truthspider seemed determined

to pin every murder on Hackett—not just Shannan and the four in burlap but the unidentified ones, as well as the ones in Manorville. The handle Truthspider belonged to a Long Islander named Brendan Murphy, a skilled researcher who dug up some court documents about Hackett suggesting that he'd been sued twice. The first case stemmed from January 17, 1989, when, according to the documents, Hackett, working as a volunteer member of the Point Lookout–Lido Fire Department, responded to a call in Inwood, New York, where an infant was suffering a febrile seizure. The suit, filed eight years later, accused Hackett of negligence, saying he failed to administer intravenous fluids, treat the seizure, document the treatment he rendered, supervise the emergency personnel, communicate with the hospital, or hydrate the infant. Hackett defended himself by saying he was protected by the Good Samaritan law; the suit was later abandoned. But before it was over, the plaintiff's attorney filed a Notice of Discovery and Inspection seeking information about "medical care providers furnishing care and treatment to [Hackett] for substance abuse for the period one year prior to the incidents at issue and two years subsequent to said occurrence." The Oak Beach doctor in rehab? Truthspider couldn't help but take notice of that.

The second lawsuit was a malpractice suit involving another infant, though details of what happened and Hackett's involvement weren't available in any public documents. The lawsuit was originally filed in 1996 against three other doctors, Long Beach Hospital, and a lab called National Emergency Services, Inc. Three years later, in 1999, the hospital filed a third-party claim against Hackett in what appeared to be an attempt to shift some or all of the responsibility to him. The original case was settled shortly afterward, in July 2000. Hackett was not required to pay any fines, nor was any judgment made against him. Three years after that, the case against Hackett by Long Beach Medical Center was also dismissed.

The meaning of the court documents is a matter of interpretation. It isn't unusual for ER doctors to be sued for, in the heat of the moment, not being able to help. Even the first lawsuit's request for a rehab record was ambiguous: Either the plaintiff was on a fishing expedition, trying to dig up dirt on Hackett, and no such rehab records even existed; or, as Murphy decided, Hackett was a drug-addled predator masquerading as the neighborhood Boy Scout. As Truthspider, Murphy posted online about how the first lawsuit demonstrated that Hackett was an addict—an unstable, unethical doctor with access to prescription drugs that he could have used on Shannan that night. Others on Websleuths promptly accused Murphy of tunnel vision, bending all facts to fit his opinion. They saw no evidence of wrongdoing in the negligence cases, and in fact saw plenty to suggest that the lawsuits had no foundation at all.

But for Truthspider, the Hackett question was simply a case of Occam's razor: the simplest explanation being the most likely. For Murphy, any number of simple explanations implicated Hackett. That early April report in the *Post* about a second man, a "drifter," at Brewer's house—could that have been Hackett? Or maybe Hackett didn't come there at all, but Shannan and Brewer went to him on their quick errand out of the house. Maybe Brewer brought Shannan there to get painkillers or other pills. And maybe Hackett, upon seeing Shannan, asked Brewer to lend him the girl for a few hours.

This was all conjecture, of course, and widely disputed. But to hear Truthspider tell it, wouldn't that have been enough to make Shannan not just frightened but terrified, afraid for her life? Wouldn't it have been a short leap for her to be convinced that her driver, Pak, was in on the deal? Wouldn't that suspicion—her own driver selling her out to another guy—have been scary enough to convince Shannan to call 911? To send her running into the dark? As Truthspider, Murphy wrote as early as May 2011 that the man with all the answers would have to be Brewer, and Brewer had to be covering for Hackett. *Everybody inside knows, they just can't say. [Brewer] was able to piece it together . . . He was [saying] to the media "the truth will come out." He just can't say what the truth is. The police told [Brewer] he has to wait until they have the proof they need.*

For his next trick, Murphy pieced together Hackett's entire work biography and tried to match it up to other bodies, deciding that many of the early nameless victims were conceivably on the doctor's commute. As Suffolk's emergency medicine chief after the Flight 800 disaster, Murphy said, Hackett would have driven down Halsey Manor Road in Manorville to get back and forth from the recovery operation at the East Moriches Coast Guard station and a secondary recovery location at Calverton Executive Airpark. When Hackett moved on to Suffolk Central Hospital in Riverhead, his commute down the Long Island Expressway from Oak Beach would have brought him past the same area near Halsey Manor Road, possibly at an ER's very odd hours. A few years later, in 2000, a torso would be found in the Long Island Central Pine Barrens, a state-protected wooded region just off Halsey Manor Road in Manorville. Portions of Jessica Taylor's body were found in the same area in 2003. Both of these discoveries, of course, were later linked by DNA to body parts found along Ocean Parkway. For Murphy, that sealed the deal. How many people on Long Island are familiar with the back roads of Manorville *and* Ocean Parkway? *For all you non-believers out there,* Truthspider wrote, *it's time to take your head out of the sand and start believing.*

Truthspider saw clues everywhere. An old *Babylon Beacon* story about Hackett speaking out against a proposal for developing the old Oak Beach Inn site led Truthspider to conclude that Hackett exhibited "territorial behavior" and that, he hastened to add, Hackett made those comments at roughly the same time as the toddler and a Jane Doe's head, hands, and right foot are believed to have been dumped by the killer. When something didn't quite fit the theory, like the dismembered legs found all the way in Davis Park, he made it fit: *I am certain they floated to Davis Park from elsewhere due to severe coastal flooding from the Nor'easter in January 1996,* he wrote, noting that the marks on the legs were consistent with the work of a surgeon.

Another prolific commenter named Peter Brendt wrote, *So . . . Truthspider . . . you tell me, how someone with one leg prosthesis and breathing problems can alone carry a body from his vehicle down to where the [four bodies in burlap] were found?*

Truthspider responded coolly: *He worked for years as an EMT with a prosthetic leg, as part of that job you have to be able to pick up victims, put them on stretchers, or boards and carry the board or stretcher possibly up and down stairs. I think he can handle a sedated 110-pound girl. From my personal experience with the Gilgo dump sites, the full skeletons were 3-5 feet into the bush, whereas the dismembered parts seemed to be buried further into the brush a decent distance from the road.*

Brendan Murphy is about thirty years old and won't divulge where he lives, except to say that he spends part of the time in a barrier-island community that is not Oak Beach. When I met him for dinner in Manhattan, he struck me as calm and reasonable but every bit as fervent in his belief that Hackett was the killer as he was on Websleuths. He said he thought Hackett might have gone into his chosen career with fantasies of being an angel of mercy, but from there it was a short leap to becoming an angel of death. He pointed to other medical people who have become mass murderers, like Richard Angelo, the registered nurse implicated in at least eight deaths during the 1980s; and Michael Swango, the doctor suspected of poisoning some sixty patients and colleagues over twenty years. Murphy's favorite comparison was John Edward Robinson, an accomplished con man and killer from the eighties, who got away with it as long as he did only because people considered him too old, too nice, too soft-spoken, and not physically capable, all while he maintained a sparkling public image as a do-gooder, a good neighbor, and a family man.

As the summer went on, Murphy developed an intricate theory of how Hackett grew up to become a serial killer. He'd read a war novel written by Peter's father, Charles Joseph Hackett—*The Last Happy Hour,* a semiautobiographical romp in the mode of *Catch-22* or *M*A*S*H,* published by Doubleday in 1976—and discovered a passage in which the main character goes on about how impossible it is to "convert" prostitutes by arguing with them, then travels the country with his young son after the war, spending nights in motels with "dancers." *It's really a very unfortunate description of a boy's early life if people are suspecting him in the Long Island serial-killer case,* Murphy wrote. He decided that Peter's mother's death in childbirth and his father's presumably strange predilections created a monster. He pointed to the car accident that took Hackett's leg, and the carnage of the TWA Flight 800 crash. He cited a theory called "Trauma Control Model," put forward by Eric Hickey, a researcher of serial killers, which argues that an early childhood catastrophe can set up a child for deviant behavior in adulthood. Murphy decided that something in Hackett's childhood—the feelings of abandonment caused by not having a mother, perhaps—got dredged up in these adult traumas, and Hackett descended into deviant behavior.

Murphy also thought that Shannan's disappearance was a turning point for Hackett, a sign that he was getting sloppy. *He did something out of the ordinary on May 1st by going after [Shannan]*, he wrote, *and it's also why she got away from him for almost an hour.* Like Joe Jr., Murphy believed the bodies of the other four were stashed locally until shortly before they were discovered. *Since his dump site—the shed beside the marsh—was undiscovered for 10+ years, he felt he didn't need to dismember and leave torsos far from his house,* he wrote. Then, in a panic, he dumped them. *He was extremely organized, but got lazy, then slipped with [Shannan] and now he is going down.*

Murphy told me that he believed Hackett started tentatively, picking up people along his work commute and leaving parts of them in parks. He noted that all the bodies along Ocean Parkway and Manorville were found on state parkland. "In the middle of the night, parks are not patrolled," he said. "I can tell someone I have a reason to be in a park. I can con them."

The same way, he said, that Hackett might have conned Joe Brewer into bringing him a victim.

On July 11, Hackett blinked. CBS aired a one-hour report of *48 Hours Mystery* devoted to the bodies at Gilgo Beach and the disappearance of Shannan Gilbert. The show featured a section on Hackett in which the doctor, after numerous interview requests, reversed himself, admitting to making two calls to Shannan's family on May 6, a few days after she disappeared.

Hackett refused to be interviewed on-camera. In two written responses to CBS, he said merely that he called Mari at Alex Diaz's request, to offer to help with the search. On the face of it, this timing would make more sense than Mari's claim that he'd called just after Shannan went missing. Hackett said the longest call lasted under four minutes. While he said he couldn't quite recall what was said, his memory was apparently strong enough for him to continue to deny ever telling Mari that he ran a rehab or home for wayward girls, and to deny that he ever saw Shannan. He said the same thing to *Newsday* just before the broadcast: "I had nothing to do with anything occurring the night Shannan went missing. I never saw her that night; she never came to my house, I never offered her assistance."

His coming forward only made him a larger target. The Websleuths world parsed the wording of Hackett's letters, making much of how he'd refused to take a polygraph, citing health issues. *If I picked this suspect out of a hat, I agree it would be coincidence, but we didn't,* Truthspider crowed. *He is one of three men directly tied to the May 1 incident, but is the only one of them who refuses to take a poly, changed his alibi multiple times, lied to everyone for a prolonged period of time, can be connected to the areas of the dump sites, and whose parameters fit that of the serial killer: classic post-crime behavior, age, intellect, capacity, knowledge of law-enforcement tactics, etc.* The police continued to maintain that Hackett was not a suspect. But for Mari, blood was in the water. The doctor had lied; how could you believe anything he said after he'd spent a year saying the phone call never happened?

On August 19, a sunny summer Sunday, Mari and a small entourage staged another offensive at Oak Beach. No family members were with her this time, just her old friend Johanna Gonzalez; the British film crew working on the A&E documentary; and some new friends from Long Island she'd made through Facebook who had become devoted to Shannan's case: a Glen Cove resident named Michele Kutner and a Massapequa native named Mike

Dougherty, who, on Facebook, darkly calls himself Jim Jones. The publicity had also brought two local psychics into Mari's life—Cristina Pena and Joe Agostinello—and they came to Oak Beach, too. Jim Jones later recalled that when they got to the spot on Anchor Way where Shannan was last seen, Joe the psychic, who is Hispanic and Native American, took out a crystal pendulum, let its chain hang from between his index finger and thumb, and watched its movements carefully as the late-day sun moved through it. "Something happened here," Joe said, his voice rich and deep. "I'm picking up a whole lot of vibrations right here."

They were standing next to the marsh.

They continued down Anchor Way to where it intersects with a road called the Bayou. This was supposedly where Shannan's jacket was found. Joe shook his head. "I felt more back the other way," he said.

They decided to walk up toward Hackett's house, a Cape-style cottage, raised high with a carport at the ground level. Mari wanted to knock on Hackett's door and confront him. Before she had the chance, the doctor appeared down the road, lumbering toward them from a neighbor's house.

Mari stood as the man she'd been thinking and talking about for over a year walked toward her, his hand outstretched. A portion of the encounter was caught on video. Hackett was wearing a deep blue polo shirt tucked in, accentuating his big belly. His white shorts showed off his prosthetic leg.

Hackett was surprised to learn the woman whose hand he was shaking was Shannan Gilbert's mother. As soon as Mari introduced herself, he grimaced, looking this way and that as she and others in her group fired questions at him.

"What I don't understand is, what happened?" Mari said. "Did you see anything? What did you hear?"

"I never saw her," Hackett said evenly. "I never met her."

Mari's friend Johanna spoke up. "You must have heard something, because everybody here has heard something, one way or another. What's the rumor you heard?"

Hackett squinted at her. "Rumor?"

"Everyone's heard a rumor here," said Johanna.

"What's been on the news," Hackett said, shrugging. "That's it."

"Yeah," Mari said, "but this is my question. You called me. And for over a year you denied it."

"I didn't deny it," Hackett said.

"When there was proof you did call me, you admitted it," said Mari.

Michele Kutner spoke next. "But you never saw her that night? You never heard?"

"Didn't hear, didn't do anything," Hackett said. "Whoever Alex asked me to call, I called. All of this stuff about a rehab or something? I don't have any rehab. I don't do rehabs."

"Then why would you say that to me?" Mari asked.

"I didn't," Hackett said, some irritation coming through.

"But my point is this," said Mari. "How can we not know in another year it will be proven that you *did* say that to me?"

That startled Hackett. "I didn't say anything!" he answered. He glanced at the camera crew. "If you want to talk, I'd be happy to chat with you, but not with whatever this is."

What happened next, as Jim Jones remembers it, amazed them all. Someone in the group wished they'd brought some water, and the doctor's wife, Barbara, invited them all inside. Mari and Jim took her up on the offer as Hackett stayed outside with the others. As they walked in, Mari's body shook, and she clasped Jim's hand for support. They saw Hackett's daughter's paintings, and detective novels on the tall bookshelves in the living room.

The doctor's wife did her best to show some sympathy for Mari. She said she couldn't imagine what she was going through. Then she talked about the pressure her husband had been under— the media assault, the constant questioning. She recounted her husband's life of selfless service: Countless times, she told them, he wouldn't make it home for dinner because he was out helping someone who needed assistance in one way or another.

Asked about the security video, Barbara said it ran on a two-week loop and got taped over automatically. That was all.

On her way out of the house, Mari finally lost control and started sobbing. In the months to come, she'd get angrier, returning for Shannan's birthday in October. She was backed into a corner. Nothing anyone said would alter her conviction that the conspiracy was real.

ALLIANCES

"That girl standing there?" Kritzia said. "She's working. And the guy in front of her is her pimp."

We were standing on Seventh Avenue at about one-thirty A.M., across the street from Lace, the strip club. She and her friend Melissa used to spend hours on end on this corner. Kritzia was tiny, plump, and sultry, with bright red lips and wild hair. But she was dressed conservatively, like a mom at a PTA meeting. Since hearing about Melissa's death, she'd sworn off working as an escort, and so far, she's kept the promise to herself. On a clear night in October, she agreed to show me around where she and Melissa used to work, to get a view of the women who have taken their place.

"Does she look familiar?" I asked about the girl in front of us.

"Yeah. She knows me and I know her."

"Why not talk to her?"

"Because the girl's pimp is there, and I don't want her to get in trouble."

When Kritzia pointed to the pimp, I saw him for the first time, even though he was under ten feet away—skinny, white, and dressed plainly, eyeing us both suspiciously over a thin trace of a mustache.

We walked away a bit, then circled back around to Lace. "I'm trying to bring you closer but so we don't look so obvious," Kritzia said.

A new man, dressed in a suit, came walking down the block.

The woman approached. "She's trying to talk to him," Kritzia said. "But he's probably not going to leave with her." She was assessing every aspect of the encounter with a professional eye. "I don't know, but it looks like he's staying at a nice hotel, and you can just tell she's a ho. But he might take her because she's pretty and she's white—you know, just because she's white and it looks more regular. But it's hard convincing men. You don't just walk up to a guy and he says, 'Yes, let's go.' 'Cause remember, you're talking hundreds of dollars."

As she finished speaking, we saw the man walk away.

"Yeah," Kritzia said, laughing. "I could always tell which guys would go with me and which guys wouldn't. Some girls talk to every man. I wouldn't, 'cause some guys would be a waste of time."

Everywhere she looked, there were memories. The McDonald's on Broadway, where they gathered in cold weather; the Batcave on Forty-seventh between Sixth and Seventh, where they hung out in the summer. The cross streets on this side of Seventh Avenue were dark this time of night, and Kritzia was muttering almost to herself, "Drug dealers. Coke. Pot. Pimp wannabes. Stone-cold fake-ass rappers."

Between the Batcave and Seventh Avenue, we saw a collection of people outside a deli on the north side of the street, and she stiffened. Then, just as though he were another bullet point on her list of what she'd left behind, Kritzia said, "That's my son's father right there. The one next to the one with the red jacket. We don't talk anymore."

Mel was in the center of the crowd, right in our path. We walked by, but not fast enough. As if to announce herself, Kritzia called out, "Excuse me!" and Mel whipped around and feinted a punch at her. She staggered back and was still reeling when, a half second later, he hit her for real this time. He made no attempt to hide what he was doing from anyone watching, but no one around him seemed to notice. Maybe they were too afraid and were looking the other way. Or maybe confrontations like that happened all the time.

I was startled, but I tried to stay close as Mel leaned toward her again, growling something only Kritzia could hear. She wouldn't let him touch her; she was weaving out, running for cover into the deli. Mel followed. The Asian guy behind the counter recognized Kritzia and said, "Oh, hello!" The shouting continued. After a few seconds, Kritzia darted out and rushed past me, down the block. I followed her.

She was trying to laugh it off. She lifted her iPhone and waved it at me; the screen was shattered. Then she locked eyes with mine. I saw a small bruise on her cheek and tears streaming down her face. She grunted. "You know, that's just the way of him talking to me, and getting to *touch* me, and feeling me up."

She wiped her nose and fixed her hair. We kept walking west, to Eighth and Ninth avenues, where she said the girls were cheaper, and where Kritzia had gotten her sad start. "You saw the way he was now? That's why nobody would ever fuck with me or Mel. 'Cause they're fucking scared of him. *There's nothing to be scared of!* Like, I got hit by him just now, and did you see me crying? Every other nigga would have been, like, running. 'Cause they're just, like, pussies."

Kritzia was smiling. I wanted to see what it was like? Mission accomplished. She raised her hands in the air and let out a long, hearty laugh.

"This is the fucking life, yo!"

Kritzia had been out of circulation for a while. Back in 2009, shortly before Melissa disappeared, Kritzia had gotten pregnant with Mel's baby, a boy she would name Jemire, and moved to New Jersey. Her life had changed for a time. The pregnancy had compelled Kritzia to connect with her parents for the first time in years. A sort of armistice was declared: Kritzia didn't have to talk about where she'd been or what she'd done. Mel lived with her for a while. "Mel was paying all the rent, all the bills, taking care of everything. My parents weren't giving him nothing. They took our living room and made it my little brother's room."

Kritzia applied to school, and Mel found a straight job, in carpentry. "I thought everything was going to change." But when Jemire was born, Mel wasn't around. Then came a rent dispute with a landlord, which Mel sat out, and a move into a homeless shelter with Jemire. "Then one day I realized, this nigga just wants to be in the streets—he don't want to be a father. He don't want to work, he don't want to do what he's supposed to do. He just wants to be free. There are people that are like that."

Alone with Jemire, Kritzia broke down. She saw a psychiatrist for depression, and without her knowledge, the psychiatrist filled out an application on her behalf for SSI, the Social Security program that supports mentally or physically disabled people. It wasn't the money that Kritzia objected to; it was the possibility that being on SSI would flag her as an unfit mother. Sure enough, along came Children's Services. "They came after me and took me to court, to take my son." She appeared before a judge and made her case. She told him everything about her life. She got to keep Jemire. And when she needed money, she returned to Times Square to work.

One night in July 2011—a few weeks after the family vigil at Oak Beach in June—Kritzia ran into Blaze, standing outside of Lace.

"Is that *Mariiii-ah*? Hi, *Mariiii-ah*! How you *doin'*?"

They exchanged a few pleasantries. Kritzia showed him a photo of her baby. Then she asked, "Where's Melissa?"

"That bitch is dead," Blaze said.

"What?"

"Yeah, a trick killed her," Blaze said. "She was one of those girls they found in Long Island. All they found was her bones."

Kritzia had been so consumed by her own life in New Jersey that she didn't even know about the bodies on Ocean Parkway. She didn't believe it until she Googled Melissa's name. Then she saw the news and the video and the pictures, including one she'd seen before, of Melissa with red hair pulled back in a ponytail. That picture transported Kritzia to a night long ago, when they were riding into work from the Bronx. She even remembered what she was wearing that night, a tight white tank top with little spaghetti straps.

Kritzia started crying and couldn't stop. Then she started breaking things, and the people downstairs knocked on her door. When she saw how scared her son was, Kritzia finally calmed down. She went into the bathroom and shut the door.

She really had thought Blaze was lying.

The next day Kritzia jumped onto Facebook and joined all the memorial groups. She got on the phone with Lynn in Buffalo— they'd never spoken; not even Amanda knew Kritzia existed— and learned how Melissa's whole family had blamed Blaze for the life she'd been leading. Melissa's family had so many questions about her disappearance that Kritzia served at least as a kind of confirmation. "They were like a lovey-dovey couple," Kritzia said. "That's how Blaze treats his girls: hugs, kisses. I mean, pimps, they still beat you when you go to work, but then they act like they love you. That's why it makes you want to stay."

Kritzia didn't stop with Lynn. She was shattered by the idea of a serial killer going after girls just like her, and she needed to talk to someone about her lost friend and the fear of being preyed on herself. She friended Missy, Lorraine, and Sherre. Unlike Kim, Kritzia was an escort who spoke out with deep regret about the life she'd chosen. "I want it to be exposed, what goes on in Manhattan, what goes on in Times Square," she said. "There are so many other girls that are out there working right now. And they don't know. I want girls to get scared and stop working—which I know is not gonna happen, but some girls get scared. I got scared."

As she showed me around Times Square, Kritzia barely stopped talking long enough to catch her breath. She talked about what she and Melissa used to do, and why they did it, and why so many other people were still doing it—by some estimates as many as five thousand underage girls and boys in New York City are working as prostitutes at any given time. She talked about being seventeen and homeless in Times Square, too angry to go home to her mother, rejected by cousins already packed into her grandmother's place. A bed at a city-run nonprofit social-service agency seemed out of the question. The city has about 250 beds available in all of New York for some four thousand homeless young people without families. When she met her first pimp, a guy everyone called Baba, Kritzia needed more than cash; she needed a reason to go on. "It's not just about the money. There are so many other things. You don't have family, you don't have friends, you don't have nobody. If you don't work, you don't eat, you don't have a place to live. When I was underage, nobody wanted to help me—because I was underage! Nobody wanted to give me a job, no one wanted to give me an apartment."

Kritzia said that escort work gave her something to do, someone to be, though selling her body meant living in a shadow world that everyone ignored. "And then you've got pimps who follow you and beat you up. And then you go in front of the judge, and they don't care, they throw you in jail." She believed that Melissa's online career was her way of escaping that cycle. "People think, *Oh, the money, the money,* but do you know how hard it is to get a guy to date you? I'm not just standing on the corner, waiting. You have to go to them, walk to them, talk to them, convince them. Then you have to agree on a price, convince them, and a whole lot of fucking bullshit."

She was crying now. "I was thinking about her all day today. That's why she didn't walk the streets—because it was so much work. It was too much walking. Like, you have to walk all over Manhattan, like, all night on these heels, and you don't know who you're gonna meet, you don't know if you're gonna make money. You just walk all night in the cold, in the heat. And that's what Melissa didn't like and why she started advertising on the Internet."

Online, Kritzia became an honorary family member, representing Melissa's memory in the memorial Facebook pages, posting constantly. She was mostly steering clear of contact with Mel, and she had no use for Blaze anymore.

But someone who knew Blaze, near the Batcave on Forty-seventh Street, was able to relay a message to him, and a few weeks after my visit there, Blaze and I spoke on the phone. Straight away, he denied being a pimp. He said he was a musician and a rap producer. Kritzia had predicted this: "Blaze wanted to be everything, but he really was nothing." Blaze, in turn, had some unfriendly things to say about Kritzia: "She probably gets a check from the state for being slow."

But he stayed on the phone. He seemed eager to get a message to Melissa's family in Buffalo. He surprised me by saying that he used to call and talk with Lynn all the time when he and Melissa were together. Though he seemed to want to meet in person and agreed to have lunch at a Caribbean place in Washington Heights, not too far from where he lived, he never showed up.

"I've got a lot of stress," he said later, on the phone. He had three kids, and for the first time in his life, he said, he was being hit up for child support. He agreed to stay in touch with me. A few months later, after a flurry of texts, he was on the phone again. In a more tender moment, Blaze told me what he loved most about Melissa: "The way that she would go hard for me. The love that she had for me. The way she was there for me, no matter what people said. Like, when we used to argue or break up, she would call me back on the phone and rush back to the house or whatever and try to fix it."

He even said his mother liked her. "My moms loved her. My moms, you know? She would come over and help the best way she can, always. Always."

He revealed a little more about himself. He said his kids were nine, twelve, and thirteen. He'd gotten out of jail recently, after serving a brief stretch for credit-card fraud. "That was bullshit," he said. In one of our last conversations, I brought up the attack on Melissa in the street, the one Kritzia said he ordered. That was when Blaze exploded. "I took care of her the whole time she was out here! Any time somebody is with somebody in a relationship, you can't tell me that people don't have fusses and fights and arguments. So if I'm guilty of fussing and fighting with my girlfriend, yeah, I'm guilty for that. But hurting her and harming her? No, no. Not at all. I've been through some stuff because of her, stuff a lot of homies could've got killed for, and I still took her back, you know what I mean?"

He shifted the focus away from himself, back to Melissa's family. This time he was less tender. "She sent Lynn the money to pay her bills, for her diner and all that. Did you know *that*? Did you? So come on. Like, everybody's putting me out to be the bad guy or whatever. But your *daughter* was the one who was in the streets doing stuff, not me. Not *me*."

Sometimes—"Well, okay, a lot of the time"—Sara Karnes thought about what would have happened if she'd stayed in the Super 8 with Maureen on Monday morning. Would Maureen still be alive? She knew the answer. "I wouldn't have let her go. We would've just ended up chilling in the room till Wednesday."

Sara didn't stop working after Maureen disappeared. She went back to New York, to the Super 8, a few times with Matt, and she and Matt hooked up. Sara tried doing calls in Connecticut, but she learned quickly how much better the johns treated her in New York—most of them, anyway. There, she felt treated like a princess. Back home, she'd say she was treated like "a fuckin' street-corner bitch, only more expensive."

She posted as Lacey on Craigslist for eastern Connecticut. One guy she met at the Two Trees Inn at Foxwoods was completely naked when she walked into the room. "Hi, I'm Lacey," she said. The guy said, "I don't give a fuck. The money's on the counter, put it in your pocket, and suck my dick." She surveyed the scene and walked out. He was naked, she was dressed; let him try to chase her.

She kept on working steadily until 2009—two years after Maureen's disappearance—when she got picked up for the first time by the police. She had a cop friend, a Norwich detective who had worked on Maureen's disappearance early on, who hadn't been very helpful to Missy but gave Sara good counsel.

Every time Sara would call him to check in about Maureen's case, he'd offer tips on where or when not to work. Unfortunately, he was telling her only about what he knew, in Norwich. When Sara arrived for an outcall at the Radisson in New London, she got caught. Normally, the bond would have been $2,500, which would have meant paying $250 to get out. But the cop who arrested her saw that she didn't have a pimp and wasn't part of some bigger drug or sex ring, so he took pity on her and released her on a promise to appear in court at a later date.

Life might have gone on fine for Sara if she hadn't been busted again for drug dealing. It was March 17, 2010. Sara claimed she was set up by the wife of a cousin who turned out to be a confidential informant. She was charged with dealing and prostitution and failure to appear in court and was sent to jail. She got out on June 11, her twenty-eighth birthday. She went into a drug program, failed it, and went back to doing calls, despite being pregnant. When she missed a court date, she earned a "failure to appear" bench warrant. When she got arrested for rolling a blunt behind the Groton Stop & Shop, that put her away for real.

The second time in jail seemed to snap Sara out of it. She decided she just couldn't do the work anymore. When she found out about Maureen, she added that to her list of reasons. "There's nothing that can convince me," she said. "I'm broke as shit right now, and if this was two or three years ago, you're damn right I'd be doing it right now. Because I don't want to be broke. But I'd rather be broke and with my daughter than what happened to Maureen."

On the day in October when we met for lunch in Stamford, where she was living in a nonprofit shelter for families, Sara was late. She had thought her daughter, a fourteen-month-old named Bella, was sick and had taken her to the hospital, but it was just a cold. Then she saw her probation officer; she had to see him monthly for another eight months, until June, when her probation for the felony was scheduled to end: "my *faaabulous* felony," as she put it. She had to mention it to every potential employer. As a result, Sara hadn't been able to get a legitimate job.

Over lunch, Sara talked about the irony of getting a free four-hundred-dollar replacement phone—the latest Droid—after getting robbed, but not being able to find a job to get out of a shelter. Then she looked down at Bella, who was playing with the phone. Sara said her daughter was the best reason she'd stopped escorting.

The night before, Missy had sent Sara a Web link to a German documentary that seemed to show video of a skeleton being discovered along Ocean Parkway. Missy was certain the skeleton was Maureen's, because the shoulders were so broad. Sara flipped out when she saw the video. She showed it to two other women at the shelter. Then she went on Facebook with her new Droid and published a screed about it. *If I would, I'd go Dexter-style on him,* she wrote. As we talked, Sara said she'd rather be Stieg Larsson's avenging Goth girl, Lisbeth Salander. Whenever she felt this way, Sara posted on Maureen's Facebook page:

> I'm soooo sorry Maureen that i didn't stay. I'm so sorry that there's a fuckin' wacko out there that thinks he can play god when he's really the devil . . . I keep praying that all of this will end, that this motherfucker will pay dearly for what he did to you all. I personally don't think that our justice system has a severe enough punishment for this creep.

Sara had known Maureen for only six months before she disappeared. Something about the emotion she brought to the loss seemed misplaced, overwrought, as if the drama helped elevate her life a little. But those feelings were real to her. Whenever she was feeling low, Sara tried not to think about how Maureen died but, rather, about how she lived. She would will herself to recall her favorite memory: that Sunday night in July, their hair done up, their makeup perfect, all eyes on them in Times Square. Sara said she believed that Maureen was put in her life to teach her to be more independent—"'Cause my mom sure didn't." Sometimes she thought that was as good as life would ever get for her.

"I made that Lacey picture my Facebook picture," she said. "'Cause it's pretty. It's my favorite picture of myself."

On each of Greg Waterman's arms are two enormous tattoos spelling out one phrase: CAUGHT UP IN / THE STRUGGLE. Megan's brother had been working construction for the same guy for seven years until the 2008 market crash forced his boss to sell half of his properties. Since then, Greg has had trouble finding work. His search was complicated by the fact that he'd lost his driver's license and had a theft arrest on his record. "That really screws things up for me," he said over dinner at the Olive Garden at the Maine Mall. "It was five years ago, it was a while ago. I just can't deal with not having a job."

Greg had four kids. Nicci Haycock was the mother of the youngest. "She's got two kids with another person. I look at them as my own kids, I raised those kids like my own for three and a half years." He and Nicci were together a long time, but at dinner, they said they were on a break for the time being. "It's not permanent," Greg said. "It's just the time is not right." He suggested that their separation had something to do with his sister's disappearance. "My anger got a lot worse," he said as Nicci stared down at her food.

Like the rest of Megan's family, Greg spent the better part of a year bristling at Lorraine, especially after her trips to New York to publicize the case. When Greg found out about the little heart-and-angel trinket she had bought the other mothers and sisters in New York, he castigated her for buying gifts for four strangers when she hadn't bought her own grandchildren a thing in years. The vigil in June compounded the problem. He and Nicci went down with Lorraine, but "she was more concerned with impressing the other family members there." He almost exploded at her when she encouraged him to drive faster. "I said, 'I'm not rushing for you, and I'm not rushing for them. I didn't come down there to show my face, I came down there to see where they found my sister.' I was so sick of her, you know? She's so worried about getting down there to get her face on the news."

Greg did explode when he got home and saw Lorraine's post on Facebook that the women at that vigil were her "new family." Even months later, he was practically shouting about it at the table, speaking as if Lorraine were right there in the restaurant with us. "You're out here again trying to get a pity party for you? I've been back in Maine for a month and a half, and you haven't called once to see how my daughter is! Everyone in your biological family knows how you are and your true colors and all these other people don't." For Lorraine to call Megan her daughter, he said, was a joke. "You never *had* her. You were *never* a mother to her. *Your* mother raised her."

Lorraine, meanwhile, was feeling as wronged as Greg, locked out of Lili's life by her mother, Muriel, and Lorraine's oldest sister, Liz. "When Megan was alive, all of Liliana's birthdays were at my house," she told me a few weeks later. "When Liliana turned four, Megan wasn't here, and we still had her party at my house. Since

Liz got guardianship, she had planned Liliana's fifth birthday party and never invited me. So I missed my granddaughter's fifth birthday party because of my sister. Her school pictures, everybody in the family has a picture of her but me. That's a tough situation."

What was more upsetting to Lorraine was that, at least according to her, Liz had next to nothing to do with Megan when she was alive. "Liz could not stand Megan!" She said that Liz asked Megan to sign over custody of Lili while Megan was alive, thinking maybe she just wouldn't want the headache of having a child. (Megan declined.) "And the minute Megan went missing, Liz and everybody in my family acted like they'd been involved in Megan's whole life."

Now it was Lorraine who had seemed to fall away again. Muriel and Liz were accusing her of being completely inaccessible, never returning calls, never making time for Lili, and yet still complaining about being the black sheep. Once, when Lili had fractured her ankle, Muriel and Greg each tried to call Lorraine, and when she didn't answer, they left messages. She didn't call back. Then Lorraine noticed the news on one of Liz's Facebook posts, and she posted: *It's a shame I have to hear about my granddaughter breaking her ankle on Facebook.* "She might be angry," Liz said, "but she really doesn't feel anything is her fault."

"You know what breaks my heart?" Muriel said. "Lorraine turning her back on this baby. Any time Lorraine even calls to see how she is, it's because I posted something nasty about her on Facebook."

All these years later, Muriel still didn't believe that Lorraine could be a good parent. Ella, Lorraine and Liz's sister, agreed. "I tried to defend Lorraine when it comes to Lili," she said, "but it's not my mother saying no. It's Lorraine just not doing it on her own."

Greg sided with his aunt and grandmother. He hadn't always seen eye to eye with Liz—he'd like to share custody of Lili; Liz and Muriel are concerned that he isn't stable enough—but Lorraine incensed him. "She acts like she wants to get to know her granddaughter, but behind closed doors, she could give two shits about it," Greg said. "She can't be bothered. She does more for her boyfriend's kid now than she does for her kids or grandkids."

A lawyer would cost Lorraine about two thousand dollars to fight for custody. That was money she didn't have, and she couldn't pull it together working at Domino's. Once she earned her medical-assistant degree, maybe she would have a chance. For now, all she could do was bide her time. "When Liliana gets older," she said, "she will learn the truth, just like Greg and Megan did when they got old enough. Liliana is going to know the same thing and realize or know that it had nothing to do with me."

One late-summer day, Dave Schaller was walking near his new home in Greenpoint, Brooklyn, when he heard the honk of a car horn. Dave looked over and his mind flooded. He remembered the car right away, an Ultima, and the guy behind the wheel, one of Amber's old johns. As he recalled, this john lived somewhere in Nassau County. Dave didn't know what he was doing in Brooklyn, or why he wanted to talk, but decided he didn't want to know. Dave dashed down the stairs of the G train to avoid him.

Dave knew he'd been running a risk by appearing on *48 Hours* in July. The police had warned Dave not to be too out in front about his ties to Amber or the case. "The cops were like, 'Listen, it could've been somebody you threw out of the house. You don't know if you once kicked this guy's ass.'" Now, Dave thought they had a point. "If the killer was so adamant about picking her up near my house, he's probably somebody I saw," he said. "So I worry about it sometimes. What if I'm a loose end?"

All fall, as Dave continued hitting the methadone and looking for work, he dreamed of Amber, of how he had failed to save her. "Every single fucking time she had somebody come or she went somewhere, I was with her," he said. "Every time except the time she left and she got killed." By day, he felt stigmatized. "Everybody thinks I was a goddamn pimp. Because why would I have two whores in my house if I wasn't fucking pimping them?" His only respite was twelve-step meetings. He despised them, but they kept him together. "I'm not going to lose my sobriety," he said. "I hate sitting there, but it is what it is."

One thing he'd managed to get over was his attachment to Kim, though now and then, he'd allow himself to vent. "I'm glad she's out of my life, that much I can say," he said. "Let me tell you, man. That girl, it's sad to say, but she's going to wind up dead. She's going to wind up dead."

I suggested that Kim might be going through a version of what he was going through, that she felt guilty, too.

"I hope she does," Dave said. "I really do hope she feels guilty. Because the way she treated her sister was fucked up."

Kim's Backpage photo showed her tan and trim and toned. Shot from behind, she was topless and bending forward, away from the camera, offering a full view of her lean bottom in a tight set of black panties, riding up. In person, though, she looked tired, worn out. The skin on her face hung a little loose. As she talked over lunch on a September afternoon in Manhattan, Kim demonstrated a lot of addict behavior—she was hyper-verbal, very friendly, constantly gauging my reactions, never overtly asking for anything. Still, all through the long lunch, she was in a great mood. She ordered a glass of red wine, and as she talked, she did her best to describe her current life as free of conflict.

Until that day, Kim had all but dropped out of the alliance of family members and friends. The more unavailable she had made herself, the more people blamed her for what had happened to Amber. In Florida, Louise Falvo—a friend of Amber's who helped take care of little Gabriel before he moved back with his mother—believed that Amber would have had a better chance at surviving if she'd never joined Kim in New York. "Kim is the biggest BS-er there is. How do you not know your freaking sister is missing?" she said. "Amber is very easily influenced, and Kim had a way of mesmerizing Amber. And Kim knew it and took advantage of it. And that's how Amber ended up the way she ended up."

Back in Wilmington, Amber's old friends Melissa Wright and Carl King had gone on about how Kim never saw her kids there, including her oldest, Marissa. "Me, personally, I can't go through a Christmas, let alone a birthday, without seeing my kids," said Carl. "I'm sorry, I just can't do it. Once I saw that Kim did that, I lost a lot of respect for her." Every few weeks, Melissa Wright posted on Kim's wall on Facebook, asking what she did with Amber's ashes or where she will put the headstone. She never got a reply. "We all just want to be able to say goodbye to her," Melissa said. "Because we were told she was going to bring her home and put her with her mom. I love Kim to death, but she needs to get her priorities straight and be honest."

Lorraine and Missy left Kim messages, too. Kim kept her distance from everyone, popping up briefly on Facebook, then disappearing again. All the drama around her might have explained why, a few days before Labor Day, Kim returned one of my messages, saying she wanted to tell her sister's story.

We met in midtown, near Penn Station. She said she had come in from Long Island, where she was living close to her old boyfriend Michael Donato's parents, John and Amy, who still had custody of the three children. I asked if John and Amy were all right with her being near the kids, considering everything that had happened. Kim nodded. "They know I come around," she said. "They do not like me doing anything like the escorting now, and if they think drugs are involved, they step in immediately. 'Let's go get tested.' And if something does pop up, they're like, 'Let's see what we can do to fix this problem immediately,' because they don't want the girls to be exposed to that shit, and I understand. They love those girls like I love them. And I love them, too—I love John and Amy."

I asked if she'd been escorting lately. "I'm not gonna lie to you. I did this up until I went to North Carolina." That would be the previous fall, before she learned that Amber's body had been found. "I always fell back on it as fast money. Even when she was living with Dave and I needed money, I did a couple calls, too. I always fell back on it because it was such a good moneymaker for me."

She reminisced about her life with Amber—how they'd bonded as children. "We weren't that wild compared to some of the kids," said Kim, who, a moment later, mentioned getting stabbed one time and seeing a group of black girls try to jump her sister. "It's not that we were raw," she said. "We just knew how to survive at an early age." In less charitable moments, Kim said she always felt put upon by Amber. "Amber, she never turned her back on me. But she was selling me out a lot. If I talked shit about Amber, I talked it to her face. I never talked shit behind her back, and I never let anyone else talk shit behind her back. And she was never like that. If somebody talked shit about me behind my back, she would never say anything. Which pissed me off, because I always stood up for her."

They were both plagued by addiction, with crazy adventures as business partners in between. "We traveled all up and down the East Coast" working as escorts: "Hilton Head, Florida, California, New Orleans." Kim kept focusing on the positive. "I tell you, I don't regret anything in life. Amber chose her path. You choose your own path. It's just the way it is. Or your path is chosen for you—I don't know, whichever. But everything has been a learning experience." She seemed determined, at least for the moment, to derive some sort of wisdom from what happened to Amber and what it said about her own life and her own choices. "I feel like, in order to make it, you gotta be able to make it on *and* off the streets. You gotta have both book sense *and* common sense. I'm not gonna say I have the best of both, but I have some of each, and it's what got me through."

When the check came, Kim insisted on paying. She pulled out a small cash-sized manila envelope packed with bills, glanced over at me, and smiled. I didn't ask where the money came from.

Using the same photo but a new phone number, Kim continued to post ads in the "adult entertainment—new york escorts" section of Backpage in September, October, and November:

> hi im 26 5ft two 115 lbs . . . brown hair honey eyes . . .
> 34c size 3 waist . . . so if u like a enjoyable non rushed expirence
> u can touch me

In the middle was an ad that Kim posted in North Carolina on September 27, about the time she'd told me she was planning on visiting her daughter Marissa in Wilmington.

Missy Cann noticed the ads while doing her usual research on the Web. No one seemed to spend more time on the computer than Missy, monitoring the conversations on Longislandserial killer.com, fielding instant messages and texts from new friends around the country, probing Joe Scalise, Jr., for the latest neighborhood scuttlebutt, planning a vigil at Oak Beach in December for the first anniversary of the discovery of the bodies. Missy had thrown her hat in with all the others who, on Facebook, were voicing concern about Kim. When she saw the ads, Missy despaired. "It really makes me want to understand why she still does this," Missy said. "I wish Kim the best. I pray every night for her safety. It bothers me to no end to know what she is putting herself into. I mean, if I knew now what I did not know before Maureen went missing, I would have done everything in my power to stop her and help her out. I just feel like there must be something I can do to help."

To Missy, Kim had become a surrogate for Maureen. Yet part of what Missy said wasn't true. She'd known that her sister worked as an escort, and she had acknowledged it later, in conversations with other family members. To say she hadn't known enough about it seemed a little off. After living with it for so long, Missy, like all of the family members, was tempted to make some small adjustments to history, to ease her burden somehow.

Within a few weeks, it wasn't just Missy who knew that Kim was back doing calls. The A&E cable documentary that had followed Mari to Oak Beach announced an airdate, December 5, and reporters got a sneak peek of Kim explaining on-camera that she was back escorting so she could lure and trap the Long Island serial killer. "From time to time I put up ads just to see what bites as far as my sister's killer goes," Kim said. "'Cause it'll intrigue him. And that's what I'm hoping I'll do—catch his eye." She was in tears, but the grandiosity was hard to miss: The police had botched the job, so why shouldn't she go after him herself?

Even people who knew Kim were stunned. "Do you think what Kim did is absolutely retarded?" Dave Schaller asked me on the phone. "I mean, what the hell does she think is going to happen? She's going to be sitting there having sex with somebody, and she's going to be able to stop this guy from strangling her?"

The full documentary, once it aired, offered a long overview of the case and a few visits with family members. Mari made vague accusations about the people of Oak Beach (though Hackett wasn't mentioned by name). Lorraine criticized the Suffolk County police. Lynn lashed out at Craigslist. Missy went on about how Maureen needed money. There were some first-time TV appearances—Alex Diaz, framing as best he could the story of punching Shannan in the jaw; and Michael Pak, behind dark glasses, laboring to explain why he'd driven away without Shannan. But the real revelation, aside from Kim, was Richard Dormer coming forward after months of silence to announce that the Suffolk County police had a new theory.

"We believe it's one person," he said. "One killer."

With this theory, the commissioner was contradicting what the district attorney, Thomas Spota, had said months earlier about multiple killers. What changed Dormer's mind, he said, were how remains discovered along Ocean Parkway were found to be parts of bodies discovered elsewhere years earlier: Jessica Taylor in Manorville in 2003; the Jane Doe in Manorville in 2000; the body parts on Fire Island in April 1996. The body of the toddler turned out to be connected by DNA to yet another Jane Doe, dumped seven miles west of where the child was found, again off Ocean Parkway. To Dormer, it seemed the same killer had been using Ocean Parkway as one of many dump sites, then settled on it as the main dump site as time went on. "The theory is that it's a Long Islander," he said, someone so fluent in the area that he'd feel comfortable dumping bodies all along a forty-two-mile stretch from Manorville to Gilgo Beach.

In Dormer's view, this single killer had refined his technique over time. First he dismembered his victims and left parts in separate locations. With Maureen, Melissa, Megan, and Amber, he held on to them and apparently bagged them, intact, in burlap. That didn't explain why so many victims didn't fit the pattern of the four women in burlap. What about the Asian man in women's clothing and the small child? The man, Dormer said, could have been a prostitute in drag. The toddler, Dormer said, could have accompanied his or her mother on a trick, something that isn't all that uncommon. Dormer said that the police's very inability to put names on those victims suggested that, like the others, they all lived so far off the grid. These last four were so similar, perhaps, because the killer had started using Craigslist and Backpage to vet his victims before meeting them. That way he could get exactly what he wanted.

The exception to the single-killer theory, Dormer said, was Shannan Gilbert. Unlike the others, Dormer said, Shannan hadn't been working alone. She had come to Long Island with a driver. That wouldn't have fit this killer's pattern. "There doesn't seem to be any connection," he said. "Everything is different. It is some coincidence that she went missing in the same area where the bodies were found. But when you look at her closely and you look at the evidence, Shannan Gilbert is a separate case."

With this, Dormer seemed to be saying not just that the killer hadn't murdered Shannan but that she might not even be a victim. Her body still hadn't been found. In the following days, even some of the officers working under Dormer were said to doubt the commissioner's one-killer theory. The only one Dormer thought wasn't connected to any of the others, he said, was the one whose disappearance started it all.

Many family members were as perplexed as they were angry. After months of silence, to casually mention on a TV show that the police didn't think Shannan was connected? Even Dormer's air of certainty—and his statement's timing, so soon before his expected retirement at the end of December—made him sound a lot like a man trying to wrap things up before heading out the door.

I wish I could grab them all by the throats and shake the shit out of them, Lorraine wrote on Facebook, *and make them talk and explain why they have lied to us.*

The night Dormer's theory made the news, Kim called me. She sounded angry, unraveling. "The cops don't know shit. They're just frontin'. If they had information, they'd have an arrest." She did not buy the one-killer theory. She'd been out there, seen how desolate it could be. She viewed Gilgo Beach as a giant dumping ground, like the swamps of New Jersey or the hills of Staten Island. It wasn't so hard for her to imagine that more than one person would pick a place like the barrier islands to leave a body. "The four girls are together," she said, all killed by the same man. "But the other girls are chopped up and don't fit the same MO. And Shannan Gilbert is a *fluke.*"

Kim rambled, sounding more vulnerable as time went on. She talked about getting sucked back into the life—not just calls but drugs, too—and she admitted it wasn't working out. Since our lunch in September, she said she'd checked herself in to Talbot House, a twenty-eight-day rehab in Bohemia, Long Island. I was surprised to hear this, since I'd noticed Kim had posted an escort ad that very morning.

Sounding tearful, Kim said she'd lost the only person who ever really understood her, more than any parent could. Now that she was alone, she thought she might be the only one with the knowhow and the connections to be able to solve the case and find the killer. But Kim said her solo investigation had netted her one lead so far: a girl who got an outcall from a guy who wanted to talk about nothing but the serial killer. The lead was going nowhere, and she was tired and frustrated. "Usually, when I bring it up, guys don't want to talk about it at all." She said she wanted to stop; if she didn't think that Amber would have done the same thing for her, she probably would quit.

I asked Kim if she'd heard from her oldest daughter, Marissa, and her tone shifted again. "Yeah, I talked to her," she said, her voice distant, as if she'd shut herself down. "I'm trying to push her away from me, so I won't do to her what I did to Amber." Kim was rejecting her for her daughter's own protection, although it was possible she simply felt unworthy of her daughter's—or anyone's—love. "Marissa is fifteen years old and gorgeous," Kim said. "And she looks like she's nineteen. He would go after her in a minute. It'd be a wrap at that point. Collateral damage. I don't doubt he wouldn't go after her." Like Dave Schaller, she felt exposed after appearing on television. "Like, I'm telling you, if he didn't know who I was, he does now. That's for damn sure."

Kim's new plan, she said, was to lay a wreath for Amber at Oak Beach. Missy and Lorraine had set a date for a vigil on December 13, 2011, the first anniversary of the discovery of three of the four bodies.

. Melissa's family couldn't afford to come, but Kritzia would carry the flag for them. Kim said she would join them all, reuniting with the families. Then she would say goodbye to Amber, stop looking for her, and stop doing calls forever.

"Every day, it eats at me," she said, determined but fragile. "I went through a really hard time, and I really gotta maintain."

Kim claimed to be working round the clock on behalf of her sister. What went unsaid was how she hadn't been there for Amber before she'd gone missing; she hadn't even called the police. "You have to understand," Bear had told me. "Kim is a fucking crackhead and a prostitute, too. That's how she gets her money. These Craigslist ads, these Backpage ads, these postings and listings and all this *shit,* man."

Amber's old boyfriend Björn Brodsky was living in Manhattan now, crashing in stairwells and on street corners around Tompkins Square Park. He was still skinny—rail-thin, really—and he slouched as he walked, loping like a camel. It takes a while to gather that he is six feet tall. Where his hair had been almost shoulder-length and dark when he lived on America Avenue, now it was short and bleached blond, poorly. He'd made the change, he said, because he'd been ejected from a court-ordered rehab, and the fact that he hadn't found another rehab had led to a warrant for his arrest. "It's like fucking Ponyboy and shit. You know, *The Outsiders*? I read a lot, you know? I read a lot of books."

The East Village neighborhood around Bear was gentrified now. Apartments went for millions, and the park even had a playground. But the southwest corner of Tompkins Square Park, near Avenue A and Seventh Street, was still known as Crusty Row. Crustys are society dropouts, and famously so: covered with tattoos and piercings, and several rungs further out of the mainstream than Deadheads or Phish-heads or those who used to be East Village squatters. Bear walked among the Crustys and was largely accepted, though he was not one of them. He could supply them with dope when they wanted it, and that counted for something. "If you're homeless in New York," he said, "no place is better than the Lower East Side. I just have enough swag to be out there on Avenue D. I get along with everyone. I'm a likable person. I'm a good person. I have a good heart. I get arrested, I'm not fucking snitching. I'll eat that. I'll go to jail. I don't deal with fucking cops. I don't do that shit."

He was not in touch with Dave, though he said he loved him like a brother. Even Kim he still liked, though he recognized her limitations. "I'm not saying Kim is a bad person, because she's not," he said. "But even if Amber was strung out, she'd still give you the shirt off her back. She'd do anything in the world." That was how she differed from her sister. "Amber cared about others. That's just the bottom line of it. Amber cared about others; Kim cares about herself."

Did Kim treat Amber well?

"Kim used Amber a lot, I think," Bear said.

How?

"To her advantage, you know what I mean? Through these postings, and these ads, you know? She used Amber to keep that house available to her at all times. A lot of manipulating. A lot of lies." He was quick to add that there were deceptions all around. Amber, he said, "would have to act like she was on the phone with Kim to calm down Dave," who couldn't stand the way Kim ignored her little sister. Even so, "Dave was so blindly in love with Kim. That man loved this woman more than you could possibly know. Like, Dave is the biggest sucker for love there is in this world."

As he went on, Bear made it clear that Kim hadn't been the only one to fail Amber. He didn't call the police, either. And yet he knew how much she loved him.

"For some reason, I was her number one priority. I wanted her to learn to love herself a little bit."

It didn't take long for Bear to turn sorrowful, and when he did, he employed the vernacular of rehab, perhaps because he thought that was the format in which I would best receive it, or maybe it was a way of connecting with the memory of meeting Amber. "My choices have ruined my life," he said. "My life is in shambles."

In his twenty-seven years, Bear had been in rehab for alcohol, Xanax, crack, intravenous cocaine, weed, and dope. "I'm no longer opiate-dependent," he said proudly—which, to clarify, meant to Bear that he was down to a bag of heroin a day. "And I don't shoot it. I sniff it. Once in the morning, every other couple of days." He circled back to rehab again and again, coming up with new reasons not to bother trying. "I've gone to every hospital, every rehab, every detox in this fucking city more than once, and it's never worked. It's rough, man. I got real bad post-traumatic stress. And that whole thing with Amber did not help at all."

II.

THE DOCTOR

In December, they started searching the bramble again. The announcement from the police came on November 30, just one day after Dormer made public his theory that one killer murdered them all except Shannan. Now the police were saying they had information that Shannan's body might be at Gilgo Beach after all—out along the parkway, not far from where the first four bodies were found.

To Mari and the others, this felt like more window dressing, a chance to demonstrate that the case was alive as the anniversary approached. Then again, they couldn't just ignore it. What if the police were acting on a new tip?

In a few days, the police settled that question when a spokesperson said the new search was about information they'd been sitting on for months. The high-resolution aerial photography conducted by the FBI in the spring had yielded a few questionable spots—"ninety points of interest," they called them—that they'd decided needed reexamination. The spokesperson said they had to wait until the brush thinned out in winter to search again.

To the families, this inspired even less confidence: Allowing a serial killer to remain on the loose is all right as long as a cop doesn't get poison ivy? Again they felt shunted aside: If the victims had been from middle-class homes in gated beach communities, the response from police, they assumed, would have been different.

On Monday, December 5, in heavy fog, seven teams from

the New York state and Nassau and Suffolk County police forces were back along the northern shoulder of Ocean Parkway, searching the bramble. Oak Beach was a media magnet all over again. No neighbors were commenting except Joe Scalise, Jr., and his father. They were hopeful about answers, even as they remained confident that the police were searching in the wrong place. If nothing else, Joe Jr. said, it put a little heat on their neighbor. "The FBI has a camera now on Hackett's house," he said. His father said Hackett had been seen at a local Chase bank branch, trying to get another mortgage. A rumor was circulating that he was planning to pull up stakes and relocate to Florida.

In rare agreement with the Scalises, Gus Coletti also suspected that the police were out searching on the highway just to look good. "If you go down there right now and you ask them, they'll all tell you the same thing: 'We're going through the motions.'"

It seemed as good a time as any to walk down Anchor Way to Larboard Court and knock on the doctor's door.

The doctor's home is small but charming, a beach bungalow with a sign over the entrance that reads BE NICE OR LEAVE. I knock a few times before he limps to the door; I can see him coming through a tall vertical window next to the threshold. He looks younger than he seemed in the photos and TV news clips, and I'm reminded that he is still only in his mid-fifties. His hair is messy and graying, but his face is boyish. The stubble on his face does little to conceal the patchiness of his skin. His eyes are wider, more spaniel-like, in person than they seemed on television. Between the limp and the potbelly, it isn't easy to imagine him as a master criminal who bewitches young women and controls a small community.

When the door opens, I see his half-smile. Maybe this is a

doctor's self-regard or a wince of pain from his prosthesis. Or maybe he's frustrated by yet another knock. He wasn't expecting me; I came back to Oak Beach because of the rebooted search for bodies, and I hoped to hear from Hackett himself about the rumors.

He seems annoyed from the start, irritated, ready to say no. He shakes his head and says he's turned down many requests for comment. He says there's no sense trying to disprove things that are so obviously not true: "What would be the point?" he says, as if it's the most ridiculous question in the world.

Then, suddenly, he glances left and right. "This is ridiculous," he says. "Come on in."

It's not at all clear, at least to me, what changed his mind. Some people simply aren't comfortable *not* talking, and Hackett seems to be one of those. The unfortunate by-product of this impulse is that he can come off as a dissembler, even when he might not be. He overanswers questions to the point where it seems like he's hiding something, because he's gone out on a limb, talking about things he doesn't know anything about. Some might say that's because he's a blowhard—or, as Laura Coletti charitably puts it, an overelaborator. Others, like the Scalises and Mari, would say it's because he *is* hiding something.

Hackett offers a tour. He heads straight back, and as he enters the next room, he snaps, "Here's my clinic." Then, quickly, he says he's joking; he's referring to the rumor that he treated Shannan here. It's a storage room, neat but lived in—he calls it "a workroom"—filled with years of boxes and tools and belongings amassed by a large family. Hackett limps swiftly through a doorway to a back room that contains a bed and an easel and paintings made by Hackett's daughter Mary Ellen, who is visiting for the holidays. Around a corner is a folded futon couch with a pillow and comforter on it. That's for his son, he says. His two daughters, both in their twenties, are living on their own now, though he'll later say that one daughter, along with his wife, was there the morning when Shannan disappeared.

He heads out of the room and up a short staircase to the main room of the house, a double-height living room that sits right in the entryway, capturing the southern light from large slanted windows. The room has a galley kitchen in the far corner, opening up to a table with barstools. The table is indeed large enough and at a good height to double as an examination table, as the doctor once said. We sit on the stools. The far wall of the room is floor-to-ceiling with books, including a copy of *Writers Market*. Hackett says offhandedly that his father was a writer.

As he talks, Hackett insists that the whole controversy about him does not usually occupy a second of his time or attention. He says that, contrary to the gossip, no neighbors called him the night Shannan went running down the street, pounding on doors. In fact, he says that days later he told Gus Coletti and Barbara Brennan that they *should* have called him; that he might have been able to help the girl. It strikes me when he puts it this way that this quite possibly could be what Bruce Anderson really overheard: Hackett saying he *would* have treated Shannan if he'd seen her, not that he *had* treated her, the way Joe Jr. believed. I wonder if Hackett had said the same sort of thing to Mari on the phone—not that he had helped Shannan but that he *wished* he had helped her.

Even that wouldn't explain Hackett denying ever having spoken to Mari, then later admitting as much. That could have been his haplessness, or it could have been a deception. Yet as Hackett answers more questions, he continues to be fuzzy on information that he should have figured out stock responses to a long time ago. He says the first time he heard anything about Shannan was several days after she disappeared, when Alex Diaz and Michael Pak came to the neighborhood with flyers. He suggests that he felt a little sorry for them. "They were nice guys, but they didn't know how to go about getting information from people." He says he told them to go to the local police where Shannan lived and to report her missing, and then he gave them his card and told them he'd be happy to help out if they needed anything. He remembers thinking that "from a police standpoint, this was not a child that has gone missing." In other words, she was a grown-up, and the police might be inclined to think she'd gone off somewhere on her own and would come back when she felt like it. It never occurred to him that anything else would come of it. "This is a twentysomething woman who has disappeared before," he says. "Or at least that's what I understood."

He remembers all of this. But he doesn't remember the call he made to Mari. At first he says he didn't speak with Mari on the phone, when he clearly admitted that in his letters to *48 Hours*. A moment later, he acknowledges that there is a phone record confirming that he and Mari had spoken.

"I don't know. It's a possibility someone called. I don't want to appear to be disputing what she said. I get thirty-five calls a day. I don't know if maybe she called me to talk. But I never saw the girl. I never talked to the girl. I don't have any recollection of talking to the mother."

Out of nowhere, he recalls something else. "Hold it," he says. "It's possible she called me and I called her back wondering who she was. It was a three-minute phone call."

In a way, you could argue that this is refreshing honesty—guilelessness. But in the middle of a murder investigation, with his name all over the news and police searching the bramble on a beach three miles away, it is also a little foolish. And yet it's impossible for me to tell if it is because he's genuinely hiding something or because he is naive about just how eager some people are to pin Shannan's disappearance on him. I can't help but think of Richard Jewell, who discovered the pipe bomb at the Atlanta Olympics only to be fingered for a long time as the bomber. Is Hackett the Richard Jewell of the Long Island serial-killer case? Or is he Joel Rifkin?

Hackett continues to insist that the whole line of inquiry is ridiculous. "I'm a family practitioner: an emergency physician, a former director of emergency medicine for Suffolk County, New York, and then emergency department director at Central Suffolk Hospital. Can you imagine my putting my reputation on the line, saying I ran a clinic?"

For a moment, it's possible to sense Hackett's plight and even sympathize. He's a talker. Maybe he said something Mari misinterpreted, something about how he works in emergency medicine and knows about rehabs. Everyone knows that Hackett has enemies in the neighborhood; maybe those enemies are only too happy to believe he's up to no good and that there's a cover-up. Is it possible that this is a perfect storm of gossip and the doctor had nothing to do with it at all?

He throws up his hands. How does one prove that one is, in fact, not a murderer? "I've been over this so many times, it doesn't get clearer with repetition," Hackett says. The best he can hope for is to be forgotten. "All you're doing is trying to tread lightly and lightly and more and more lightly until you recede into the background and eventually no one can see you anymore."

I ask about the security video. Hackett sighs. "The police wanted the security video. The police took the security video.

Being on the board, I saw when the police told the board they wanted it. So yes, we gave it to them."

Did he have a look at it beforehand?

"Of course, early on we said we should be looking at the security video. But that would be tampering with evidence."

I stay an hour. He answers every question. The doctor and I shake hands. We agree to stay in touch.

And twenty-four hours later, the police find Shannan's belongings in the marsh behind his house.

THE MARSH

The largest marsh in Oak Beach—forty-nine acres, about the same size as the inhabitable portion of the community—borders Anchor Way, where Shannan was last seen, and Larboard Court, where the Hacketts live. With every storm, the marsh fills up like a bathtub with rainwater, then drains through pipes beneath the roads of Oak Beach, down toward the old Oak Beach Inn parking lot and eventually into the Fire Island Inlet. At least that's what is supposed to happen. In reality, the pipes get crushed by storms or clogged with sediment, and the marsh fills even higher, until the ground starts to look like muck and the cordgrass and reeds and poison ivy grow so thick that no resident would ever try to hack through it.

The mosquitoes come next. They like nothing better than a freshwater marsh. The mosquitoes multiply, and so do the ticks, and the people of Oak Beach cry out for help from the town of Babylon. Every few decades, the town acquiesces and sends a team from Vector Control to dredge the marsh, building and repairing drainage ditches. You can see the trenches in aerial view: a long one down the middle and short splints off to the sides, like a spine with little ribs. As Joe Scalise, Jr., pointed out, one of those ribs runs right behind Hackett's cottage—a trench that anyone running through the marsh at night wouldn't see.

The marsh and the people of Oak Beach have coexisted this way for over a century. In the early nineties, the town of Babylon ceded control of the marsh to the state of New York in a land swap; in return, the town got control of a portion of the Oak Beach parking lot, which it intended to transform into a public park. Just before that happened, in 1989, the town dug out the mosquito ditches one last time. A main drainpipe to the inlet was replaced with a new pipe that lacked a flapper valve—meaning that in the decades since, salt water has drifted up into the fresh-water marsh. Salt meadow cordgrass followed. So did salt grass and common reed, along with the seaside lavender, black grass, marsh elder, groundsel bush, and more poison ivy.

The marsh became a Frankenstein of plant life, universally avoided by the people of Oak Beach. Everything grew there, and no one ever seemed to go in. Until, on a cold morning in December, eighteen months after Joe Brewer's last party on the Fairway, the police, John Mallia and his dog, Blue, among them, discovered—nearly fully intact, just steps from the shoulder of Ocean Parkway—the remains of Shannan Gilbert.

They found her purse first, with her identification inside. Then they went back and found a phone, some shoes, and a torn pair of jeans. They could get in now because of the repairs, which had drained the marsh for the first time in decades. Inspector Stuart Cameron of the Suffolk County police said that the pipe "drasti-cally increased our visibility in there and assisted us in being able to find things."

The police chose that day, December 6, to search the marsh because the tide seemed low. They used a large amphibious ve-hicle for the densest areas and cut new trails with a brush hog, a rotary mower with blades on hinges so they bounced up and over rocks and stumps. Ten officers went in on foot behind the vehi-cles, using brush cutters—high-powered WeedWackers—to clear paths. A dozen more came in with dogs. Rounding out the search party were six emergency services personnel and three members of the crime-scene unit. A few of the officers used metal detectors in the muck. Some of them reported working in waist-deep water and getting stuck.

"She's in there someplace," Dormer said at a press conference in the Oak Beach parking lot. It was late afternoon and misty and rainy and cold as the commissioner spoke, vowing to keep looking "into the foreseeable future . . . Hopefully, we will find the remains."

With Shannan's belongings as his first solid clue but still no body, the commissioner wasted no time fitting it into his theory. He said that Shannan was high that night, and paranoid, and she ran into the marsh, seeing the lights of the cars from Ocean Parkway beyond it. But in her condition, he said, Shannan had no concept that those cars were as far as a quarter mile away, and since she didn't know the area, she had no idea that she was about to fling herself into a dense, murky marsh that even the neighbors avoided. So, Dormer concluded, Shannan tripped—most likely in a drainage ditch—and drowned.

If this was true, it would be amazing, almost poetic irony. First Shannan's disappearance leads to the discovery of ten other sets of remains, and then the hunt for the serial killer makes Shannan's case so prominent that police have to come back to Oak Beach and search for her. Without the serial-killer case, they might have called off the search for Shannan. But without her, they might never have known there was a serial killer.

The girls all found one another.

Even if they did find Shannan's body in that ditch, there were many questions—chief among them, who killed the other girls? The people of Oak Beach would still have a lot to answer for. What happened in Joe Brewer's house that made her feel so threatened? When she and Brewer left the house briefly, were they buying drugs? If so, from whom? Once she came back, what happened that made her want to run away not just from Brewer but from her own driver? And did some neighbors—if not Hackett, then anyone—see her before she disappeared in the marsh?

Most of the people of Oak Beach had spent the better part of a year denying that she was there, behaving as if something horrible hadn't happened in their secluded beach community. Now there was proof that something had.

The police showed the belongings to Mari, who confirmed that the pocketbook and phone were Shannan's. Then she hunkered down at home, avoiding reporters, consumed with grief. Her family and friends were puzzling over the convenient timing of this search and the discovery, so close to Dormer's retirement. Some were wondering about Hackett. Mostly, they didn't want to believe that Shannan just wandered off and got lost and tripped and died. They wanted her death to mean something, and they wanted a culprit.

A day passed, and the police found nothing. Another day passed, and Shannan was still missing. When the weekend came, some of them harbored hope that Shannan wasn't there; that she wasn't even dead. "I'd rather her be alive somewhere," said Shannan's sister Sarra.

All the families were angry and bound together by that anger. Soon they were all declaring love and loyalty for one another. The most prolific was Kritzia Lugo, who, never having met any of the women in person, told the story in a long string of Facebook comments on how each one of them had saved her. Many of them replied to Kritzia, and soon they were all feeling it.

KRITZIA LUGO   It's weird but I learned from you guys one night I was so sad it was late I called Melissa Cann and she was there for me!

MELISSA CANN   I will always be there for you . . . And I know it is likewise with you also. :)

KRITZIA LUGO   That time I cut my wrist and was in the hospital for like a week Melissa Brock Wright was there for me it was late but I got to tell her all I was feeling

KRITZIA LUGO   Dawn Barthelemy talks to me once in a while and gives me advice

KRITZIA LUGO   Mari Gilbert showed me that there are mother's out there who do love their children

MELISSA BROCK WRIGHT   None of us will ever have to fight any battle alone! We are all a unit, and if one of us is having a hard time then we all are. If someone messes with one of us then they're messing with all of us!

KRITZIA LUGO   Kim Overstreet showed me the power of sisterhood when she is willing to sacrifice her life to get her sis justice

MELISSA CANN   Yes I agree

KRITZIA LUGO   Sherre Gilbert showed me children are a blessing—don't be so uptight—love them and learn how to have fun with them and enjoy them

Mari hung Christmas decorations around her place in Ellenville: garland around the fence, lights hung from the porch, and giant plastic candy canes on the lawn. In the middle was a pink sign: ALL I WANT FOR CHRISTMAS IS YOU. "Christmas is about dreams, dreaming, wishes coming true," Mari told a *Newsday* reporter. The sign included a map of the Gilgo Beach area and a list of names: Jessica Taylor, Melissa Barthelemy, Megan Waterman,

Maureen Barnes, Amber Lynn Costello. "They're my extended family now," Mari said.

Mari's youngest daughter, Stevie, was there, too, helping to decorate the home. She told the reporter that the family would put up a stocking for Shannan, and that she believed Shannan was still alive. Even if Shannan's remains were found, Stevie said, "there's never going to be closure unless I have her home. I'm just praying that Shannan comes home."

Taking advantage of the press attention, Mari noted a few inconsistencies in the search. She said she wasn't able to confirm that the shoes belonged to Shannan, who'd been seen in strappy sandals earlier that night, and the police had found what looked like ballet slippers. She said she believed that Shannan's things were planted in the marsh—by whom, she wouldn't say. She couldn't be sure of anything until Shannan was found, and even then, she vowed to fight. "I think Dormer just wants to find the remains, say she drowned, and close the case before he retires. That's what I feel, but I'm not gonna let that happen."

The question hung over every Facebook thread for days: Could Shannan really have run into a marsh and died?

"I mean, that would just be *my* fuckin' luck," Kim said.

On the phone that week from her place on Long Island, Kim said she could see Shannan being coked up and paranoid enough to run away from Michael Pak; Kim had been in situations a little like that. "And she's bipolar," she said. "Whatever meds she's taking for that, there are just some things you can't mix together. I know that through experience, with myself and my sister. My sister would have drug-induced seizures. Some people have drug-induced schizophrenia. I've seen that shit."

Which brought Kim to the purpose of her call. She'd been thinking of calling the detectives and turning them on to a menacing trick she'd had not long before Amber disappeared. "It weighs on me heavy," she said. "My instincts are usually not too wrong." The john was all the way out on the East End of Long Island. He gave her five hundred for the hour and wanted full service. Dave Schaller was with her, so she said no to the date. But the next day he called and offered another four hundred, "and he says he's going to score some rock."

She went. He was a white guy, he drove a truck, and he said he owned a tugboat business. He lived in a basement apartment, nothing spectacular. Inside, he showed Kim a box of dildos, "probably a hundred different vibrators and women's shit. And that struck me as weird at first, but some guys get off on it, so it didn't strike me too hard." Where things turned scary, she said, was when she gave him full service; that was when he reached for her throat. "Some guys do this," Kim said. "Some guys like to do it, but I don't like it. You're not going to do it to me. That can change the situation real quick. And I didn't let it go farther than it did, so I got up and told him, 'I'm not comfortable, I'm leaving, and you're not getting your money back. That was uncalled for.'"

Kim said she left and didn't think anything of it. They texted afterward but never met up again. A few days before Amber vanished, Kim said she told her sister about him and passed along his number. "I told her I had some guy," she said. "I'd seen him twice and I made a G off him in two days. I was like, 'I'm not guaranteeing anything, but you can try it.' I told her that he was kind of an asshole. But we never said anything else about him." Now she can't help but wonder: "Did she call him that week, or maybe she called him and he called her back? You know what I'm saying?"

The story, as she told it, seemed a little wobbly: Kim had been afraid of this john at the time, but not so afraid that she wouldn't pass the lead along to her sister? No matter: She wanted to find him again, confront him directly: "How do I know you didn't do it? What were you doing that night?" So far, she hadn't been able to find anyone to go with her to find his house. Ever since she'd appeared on the A&E show, all her crack and escort connections had been avoiding her. "They think I put myself out there too much," she said. "My dealers are like, 'What the fuck?' I'm like, 'My sister got killed! Every man for their fucking self at this point. Shit!'"

The killer dominated her thoughts. She'd decided that he was thinking about her, too. "It eats at me every day. I dream about this fucking guy. It's a war right now between him and me." She was talking even faster. "This is the rest of my life. It's all I think about day and fucking night. I cannot shake it. I can't. Because if it was Amber here, that bitch would be on TV every two days, they would lock her up just to keep her from getting the publicity. I'm telling you, that's how she was. She was a crusader. She was a moneymaker. If there's something to make from it, she's going to make it. And I'm telling you, she would fucking do it. So how can I not, you know what I'm saying? It ruined my life. It took almost my whole heart out of my chest. It's ruined my fucking life. It's put me back out on the streets. I'm running as hard as I was from day one."

She'd been fighting some version of this war long before the killer entered her life. She'd been running since she was a little girl, since Coed Connection and maybe before that. So had Amber. They ran together. They hustled together. Those guys Amber and her friends robbed, they had it coming. "They got treated the way they treated her, and that's just the way it is," Kim said. "That's life. A lot of people don't understand that. But it's because there's war in the streets, for any type of hustle, whether it's drugs, whether it's guns, whether it's ass, whatever, it doesn't matter. It's the same war. It's war. And people don't realize that, and they live their normal little lives and stuff. Girls on the Backpage, it's not a fucking choice, it's a last resort. It's a white-knuckle way of survival. It's just the way it is."

I told Kim that her friends were worried about her. They didn't want another victim. They didn't want another death.

"And God forbid," she said. "But it'd be better than living my life like this every day. I'd rather be dead than have to live the rest of my life every single day like this."

"She's gotta be there someplace," Dormer said. "Or parts of her, at this point."

It was Monday, December 12, six days into the search, and the commissioner had agreed to see me in his wood-paneled office in Yaphank to discuss the case. As he talked, teams of cops thirty miles away were searching the marsh for Shannan. They knew the window of opportunity was closing, that they had to find her before the tide came in and water bubbled up into the marsh again. Dormer strained to explain why she hadn't turned up yet. "You know, she's been out there for over a year and a half, two summers, heading into the second winter," he said. "It's a wild area, swampy. People don't go in there. You need a machete to get through this stuff."

His chief of detectives, Dominick Varrone, was on his way—Varrone was the details man, while Dormer was the big-picture guy—but while we were waiting, Dormer took the opportunity to tell me why he thought Shannan's death was accidental. "Where she went in, it's like a little path. I was down there, you could make it through there. So she went in, and now you're in that area, disoriented." The things of Shannan's that they'd found weren't far from the little path. That made Dormer think she'd headed in there and hadn't come out. "But it's very difficult to find anything in there. A lot of animals in there, muskrats and that kinda thing. A lot of wildlife in there that would obviously feast on the flesh."

Dormer sounded so certain. But the next second, he shrugged and said it was just a theory. "If you've been in this business for a while, you start to get a sense," he said. "You can pick out what's real and what's not. They don't teach this in college. It comes through life experience from dealing with this stuff, dealing with people, and dealing with investigations. And looking at it logically, keeping an open mind—always keeping an open mind. I say that all the time, 'Never close your mind on something, never throw something out.' I always keep it there. Keep it on the table. You may have to go back to it. You know, investigations evolve as you move forward."

Why did they go back to the marsh after all this time? Dormer credited John Mallia, the cop who found the first four Gilgo bodies. Mallia, Dormer said, "had already searched the area there, but there was a lot of water and we really couldn't get a good search. In fact, he had told the guys, 'I think we should go back.'" With Varrone still not here, Dormer decided to clear up a lot of gossip about the case, starting with the rumors about a second person at Brewer's house. He said they had no indication that anyone besides Shannan and Brewer were inside. He mentioned the twenty-three-minute 911 call, noting that Shannan got switched away from Suffolk County when she couldn't say exactly where she was. Once the police got the 911 calls from Coletti and Barbara Brennan, he said, they arrived "within eighteen minutes."

And he scoffed at the rumor that the killer had special knowledge that only a cop would have. Anyone who watched *SVU* or *Criminal Minds,* he said, would know anything this killer knew about using disposable cell phones and avoiding detection.

Dormer detailed how he came to believe all the others had the same killer. "Maybe the killer evolved," he said. "Maybe he didn't go through the trouble of dismembering them now. The experts tell us that that happens. They evolve over time. So you put all these things together, and it looks like one person." He saw more circumstantial evidence in the fact that five sets of remains still hadn't been identified. "If a young woman from college went missing from the shopping mall, their parents would report them missing. And they would put them in the database. The fact that the others are not in there is an indication to me that they were estranged from their families, nobody missed them, and therefore they didn't go into the database. Which would indicate that they're probably sex workers."

Dormer, in other words, had no special knowledge about these victims. He was playing the averages—working from a set of accepted assumptions made by many people in law enforcement about who typically goes missing and who gets murdered by serial killers. University of Illinois criminologist Steve Egger, author of a popular 2002 study called *The Killers Among Us,* has asserted that nearly 78 percent of female victims of serial murderers are prostitutes. That finding does not seem to have been replicated in any other research, but it's become received wisdom. Dormer no doubt assumed that in general, prostitutes who are murdered by serial killers aren't known to be missing until their bodies are discovered, and sometimes not even then; often the killer has to identify his victims and guide the police to the remains. In the case of Washington's Green River Killer, Indiana University criminology professor Kenna Quinet has found that eleven of the forty-eight victims—or 23 percent—were so-called missing missing: victims with no active missing-person case. Faced with a string of bodies along a beach, Dormer decided to work with the assumption that they, too, were missing missing.

None of that explained the toddler. "It's particularly puzzling," Dormer said. "Because even if the mother was in the sex business, somebody would know that she had a toddler. But people that I've talked to in the business tell me these girls move around a lot. They're in New York two weeks, they go to Atlantic City, Vegas, Florida, Buffalo. So they're moving around all the time, a lot of them. And so they go missing, and nobody notices."

What really convinced Dormer that the victims were prostitutes targeted by the same killer was the low probability that two killers would dump in the same spot. Then again, it could be an unusually good spot. The more he thought about it, the more Dormer couldn't see any possibility other than one killer. "Do they have a society of serial killers that meet once a month, and they sit in the diner in the back room, and they say, 'Where are you dumping the bodies this month?' And they say, 'Oh, well, Ocean Parkway, down near Gilgo Beach'? I don't think we have that. They don't usually work in pairs, either. They're individuals—psychopathic, the whole bit."

He was all but certain that Shannan was not one of the killer's victims. "The MO is different," he said. "The driver drives her out there. Brewer's very open that he contacted her through Craigslist. He makes no bones about that, it's what he does." The others, he said, "were strictly one-on-one contact. There was no john involved, no driver involved, that we know of. All these gals were contacted by the killer."

That was when Varrone walked in, a grim, guarded figure

with receding hair and a bushy mustache. Varrone talked about the marsh. "It's a massive search," he said, "and it's a search that we really couldn't do earlier, because of the amount of water in here." Had there really been enough water for her to drown? "Well, she was exhausted, she was up all night," he said. "You talk about cocaine psychosis—she could have just succumbed to exhaustion, and she could have drowned in six inches of water."

Then Varrone surprised me by saying that at first, he hadn't believed Shannan was hysterical enough to run into the marsh. "Despite the fact that she was acting irrational, she was rational enough to be running apparently to houses that were well lit," he said. "Some people have cocaine psychosis, and they jump into a lake or something. But we didn't think she was irrational enough to go into here. But apparently, she did."

He talked about the killer of the others. "First of all, he probably makes them an offer they can't refuse. Like we speculated he'll pay the whole night—a significant amount. And with certain demands, he doesn't want to be interrupted." Varrone thought it was strange that Amber had left her cell phone behind. "It's probably the demand that he has made on some of the victims." And then Varrone came close to blaming the victims. "And this guy—this killer—is making them an offer that they find very hard to resist. And greed gets the best of them. In fact, most of them are in the business that they're in because it's an easy way to make money, and because they're greedy."

Not the most compassionate or PR-friendly thing for him to say about the victims of the department's most famous unsolved mystery. But Varrone, like Dormer, was a lame duck. It's customary for all the chiefs to leave with their commissioner, and he didn't seem at peace with that. There was an edge to Varrone's comments—irritation at, if nothing else, the pressure brought by the families. As he talked, it was clear that he didn't have a high opinion of them, either. "In a high-profile case, it becomes difficult," Varrone said, "because everybody is pounding on their doors for information. They're not sophisticated enough. After a while, you could almost see—I don't want to pick on one family—but some of the family members start doing their hair and dressing up. They rise to the spotlight. And they criticize us."

With Mari in particular, he'd been reminded of another famous case he worked on long ago, the 1992 kidnapping of nine-year-old Katie Beers in Bay Shore, Long Island. The girl's mother, Marilyn Beers, "was a taxicab driver," Varrone said, smiling at the memory. "And then she got her hair all done up."

Dormer chuckled.

It was time to go. Varrone left first; he was heading to the marsh. On his way out, I asked about Hackett. "He's somebody we've taken a look at, and we continue to," he said.

When Varrone was gone, Dormer answered, too. "He's a kook," he said. "Have you met him?"

I said yes.

"Does he look like he could commit murder?" Dormer asked rhetorically. "No, he doesn't." But then he caught himself. "Unless he did."

His smile was unreadable. Or rather, it could be read any number of ways.

The bones—an almost fully intact skeleton—were found on the far side of the marsh, about a quarter mile from Shannan's belongings. The police didn't wait for a medical report. The metal plate in the jaw gave them all they needed. Mari got the call early in the morning. And at eleven-thirty A.M. on December 13—a year after the discovery of three of the four bodies—the police announced that they'd found what they believed were Shannan's remains.

They found her on the far side of the marsh, about as far from where they found her belongings as she could be. The remains were close to the southern edge of Ocean Parkway, surprisingly, which brought her a little closer to the other victims. Even though Maureen, Melissa, Megan, and Amber were dumped on the northern side, it was possible that Shannan had been dumped off the side of the road like the others—at least as possible as her clawing her way through a quarter mile of marsh before dying.

The inconsistencies didn't faze Dormer. When he spoke to the press, he doubled down on the theory that Shannan wasn't a murder victim—that she'd died after collapsing in the marsh. "It appeared she was heading toward the parkway, toward the lighting on the causeway," he said. Why were her belongings found so far away from her? "That's explainable," Dormer said, "because she's, you know, hysterical. And she's discarding her possessions as she moves along . . . Her jeans could have come off from running in that environment. And that is a possibility."

Dormer was out on his own. Within hours, a former chief medical examiner from New York named Michael Baden, who once worked in Suffolk County, was telling reporters how absurd it was to think that a woman who weighed not much more than a hundred pounds could thrash her way through a marsh that the police were afraid to walk into. "The circumstances are very impressive that the mother is right and she was murdered," Baden said.

Soon after that, the DA, Thomas Spota, tossed a bucket of water on Dormer's other theory: that the rest of the victims all were killed by one person. While Spota allowed that everyone involved in the case believed the first four bodies were the work of one killer, he said the others had displayed gruesome tendencies that were all over the map. He also suggested that Dormer had been off the reservation with his theory all along. "I don't think it's healthy for us to be talking about a single-killer theory," Spota said. "[Dormer] has never mentioned it to the prosecutor and, to my knowledge, none of the homicide investigators who are assigned to the Gilgo investigation."

Some of his motivation was political. Spota was a foe of Dormer's boss, Steve Levy. Spota hated the way that Levy and Dormer had gutted the police budget, and his investigation into possible campaign-spending improprieties had helped convince Levy not to run for another term. Still, any time a district attorney and police commissioner openly clash over a high-profile unsolved case, an investigation can seem compromised. It was almost as if, by floating two conflicting theories, they were giving a gift to any future defense lawyer handling the Gilgo case at trial. Which might have explained why the incoming interim commissioner, Edward Webber, would announce that the department no longer was pushing any theory of the Gilbert case or any of the Gilgo Beach cases. "The theories are open," he'd say. "There's no fixed theories at the moment."

Mari's family and friends couldn't stop picking apart what Dormer had said about Shannan's death. Would a crazy person call 911? That's not a psychotic break, they said, that's genuine terror. How could she be crazy enough to pull off her jeans in the marsh, yet rational enough to keep 911 on the phone for twenty-three minutes? They started teasing out other explanations, conspiracies to explain everything. It seemed to them too coincidental that the police would suddenly look there and find Shannan months after not searching there at all. Some said the body must have been placed there recently. How else could the

FBI Black Hawk helicopter not have spotted her on its flights earlier in the year?

And they all marveled at the most poignant coincidence: that Shannan's body was found on the same day that the rest of the families were convening at Oak Beach for the first-anniversary vigil.

Missy and Lorraine had been at Oak Beach for two days already, camping out in the rain, trying to get press attention. Missy had put her family's forty-six-inch Sharp LCD TV up for sale to pay for the trip. But that day, hours after the police announced they'd found Shannan, the fog and misty rain had cleared just in time.

It was bright but cold and windy when the reporters and camera crews started rolling into the parking lot. Kritzia joined the others, a good distance away from the media. Michele Kutner, the girls' biggest Facebook fan, was with them, telling everyone that there was no way Shannan just drowned. She and two others had spent a few days determining the exact site of each victim, then marking each location with spray paint on the side of Ocean Parkway so that they could erect four crosses before the vigil. Each family made their own except Kim. Melissa Wright in Wilmington made a beautiful white cross for Amber and had it shipped there for the occasion.

As they all waited for Mari, they were crying, embracing, and marveling at the coincidence. The reporters, watching from a distance, weren't quite as amazed. They'd been coming to Oak Beach for a long time, and cynicism was taking over. "I can't believe they're doing all this for a whore," said one member of a TV crew.

Kim turned up, too, as promised. She brought a friend, a woman who was helping her stay sober. But she had dark circles under her eyes, and the tears never stopped flowing. When Missy saw Kim, they hugged, but then Missy looked at her like she was a dead woman walking.

Gus Coletti came by. Michele Kutner broke away from comforting the families and gave him a hug. "Where's Hackett?" she said.

"He's in my living room," Gus said.

Kutner took that to mean that Hackett was hiding from reporters. But a little while later, Hackett came out, too. Kutner went over to him. "Thank God they found her. Aren't you happy?" she said.

"Yeah," Hackett said, smiling a little. "You guys thought I did it."

Michele saw his hands shaking.

Finally, Mari arrived, wearing a black leather jacket and sunglasses, her blond hair flowing. She locked into an embrace with Missy and Lorraine as the camera crews closed in on them.

Kim refused to get up with the other three. "I'm not doing that shit," she said. "I fuckin' hate these people. I'm here for my sister."

Soon there wasn't room for her, anyway. The other three were frozen in their hug for minutes on end as the reporters crushed in, snapping away. A minute or two later, they gathered behind a collection of microphones, Mari in the center, Missy to her left in a plaid flannel jacket, Lorraine to her right in a blue parka. Mari's arms were around the others, clutching them for support. There was more media today than ever before—more than the June balloon release, more than any of Mari's guerrilla attacks on Oak Beach.

Mari spoke. "First of all, I'd like to say this is a sad but yet happy moment. Today marks the one-year anniversary that the bodies were found, and I want to be here to support the families and to be with them. And as much as today may be Shannan, it's not just Shannan. It's all of us. Every one of us and our families and friends and everyone that was affected by this." She trailed off. "It's too hard," she finally added. "I can't even talk. I don't even have words to say how I'm feeling right now." Then she looked to either side, at Missy and Lorraine. "But I'm sorry."

"Don't be sorry," said Missy. They all hugged.

"Don't be sorry," said Lorraine. "Like we told you, Mari, don't ever be sorry."

"And just like you're here to support our girls," said Missy, "we're here to support Shannan. And we've been here since the day that we found out that Shannan was a part of our girls. And we won't ever leave. Please believe that."

The three embraced again.

The reporters were surrounding them, video cameras in the back, photographers down low in front. When the embrace lasted longer than a few seconds, the reporters took that to mean it was time for questions. The first question was the one everyone wanted to ask: "Do you believe it was an accident?"

"No, no," Mari said, running a hand through her hair. "I will not believe that, for the simple fact that Shannan was a strong woman."

The next questions baited Mari into unloading on the police, and she was more than happy to oblige. She wondered why the police seemed so certain it wasn't murder when they hadn't even conducted an autopsy. And she blasted the entire investigation as too little too late. She ripped into the 911 call again—the time it took the police to come after her call. "I believe that when she was initially reported missing that they didn't care. They treated her like her 'job' and not as a person and as a human being. And

I think if they started to search early and continued it longer than they did the first time, we would have found her sooner, and this case would be so much further ahead than it is."

Another question, posed tentatively by a reporter in the back: "Is there any thought that this guy is . . . uh . . . is still . . . doing it? I mean—"

Lorraine spoke up. "I almost a hundred percent guarantee that this man is sitting in his home right now, watching what is going on on the TV, getting the biggest thrill of his life, seeing what he has done to these families."

There was one last question. "Mari, if the autopsy proves the police's theory"—if it indicated that she'd fallen and drowned, as opposed to sustaining any obvious wounds—"do you feel like Shannan had a purpose to solve this case?"

"Oh, yes, absolutely," Mari said. "She brought loved ones home."

"She brought us together," said Missy. "Because *this* is our family, you know? Our bond."

A few police cars led an SUV filled with family members to visit the sites along Ocean Parkway where the bodies were found. Counting Kritzia, at least one person who knew and loved each of the girls had come to visit the crosses. Mari came, too. On the way there, it was lost on none of them that they were tracing the killer's route and making the same stops.

These were their only few minutes alone, without the media on top of them. In the car, Mari was subdued, fuming about everything that she'd been put through, and now this. She whispered that there was no way Shannan had died by accident.

Missy asked Kim, "Where've you been?"

Kim's answer chilled her: "I'm trying to catch our girls' killer." Missy didn't know what to say after that.

Kritzia went to work on her. "I know you think this is never going to happen to you," she told Kim, "because you think you know what you're doing, but guess what, your sister thought like that, too." Kim just looked at her.

At each stop, they crouched down in the bramble, laid flowers, and tied a bright red heart-shaped balloon. Missy was the only one who didn't cry. She'd been there for two days, and mourned her sister for four and a half years, and was all cried out. Not so for Kritzia; when she saw Melissa's cross, she threw herself to the ground. "Get up," Lorraine said. "What are you doing? Get up."

When Kritzia finally stood up and looked around, something clicked. This stretch of Ocean Parkway was like a little netherworld. Nobody lived there, and there were no stores. It was the perfect place to dump a body: no signs, no streetlights. That was why he felt so confident that he could throw the bodies right there, she thought, right in the street.

Call Joe Jr. biased, call him vindictive, but he had been right all along about the marsh. As Flukeyou, he spent the next several days crowing about it online. *They found Shannan's personal items right behind the doc's house,* he wrote.

The Hackett theories abounded on Websleuths. Some commenters said he was completely innocent. Others said he was a calculated killer who called Mari after the murder in order to lull her into a false sense of security and give his partners more time to hide the body. Others split the difference, saying Hackett was just a patsy who tried to respond to a hysterical, incoherent girl, and when Shannan panicked and ran into the brush behind the house, he was left with her belongings and forced to stash them in the marsh. Still others said he gave her a sedative that interacted badly with the drugs she'd taken earlier, leaving Hackett with a corpse on his hands.

Now Joe Jr. was waiting for the police to connect the dots to Hackett, saying it was only a matter of time before the police had him in cuffs. *They only get one shot at this punk in court,* he posted, *so they're taking their time to build a case.* He built new theories all the time online, as Flukeyou. *Shannan was placed there after she died . . . They can put a man on the moon, but take eighteen months to find a girl in a field? . . . Barbara H was not home the morning that SG disappeared . . .*

The day after the vigil, Mari was in anguish. *Not knowing hurts but knowing really hurts!!* she posted in Shannan's Facebook group. As Missy, Lorraine, and others tried to support her, Mari worried about what the autopsy might reveal. She started doing damage control preemptively. *If there are any chemicals in Shannan's body, and if they are NOT "street" drugs, then who gave what to her?* She called the cops "liars or stupid," concluding, *I KNOW Shannan WAS Murdered!!!!* And she made a pledge: *Shannan will have Justice AND so will Maureen—Megan—Melissa—Amber!! If NOT by $ than by they way the SCPD CHANGE how they treat escorts!!!!*

Two days later, she was even madder. *F Dormer!!!!!!!!!!* she wrote. *Let me go running, and see how fast my jeans fall off my body!! Give me a F*in Break!!!*

On Facebook, Mari posted an illustration of Jesus holding a photograph of Shannan. Others in her group posted photos of Shannan as an angel, and angels holding Shannan, and Shannan ascending to heaven. Johanna Gonzalez got a new tattoo of an eye, modeled after one of Shannan's wide anime eyes. Another friend suggested that Mari could be the next John Walsh. Still another called her "Mama Mari."

A week after the body was found, Mari convened another press conference in the Oak Beach parking lot. Dormer, days from retirement, shrugged when he was told about it. "The thing'll never die down," he said.

Mari asked all her friends to wear blue in honor of Shannan. When she emerged from her car, she was head to toe in bluish-purple velour. Another car pulled up with her, and out stepped Mari's new lawyer, a Long Island plaintiff's attorney named John Ray. A notorious dandy, Ray was wearing a derby hat and a plaid vest with a matching suit and a long plaid overcoat. As a final flourish, he was carrying a gnarled corkscrew-shaped shillelagh. Following Ray's sartorial lead, his younger associate was wearing a well-tailored brown suit with his own matching derby.

Ray's remarks were stagey, almost Sharpton-esque, designed for maximum impact. He likened the Suffolk homicide squad to something out of Mayberry, and Dormer's investigation to a *Pink Panther* movie. He said the police had dropped the ball with Shannan from the very start. He tore into the 911 call. He said that it didn't matter if the autopsy said she'd drowned—who had drowned her?

As he talked, his associate circulated copies of a letter Ray had sent the police on behalf of Mari Gilbert and the other victims' families. The letter called upon the police to hand the case, which Ray considered hopelessly botched, to the FBI. It closed by saying that if the FBI didn't take over the case, Mari would sue.

Then Mari spoke. Her sentences were clear and short, perfect newspaper quotes. "Ask yourself what you would do if this was your daughter," she said. She was more composed than she'd been the day they'd found Shannan. Now she was resolved, a crusader. She took just one question: Did she believe Shannan was a victim of the serial killer? "Yes," she said, her head jerking forward.

The news crews were breaking down their equipment and packing when Gus Coletti pulled up in his car. He was ready to shoot the breeze with reporters, as usual. Before he could get out, Joe Jr. approached the driver's side of the car and started screaming into Gus's face. "You're the mayor of Oak Beach! There were two 911 calls that night! *Why didn't you save the security tape!*"

It was quite a sight: young, handsome Joe, completely unhinged, shrieking at a stooped old man, sitting in a car. Mari's lawyer was upstaged. The news crews rushed over. Joe kept shouting. Gus gave as good as he got: "The only thing wrong with Oak Beach is *you!*"

Gus couldn't drive off—there were too many people around it—but he made a show of pulling out his cell phone and calling the police. "I don't have to put up with that," he grumbled.

Joe was still yelling as the reporters followed him. "What are you gonna do now, Mayor? Are you gonna do your poor-little-old-man act? You're the mayor of Oak Beach! *What about that tape! Why are you covering up for the doctor!*"

Missy Cann watched the press conference on the Web from her home in Connecticut. She had trouble understanding what she was watching. All she'd known ahead of time was that Mari was going to announce she had a new lawyer. "He hasn't talked to any of us," she said.

Mari had acted unilaterally. None of the other families had been told a thing about her new legal strategy. No one had shown them the letter to the police that John Ray supposedly had written on their behalf. The request to get the FBI involved particularly threw Missy. "The FBI already is assisting. If Suffolk County wasn't doing their job, the FBI would have already stepped in." Missy thought criticizing the police was a misguided strategy—that the police knew more about the case than they were letting on, and for all anyone knew, they might not be bungling it at all. The best guess Missy could make was that the tactic was just a lot of posturing. "It's a little premature. I'd have waited until the autopsy came back before I said this."

Once John Ray's office passed Missy a copy of the letter, she became furious. "'On behalf of the sex worker murder victims'?" she said a few weeks later, quoting the letter. "So Shannan is *Shannan,* and the other girls are *sex workers*? I never talk to that man for a day, and he's working on behalf of my sister?" She couldn't believe what Mari had done, how she had decided to stick a thumb in the eye of the people investigating the case. The police, Missy said, arrived ten or twenty minutes after Barbara Brennan called, not counting Shannan's call as the start of the response time. "They did way better than the police did for us or the other girls. She should be a little grateful." If you thought about it, she said, Shannan had more resources than any of the other girls. She'd been treated better, too. "They didn't bring anything of *Maureen's* belongings to my mom or *me* to look at."

Missy had been holding her tongue for a while about Mari: her volatility, her vanity, her need to fight everyone who threatened to pull attention away from her. Now she was unburdening herself. She made a crack about Mari's "groupies" on Facebook, winding Mari up, feeding her ego, egging her on. She called them all "yes-men" and suggested that any dissent ended with being punished—banishment from the group. "We have to walk around eggshells around her, too," Missy said, "which is kind of bullshit. Me and Lorraine have been avoiding her. She changes her theories more than anyone. I just try to be as supportive as I can be and go on my way. 'Cause Mari's the type of person who, if you disagree with her, she starts blasting you to everyone."

She was fed up. "Six days after Shannan is found, she gets this lawyer and goes on TV? I was talking to Lorraine, and she said, 'Sorry, but she does not act like a grieving mother.' When my mom found out, my mom talked to nobody. I felt the same way. I guess everyone's different, but I know I would have waited for my daughter's autopsy before saying anything. And then she switches and said she thinks Shannan is part of the serial-killer case? I think she just wants attention for Shannan. That's so sad. I'd rather just know it was an accident."

Her voice had flattened as she spoke. She was so immersed in every detail of the case that stoicism had set in. For Missy, all the questions that obsessed other people about Shannan's disappearance were not quite so mysterious. Of course Shannan died accidentally, she said. Of course she wasn't connected to the others. "I definitely *don't* think Shannan got murdered by the same serial killer," she said. After repeating some of Dormer's arguments— none of the other girls had drivers; they didn't have anyone with them—she added one more: the time line of the murders. Shannan went missing after Maureen and Melissa but before Megan and Amber. If the killer got Shannan, too, Missy said, "she would have got placed in the same place, in burlap bags." The theory that the killer changed up his pattern for Shannan—pressured by her attention-getting dash through Oak Beach—didn't hold water with her.

The thickness of the brush, she suggested, could be why Shannan took off her jeans—"because they were weighing her down," she said. "You'd be surprised what a person would do to survive."

Besides, she added, "I don't think anyone could put her body where it was."

Missy didn't necessarily agree there was a police screwup in Shannan's case. The 911 call had jurisdictional problems; things like that just happen. "I'm sorry, but I think this is ridiculous. They couldn't search that area because it was engulfed with water at that time. They couldn't bring dogs in. I think they did the best that they could, given the situation. They treated Shannan as their own separate case, which was good. And then they worked on the serial-killer case. But when they found these girls, they didn't just forget about Shannan. They just kept looking."

If Shannan's death had been an accident or a crazy coincidence, Missy thought the serial killer was a john who was a regular to all four of the girls. "I think that he knew them, gave them trust," she said. "Amber was very experienced in that field, and she obviously knew this person very well. She let her guard down."

What upset Missy more than anything was the disagreement between Dormer and Spota. "It makes you wonder how close they are to catching this guy if they don't know if it's one or more killers." The only certainty, she said, was that the first four girls to be found were connected. Until someone could prove to Missy that Shannan was connected, too, she said, she'd believe the police and not Mari.

As a new year began, the disagreement created a schism—Mari and her Facebook followers in one camp, Missy and Lorraine in another. Missy started planning Stunts 4 Justice, a stunt-bike show, in collaboration with the old motorcycle club of her late brother, Will, to raise money for the Crimestoppers reward for the case. She scrambled to get local DJs to attend. She wanted to raise five thousand dollars. As soon as it was announced, Mari made it known that she was hurt that only the four girls' names were being mentioned in the publicity, not Shannan's.

Missy didn't know how to respond. "I really feel like crying," she said. "My sister got murdered. I'm just trying to do one positive thing, and I hear it's wrong. How is it wrong? Just because Shannan was found, I can't jump up and say the killer did this, too. It's not like I can change things because someone's acting like a child and kicking and screaming. It's too much drama."

On Facebook, Lorraine showed off a photo of her latest tattoo: four interlocking hearts, each a different color, each with an initial inside—*M, M, M,* and *A.* There was no *S.* When Mari said she was angry about this, too, Lorraine responded dryly that when Shannan's death was proved a murder, she would add the *S.*

On January 14, Mari and Sherre returned to Oak Beach for another press conference. No one from any of the other families attended. "It's been a very hard eighteen months," Mari said. "Half the battle is over. We still have another battle ahead of us. Our worst battle, our strongest battle. But we're not gonna give up, we're gonna have faith and gonna pursue this, no matter how long it takes and no matter what it takes. To find out the truth about what happened to Shannan and to bring the killer to justice and everyone who is involved."

Mari pulled out a piece of paper. "I'd like to read this on behalf of our family and I." She looked down. "'We are not close to accepting the loss of our daughter and our sister Shannan. We don't know if we will ever fully be well inside. How hollow we feel, lonely, sad, confused, and bitter. There will never be closure because there will be an emptiness inside. And the thought of Shannan never coming home for birthdays, holidays or births or just because, is more pain than anyone can imagine unless you've lost a child yourself.'"

A tall white cross—over twice the height of the crosses for the other four girls—had been placed in the spot in the marsh where Shannan was found. Sherre put some red flowers around the base. Mari added yellow ones. In front of the grave, they both broke down as the photographers snapped away. Mari didn't get up for the longest time. In front of a lit candle protected from the wind by glass, Mari sobbed loudly. A few days later, she posted to Facebook a photo of herself kneeling there, wailing. The caption read: THE DAY MY LIFE CHANGED FOREVER.

THE JOHN

When Joe Brewer answers the phone, one of the first things he does is ask for money. "I mean, you can write your story," he says, "but nobody can write it like I can, because I lived it. And it's even more sensational than anybody's saying. That's why I've kept my mouth shut for this long."

I tell him I don't pay for interviews. Joe keeps talking anyway, for close to a half hour, his voice overrun with laughter. In fact, the more Joe talks, the more his laugh is all that I hear, coloring everything he says, a roiling, rolling, life's-a-party laugh that he means to sound coy and knowing and smooth but more often seems bafflingly out of tune with the subject he is trying hard not to discuss.

"I think it would be important for you to meet me and get a feel for the kind of guy I am," he says. "Like, I'm a huge, *huge,* extreme liberal. You know, I couldn't hurt, I couldn't kill, a fuckin' small mammal. The whole of who I am is so disproportionate to people's perspective of me, it's hysterical to me. So why don't you meet me and see who I am as a person."

That would be great, I say.

He talks right past me. "Yeah, what kind of human being I am and how much compassion I have for the entire human race. And any living individual." Then he second-guesses himself playfully. "I *guess* I would kill a mouse if I had a mouse in my house. So I can't say I wouldn't kill *any* mammal." He laughs. "But it's insane that I was shown as a serial killer!" He laughs again. "I don't mean to disappoint you. It's funny."

He is still living at his mother's house in West Islip. The Oak Beach place was on the market for $439,000, then reduced to $399,999, then pulled off and relisted for $375,000. Joe says he is staying in West Islip for now. "At first I thought I had to relocate. But people who knew me and knew me in this town, it's like, the one thing people who grew up in this town, the first thing people said, is of all the people, I'd be the *last* person on anybody's list who would ever be suspect of anything!"

Another laugh.

"Not that I was suspected! The police, I was never a suspect. I'm sure there was a brief time in the beginning where I was a person of interest, of course. But as soon as I ran to them and made it clear to them I had nothing to do with any of this."

As soon as he says that, he corrects himself. He says he does know something special about the case. "Dude, there's something you don't know, something really big. I do have some big chits on that, but I've got to hold them back. You want to know the truth, I mean, honestly, everybody would say the same things I was saying, even if they were guilty. But there's a lot out there I know, I don't want to say this because a lot of them are my friends, but at the end of this, the police are going to have a lot of pie on their face."

When I ask why Shannan called the police that night, he laughs his biggest laugh so far.

"I'm sorry to laugh," he says. "That was, like, the easiest— you know, it's so funny—sometimes the most obvious answer is the most easiest one to figure out. And, like, that is the question I get more than any, and that is the most easy to figure out." He pauses. "No, I'm sorry, I'm gonna take that back. The easiest one is I must have scared her, I must have threatened her, you know, obviously, that's number one choice. But that is far from—I was ready to help her. And you know what, dude? If they ever release that 911 call, I know my voice is in the background. And I know I'm the only voice of reason, and I know the police know that. I would never harm a *soul*. If you actually read through, you can put it together why she ran crazy into the night. You know, the answer's there. Yeah, I know everybody wants a bad guy, they want a villain, and they want me to be the villain. It's not that sensational, buddy, it's not what happened."

The first thing I think of is Joe's transvestite story—that he wouldn't pay her because he thought she was a man. That was hardly the most obvious explanation, though it was pretty sensational. It was also ludicrous. So I decide not to bring it up. Then there is the question of the drifter reported as being at Joe's house that night. Though the police would continue to say that Brewer was alone with Shannan, a few months after my talk with Joe, the drifter would finally surface, self-publishing a memoir under the pen name "W." *Confessions of the Oak Beach Drifter* does not deliver on the promise of its title. The author, a West Islip native, confesses to a life of burglary, drugs, assault, rape, and one shooting. What he doesn't offer is any insight into Shannan's death, just a few swipes at Joe for liking rough sex with prostitutes (something the author doesn't seem exactly against) and for, he believes, telling the *Post* about him as a way to divert suspicion from himself. As a houseguest of Joe's not long before that night with Shannan, the drifter, in the book's sole accusation, recalls "one particular night I was awakened by a woman screaming, 'No! Please stop! Please, don't do that!' and that was followed by a loud thud. And then there was silence." But he also says that his memoir is partly fictionalized, and he offers no date for the incident in question, and he allows that his drug and alcohol problem "was at an all-time high" during his stay on the Fairway and that he "had quite a few blackout nights." All in all, the drifter's account is a wash for Joe.

I tell Joe that it sounds like he's saying Shannan had a bad re-action to a drug that night.

For the first time, Joe is less playful. "No, I'm not saying that."

Then I'm not following you, I say. What is the obvious expla-nation?

"No, I'm not saying that at *all*," he repeats. "I did not say that at *all*."

I apologize.

Joe chuckles. All is forgiven. He seems to be thinking over whether to say something.

"I mean, it would be shocking to you," he says. He laughs again. "Well. I'm sorry, I don't mean to laugh. First of all, Shan-nan was a nice girl. I spoke with Shannan. I met Shannan. I knew who Shannan was as a person. And she was a sweet—And you know, she had a rough life, I'm sure. I think there are some people who choose that profession. Some people are kind of forced into it because they have a family or lost their job. And some people are kind of thrown into it, and I've got a feeling that Shannan was one of those who was thrown into it."

He is not-so-subtly turning the focus away from himself and toward Shannan's family.

"And I've got a lot of compassion for that. She took care of a lot of people, you know? She supported her mother. She sup-ported her family. They knew what she did. You know? That's why she needed the rent money for her mom. You know? I feel bad for that situation. There was a very poor, sick girl, and people want to point at me for blame, and that's not how it was."

Joe won't answer the question of why Shannan called 911, at least not directly. The real story, he says, is that he was trying to help her that night. "I was the only one trying to help her till the very last moment," he says. "Until even *after* when I knew she was gone, I was reaching out. And I was *nobody*. I was just some guy, she was in my house that night, I don't know what to call it, I wasn't a person of interest, I had no connection to her, I was nobody. It's a strange thing. But, uh, why she left my house? That is the million-dollar question. To be in a rage and fearful of her life?"

He's back to teasing it out, playing up the drama. "Well, that answer will come. I have that answer."

A pause.

"Well, to be honest, I *don't* have it a hundred percent."

Another laugh.

"But basically, based on what I heard, I have more pieces to the puzzle than anybody. And I think my theory is pretty good."

I don't want to misrepresent you, I say.

At this, he laughs very hard. "What's gonna happen? Another pile of sand is gonna go on my face? *That's* gonna make me do something at this point? I know who I am. I don't need anybody, I don't need to plead to anybody who I am. I answer to one person. I'm not really Catholic, I'm more agnostic, but I believe in God, I believe in morals, I believe in yin-yang and karma. I'm a huge—Well, maybe this happened for a reason. I'm in tune with myself. I don't need the money, let me tell you. Any money I make, I'd donate some to some kind of charity for some girls who are stuck on the streets. And I'd put it away in a college fund for my daughter. Money isn't my motive. I wouldn't want a five-hundred-thousand-dollar contract movie deal, because that would probably break my family apart even more. But my story will come out."

He starts to beg off. "Ask about me. I'm a pretty well-known guy in town. I've been lifting people when they're down my entire life. So, I mean, it's just, it's such an odd time. It is so—What is this a test? What, you know? Maybe it was given to me because I could handle it, 'cause I wouldn't crack. And these girls needed to be found, and maybe some higher power up there—not that I believe in that stuff, necessarily—but maybe Shannan had a purpose, and I had a purpose, and she was on a path to destruction, and I, you know, I could handle this kind of thing. I don't know. I don't know what made these two asteroids hit in the sky, but this is a *straaange* fuckin'—this is a strange event. It is."

Joe decides he's said enough. "God, talk about a trillion-to-one shot. But I went through a lot, dude. I mean, my life is—I won't say *destroyed,* because I won't let them beat me. It actually made me a better person. How's that? There's a quote for you. So if I had to do it all over again, I'd probably let it happen again, because it's probably made my life better."

A pause.

"Except for the fact that any girl had to suffer," he says. "But anyway."

THE REMAINS

They found two more bodies after New Year's. On February 17, 2012, a man and his dog discovered a new collection of skeletal remains in the pine barrens of Manorville, a short distance from where two of the Gilgo Beach victims' body parts had been found years earlier. On March 21, a jogger stumbled on yet another set of remains, also in Manorville. Each set of remains had been left in two distinct areas, both remote and densely wooded, the perfect spots to dispose of a body. The police urged the public not to assume these discoveries were connected to the Gilgo murders.

These discoveries didn't seem to register with the media, either. New stories upstaged the serial-killer case. In Manhattan, the police had raided a posh Upper East Side brothel, and the madam, Anna Gristina, made the front page of the *Post* after threatening to reveal the names of some of her more famous and powerful johns. In Nassau County, three high-ranking police officials were indicted on bribery charges, sending the Websleuths world into a long discussion about whether the police in Suffolk were any better. Those following the serial-killer case saw conspiracies everywhere: Could the cops in Suffolk have been bribed by powerful interests in Oak Beach to call Shannan's murder an accidental drowning? Even the brush fires that plagued Manorville all spring seemed suspicious, a perfect way to obscure the investigation even more.

By spring, Suffolk County's new homicide squad chief, Detective Lieutenant Jack Fitzpatrick, suggested another change in strategy, saying that "The case is going to be looked at again, from perhaps a different perspective." At the same time, he went out of his way to knock Dormer's single-killer theory, saying he believed "it's very unlikely that it's one person." Over in the DA's office, Spota was pleased. "We are in sync again," he said. "Not one detective familiar with the facts of this case believes one person is responsible for these homicides."

Mari, in a turnaround, went back to Oak Beach to voice confidence in Fitzpatrick. Michele Kutner, the families' local booster, explained that Mari was trying to be a little less down on the police and more positive in general. Possibly, Mari realized she'd overplayed her hand with her threatening letter to the police, and that she still needed them to share the results of the medical examiner's report.

Lynn tried not to get her hopes up. "I just hope it's not too late," she said, "because it's been a long time."

On May 1, 2012, two years to the day after her daughter went missing, Mari, her lawyer, John Ray, and Shannan's three sisters drove to police headquarters in Suffolk County for a private meeting with the Suffolk County chief medical examiner, Yvonne Milewski, to learn the findings of the medical report.

The meeting lasted two and a half hours. Milewski and new detectives assigned to the case were mostly quiet as Hajar Sims-Childs, who had performed the hands-on work, did most of the talking. Sims-Childs, according to Ray, was the medical examiner who had told Dormer in December that it was possible Shannan had died of exposure. At this meeting, she told the Gilberts that after over four months of analyzing Shannan's remains, they knew little more than they did before they started; in a sense, they knew less.

The cause of death remained a huge question mark. Sims-Childs said Shannan's skeleton had been discovered almost entirely intact. All that was missing, besides a few finger and toe bones, were two of the three hyoid bones—the small, fragile bones in the upper part of the neck. A broken hyoid bone is a hallmark of strangulation cases. That the bones were missing suggested that Shannan, like the first four victims, was strangled. But Sims-Childs said that without knowing whether those bones were broken or just never made it out of the marsh, it was impossible to tell for sure. The medical examiner tried to explain that away by saying it was common for small bones to disappear; the hyoid tended to come loose quickly, and it was small enough for, say, a rodent to take away. On the other hand, there are 206 bones in the body. How likely would it be that the only bone selected by an animal happened to be the one bone that could link Shannan's cause of death to the other murders?

The drug question also remained only partially answered. Sims-Childs said they had some challenges analyzing Shannan's remains. They needed bone marrow but couldn't find any in a femur bone, and for reasons she didn't explain, they didn't crack open any other bones to search for marrow. Instead, they used a smattering of tissue from the brain and a small clump of hair, which they tested for signs of cocaine use. The tests were negative. While that didn't eliminate the possibility that Shannan had done coke—especially since the hair had spent eighteen months deteriorating in a saltwater marsh—it did make it less likely that she had. Even if nothing she'd taken that night had seeped into her bones, the theory that she was high that night, and a drug addict in general, was less plausible if Shannan didn't have traces of some cocaine in her system.

What stunned Mari and her lawyer was that the medical examiner didn't appear to test for any other drug, not even pot. Bone marrow might have yielded more information about any number of drugs: pot, meth, psychotropics, everything but alcohol, which evaporates. Based on what Sims-Childs was saying, she hadn't searched for marrow beyond that one femur bone. In light of the assumption that Shannan was hysterical and irrational that night, wouldn't they want to test for any psychotropic or psychedelic drug they could think of in order to confirm their theory? Sims-Childs did not have an explanation.

Then there was the matter of Shannan's clothes, which the police had yet to test for anything—blood, DNA, semen—that might indicate who was with her that morning. Ray and Mari had to wonder what the police had been doing for five months.

After the meeting, Mari spoke to reporters. "I'm more frustrated and angry than ever," she said. "I was hoping for something more substantial and solid. But all I got was . . ."

She thought for a second or two before settling on the right word.

"Betrayal."

A few days later, John Ray and some members of his law practice went to Oak Beach at five A.M. to retrace Shannan's steps in the marsh under what he believed were ideal conditions: the same time of day and the same time of year when Shannan made the trip. He'd been told by the medical examiner that the marsh was in roughly the same condition now that it would have been two years earlier—most important, the water level was the same. To try to keep the conditions as close to the real thing as possible, they walked through the parts of the marsh that the police hadn't mowed, just to see how hard it would have been for Shannan to run through there. Ray even brought a woman about Shannan's size to simulate what she must have experienced, what she could and couldn't see.

It wasn't hard at all to walk in the marsh. The soles of Ray's shoes barely got wet. It was easy to see, too. Ray and the woman with him found that their sight lines extended past the reeds. From the thick of the marsh, they could see houses, the highway, everything. It was difficult to believe that Shannan was lost at all, and even harder to believe that she might have drowned or died of exposure. Ray remembered the ME saying that all of Shannan's bones had been bleached by the sun in such a way that her body seemed to have been lying down for a long time. When Ray asked if that meant Shannan could have been placed in that spot after she was dead, Sims–Childs would neither concede nor deny the point.

How else might Shannan have died? Sudden heart failure from drugs? They couldn't know, because the remains were tested for only one drug. Strangulation? They couldn't know, but the absence of two hyoid bones sure was suspicious. Granted, Mari was Ray's client, and he had a vested interest as her lawyer, and he had gone to the marsh already suspecting that Shannan had been killed and dumped there, her things flung in the marsh at a different time. But after his morning stroll, Ray was more convinced than ever that the police theory was wrong. The police explanation of hysteria not only didn't make sense; it was practically Victorian in its view of prostitutes, as if Shannan had died of sorrow, or fright, or sadness, or heartache. Against all common sense and with willful ignorance of Shannan's own words that night, the police seemed to be saying that Shannan Gilbert had died because her soul had been rent asunder by a life in the streets.

It was left to Mari to champion her daughter. Months after Lorraine and Missy spurned her, some of the most devoted followers of the case would also drop out of Mari's Facebook group, even the steadfast Michele Kutner. "I hung by her," she said, "but I'm not going to stay there and be abused." None of the conflict seemed to rattle Mari, although conflict had always resembled her natural state. She spent the summer ushering in new Facebook friends who had heard about the case through repeats of the *48 Hours* episode. She was casting about for a way to get Shannan's case on John Walsh's TV show, *America's Most Wanted*. During a midsummer visit with John Ray on Long Island, Mari went out of her way to be kind about Lorraine, if a little patronizing. "Lorraine is sweet. She's a little slower at talking, because she wants to make sure it's right." And she didn't resist the chance to judge Missy, suggesting she hadn't done enough to help Maureen while she was alive. "I hurt for her the most," Mari said. "Because I hope it's not haunting her, the choices she made."

Mari was more comfortable forgiving herself, even if it meant not questioning what part, if any, she might have played in her daughter's tragedy. "I can't be plastic," she said, adding that she wished Shannan had been a little more like that. "I think if Shannan inherited anything from me, it was being able to do what she chose to do and not care what people thought. I wish she were more street-smart." Mari was trying hard to be philosophical, in her own way. "Sooner or later, things will catch up to a person. You do the best you can when you're in that situation. And everything is meant to be. You cannot disrupt the order of life. You just can't, because it's gonna happen anyway. So you do the best you can. You roll with the punches. You get knocked down, you dust yourself off, you keep going."

By then even Sherre had lost patience with Mari. They didn't speak over most of the summer. "I think my mom's a hater," she said one afternoon in a park near her home in Ellenville. "She's lost a lot of her friends. She's closing herself off from people. We've always had our ups and downs, but it's gotten much worse since Shannan's been gone." Sherre spent much of her time carefully vetting all the coverage of the case, protesting whenever anyone used the word *prostitute* to describe her sister. *This wasn't the life she wanted,* she wrote in a message to friends. *The world can't see if she would've changed, what her life may have become . . . Before you judge her or judge us, make sure your life is perfect because none of our lives are!* Privately, Sherre didn't spare herself any criticism. "I just feel bad because I never really tried to stop her. I never talked about it with her."

Despite staying active online, Sherre felt isolated. Not talking to Mari meant having fewer people with whom to mourn Shannan. Even before she vanished, Shannan had such an ephemeral place in her family's world—living at home on and off, making such foreign choices—that Sherre couldn't stop wondering, almost in an endless loop, what might have made her sister's life so different from her own. "I just feel like Shannan always wanted to be loved," she said, fighting back tears. "And she never felt like that. And I think her doing what she did, it was something that she didn't really care about. You know how you're supposed to cherish your body? Maybe if she felt loved. But I don't think she did."

What seems to hurt Sherre and Mari the most—the complaint they share with Missy and Lorraine and Kim and Lynn—is the way the police's theory of the case blamed Shannan at the exclusion of everyone else. Joe Brewer was still a free man. So was Michael Pak, who, as her driver, posted her calls, which to some made him a de facto pimp. Why was Shannan the only one to answer for what happened that night? Murder or no murder, Shannan and all of the others were failed by the criminal-justice system not once but three times. The police had failed to help them when they were at risk. They'd failed again when they didn't take the disappearances seriously, severely hobbling the chances of making an arrest. And they'd failed a third time by not going after the johns and drivers. Sherre and Mari know that no matter what happened in Oak Beach, Shannan's profession had sealed her fate. Even before she disappeared, she ceased to matter.

Alex Diaz said he hadn't been able to get and stay with a girl since he lost Shannan. "It's always in the back of my head. I want to know what happened to her. It's kind of hard to move on, not knowing." He got a straight job, earning three hundred dollars a week as a dispatcher for a valet company. Michael Pak, still living in Queens, said he'd gotten a job, too, though he wouldn't say where.

Alex's life was further complicated by the way he was perceived by people aware of Shannan's case. "The media tried to make it seem like I'm a pimp," he said, "because they found out I didn't have a job. And the family used to trash me and say I was using her."

Mari and her family were happy to let Alex twist in the wind. He was matter-of-fact when he defended himself, much the same way Blaze was when talking about Melissa Barthelemy. "If I was using her, you guys are just as guilty," he said. "They knew what she was doing. And the mother would take the money, the sister would take the money. And they would judge me? You want to put me in that category, then we're all bad people. We're taking the money, and we know where it's coming from."

In the summer, Peter Hackett's neighbors at Oak Beach noticed that his car had a brand-new set of Florida plates. The doctor spent much of the year on Sanibel Island in Florida. Back in December, Hackett had told me that had been the plan for some time. "I've been hurt so many times in my life that I've had to use the money to help my children with their habits—like eating," he'd said sardonically. "You've caught me in the last couple of years of making sure my kids all grow up in the same place, have the same memories. Now I need to move somewhere warm so I won't slip on the ice."

When he came back, Hackett put his house up for sale, listing the four-bedroom, two-bathroom cottage for $399,000. "Our plan is to see if we can sell the house," he told me in October. "Or we'll just stay right here. We're just taking a shot in the dark. I've been disabled, and now because of this miserable story that the Gilberts and everybody else have made up, I'm essentially unemployable. I've already missed getting a job because somebody went on the Internet and saw my name."

From his cottage in Oak Beach, with the autumn sun low in the sky, Hackett was more talkative than he ever had been, eager to discuss the damage the case had done to him. "My family's been threatened, people have called me to threaten me. I have no apologies to make. I've told no lies." He insisted yet again that he'd never seen Shannan, never treated her. "My daughter and wife were home. That would be pretty difficult, to treat somebody." He reiterated that no neighbors called him that morning. "Just check my telephone. Anyone like the police can just check my phone and see that. I would have known more about it on Monday when I met the boyfriend and the driver."

What about the neighbors who apparently heard him say that he saw her?

"I told neighbors like Gus and Barbara, 'If this was you and your wife, and someone was hurt, who's the first person you'd call?' They said, 'Oh, you.' They said, 'Oh, we didn't want to bother you.' I did say to people, 'I wished somebody had called me.' Having started the trauma program in this county, I would have been able to get her to the right trauma center. And I did say that to people, because I was annoyed that somebody was missing, sitting outside people's houses, and they bothered to call the police, but normally, if somebody were hurt, for twentysomething years I've gotten up many, many nights to take care of them when they were sick and injured. I felt poorly that they didn't think to call me to help Shannan out."

That didn't jibe with Gus Coletti's denial that he'd talked with Hackett at all. But Hackett continued to profess bafflement at how anyone would think he was capable of anything like this. "They seem to imply I chased after this girl or something? I can't catch up to myself walking backwards. What I've found with the press is if you don't talk to them, they make it up."

He'd denied making the calls to Mari at first, he said, because "I'd forgotten I'd called her" until he'd checked his phone records. Recently, he had looked at the notes from his meeting with Alex Diaz and Michael Pak—notes that, he mentioned, were the main reason the police wanted to talk to him about this case— and remembered that they'd been concerned because Sherre told them Shannan's cell-phone account was turned off. Hackett said he thought that the police might be able to track Shannan better if her phone were active. That, he said, was why he had called Mari. "My downfall only started because I didn't want my community to be seen as uncaring—rich people who didn't give a damn," he said. "I tried to do what I could for the family, and then I guess the family did what they could for me, which was to make up a lot of hooey." He talked about his physical limitations—the false leg, the back pain, the pacemaker and implanted defibrillator— and he wondered aloud why, if he was such a suspicious character, the police never so much as wrote him up or booked him.

He'd tried not to pay attention to the blog attacks, but that proved impossible. "This Internet mechanism of prosecuting people. Where do these people come from?" The malpractice cases that Truthspider dug up, he said, were practically pro forma. "I'm not going to deny I've been sued for malpractice, but I'm an ER doctor in New York. ER doctors in New York are sued once or twice a year." The question of a rehab raised by one court document, he didn't answer directly. "This is just mean," he said. "If I were intoxicated or whatever it was they said it was, why didn't I lose my license?"

For the first time publicly, he talked about the Scalise family. "They're using this as an opportunity to make me look as bad as possible," he said. He couldn't understand why. He claimed to have been on the Scalises' side during their battles with the association, though he allowed that "if I were to go over there and tell them that, they'd never believe me."

That said, Hackett wondered if the bad blood would ebb. His term as a board member was ending. Taking one of the free spots on the board was Joe Scalise's sister. "Maybe things will change," he said. Meanwhile, he and Barbara, now empty-nesters, were contemplating starting over in Florida. "I'm trying to get a job with the VA program to work with the doctors there. I'm writing a book about people coming home from war who have lost their legs. My dad was a writer. He said never tell anyone what you're working on." Putting all the rumors and accusations behind him, he said, would be the hardest thing he'd ever have to do.

What did he think had happened to Shannan? Hackett said he believed the police. Years as a trauma specialist, he said, confirmed it. "People on coke," he said, "if they hit their head, they're going to get intracranial bleeding and get confused and run in some random direction." The marsh was right there on Anchor Way. She saw the lights from the highway. She ran. She fell. End of story.

"I mean, just think about it," the doctor said. "If I was involved in this thing—if any of this had any substance—would the police be so stupid to miss somebody as obvious as me?"

That same day in October, Joe Jr. was doubling down on his suspicions. "The guy's no good," he said triumphantly. "Around the Oak Beach community, he's been thought of as this hero personality. Now they can't wait for him to get the hell out of here."

Did he still believe Hackett killed Shannan Gilbert?

"I know he killed Shannan Gilbert," Joe said.

He kept going, offering more rumors, all unsubstantiated: Shannan's hyoid bone had been crushed because the doctor thrust his knee into her neck . . . The police never investigated the morning Shannan vanished; they were waved off by a neighbor, and now Gus and everyone else was lying to cover up for the doctor . . . Hackett was seen making someone erase the security video . . . Neighbors suspected Hackett of mistreating his local patients . . . "Don't you think it's strange that all these supposedly God-fearing people were invested in saying she ran off to the beach, she ran to the water?" Joe said.

It was just like Richard Dormer had said. The thing'll never die down.

The barrier islands are supposed to be the rest of Long Island's first and last defense against ocean storms. On October 29, 2012, Hurricane Sandy turned that axiom on its head. The trajectory of the storm brought the whirlwind in from the west, hitting the South Shore inland towns before the barrier islands. Ocean Parkway had buckled and crumbled into pieces, but in something of a miracle, all the crosses on the north side of the highway were still standing after the storm passed. The bramble had protected them, just as it had protected ten sets of human remains. Oak Beach fared better than many inland towns, such as Massapequa or Seaford. Dunes were flattened. Houses all along the Fairway and the Bayou and Larboard Court were flooded and lost power. But the people of Oak Beach were always ready to lose power and deal with a little water. Besides, they had been through a hurricane of their own a year earlier.

Two weeks after Sandy, on November 15, Shannan's family filed a wrongful death lawsuit against Dr. Peter Hackett. With distinct echoes of the scenario that Joe Jr. said he'd heard from Bruce Anderson, the complaint alleges that Hackett gave Shannan drugs that morning, implying a doctor-patient relationship, and then let her leave his home, demonstrating negligence. Mari and John Ray held another press conference, accusing Hackett of controlling the security video and tormenting Mari with his phone calls. "The words he chose, his tone of voice—it made me feel like he was more concerned about himself instead of truly wanting to know where Shannan was," Mari said. "And it was already proven that he was a liar once by denying he called me for over a year." As a new smoking gun, Ray finally unveiled Mari's phone records, which showed that the doctor had made a five-minute phone call to Mari on May 3, 2010, two days after Shannan disappeared and three days before the calls he'd previously admitted to. "Hackett told *48 Hours* the first conversation was May 6," Ray said. "And he claimed he and his wife searched their records and this was all they came up with. Hackett is deliberately lying."

Like the civil suit against O. J. Simpson filed by the family of Ron Goldman, Mari's lawsuit was designed as a wedge to force Hackett and others to be deposed in court. "Our intent is to uncover what happened in detail," Ray said. "That has not been done by the authorities to date. So we're just going forward with every legal means that we can find to accomplish that."

What the complaint didn't have behind it was anything other than Mari's phone records. Ray explained later that he had no affidavits from neighbors, neither Joe Jr. nor Bruce Anderson. When reporters at the press conference brought up the fact that the police didn't think Shannan had been murdered at all, Ray brought the questioning to a close. "There's no direct evidence as to who killed this lady," he said. "But circumstantial evidence can be very strong. And the circumstantial evidence right now is very strong to support what we're doing here. And I don't care what the police believe. The facts are the facts."

※

Sometime after Melissa's funeral, Lynn Barthelemy got a call from the coroner's office in Suffolk County, saying they had found more remains along the side of the highway with her daughter's DNA. She wasn't told exactly where these remains were found, and it never was made clear to her what had happened: whether the body had been dismembered or an animal had gotten to Melissa's remains before they were discovered. She wasn't told what it meant in terms of the case theory, whether finding part of her daughter elsewhere meant one more link between the four bodies in burlap and the other six found along the beach.

What it meant, first and foremost, was the need for another cremation, another interment. Lynn and Jeff arranged to pick up the remains in New York. They found a funeral home that wanted to charge them $3,400, but Bill McGready, a detective who had worked Melissa's missing-persons case when it was still an NYPD matter, had a friend who ran a funeral parlor and got them a cheaper rate.

When Lynn came to Bill's office, she saw that he'd draped an American flag over the container. Bill had on his white dress uniform gloves when he handed the container to Lynn. When she took it from him, he started crying.

Melissa's friend Kritzia Lugo and her son, Jemire, had started the year in their third-floor apartment in a walk-up in Newark. In January, Kritzia was set to start classes at a community college to earn a certified medical aide degree when she was told at the last minute that she wouldn't be able to enroll: They needed her birth certificate, and she didn't have a copy. She took it hard. She couldn't stop crying. Then she took a whole bunch of Tylenol and some sleeping pills. The day she was supposed to start school, Kritzia was admitted into a psychiatric unit at Clara Maass Medical Center in Newark. After eight days, they let her make calls again.

On the phone, she sounded tired but resolute. She'd been on this detour before. "I'm thinking I'm going to go down to city hall and find some judge and get a court order or something to find my birth certificate," she said. "They're trying to put me in some program. My first day would be tomorrow. But I'm going to go to school. Because that's what I want to do."

A Facebook status from Dave Schaller on February 10, 2012:

> Today is my friend Ambers birthday she was taken by the cowardly piece of shit "serial killer" on long island from me casa! He will pay for what he did. It just hurts to have to live this everyday that I could have stopped u or remembered him if I wasn't so high. I'm sorry!

The last time I saw Bear in Tompkins Square Park, he said he was planning to move to Las Vegas with a friend, "a junkie that turned his life around." Bear said he thought he could get straight in Vegas. "I'm not going to get any better if I don't get the fuck out of this neighborhood. I am not well. I'm twenty-seven years old, and I have stage-one cirrhosis. My liver is shutting down. Some other guy could end up raising my kid. And that's my worst fucking nightmare—that people tell my son that his dad was a junkie who's dead because he chose drugs and alcohol over you. I can't deal with it."

A week later, on the phone, Bear sounded different, less manic. He said he'd asked his parents for help, and they'd found him a bed at a detox on Long Island. The Vegas plan was off the table for now. Bear had been welcomed back into his family for as long as he stayed sober.

In a rest home in Wilmington, Al Overstreet said a miracle had happened. "I come in here and I get all kinds of stuff. I caught pneumonia, I almost died from that. I got cancer, tumors, six of them. Five in my lungs, one in my chest. But you know what? The five in my lungs disappeared. No treatment. I think it was Amber, praying. She told me one time, she said, 'Dad, you're not gonna die from cancer.' She went to church. I mean, even with the lifestyle she lived, she was really religious."

Al wanted to come live with Kim on Long Island. Kim refused. "I can't take care of him physically," she said. "His skin is literally so paper-thin that it's like a wet paper towel." Once, he did live with her and Mike, and he fell backward into a coffee table. They found him sitting in a pile of glass shards. "It takes someone being with him all day, because sometimes he just falls."

Sitting on his bed, Al asked for news about Kim. He knew she was still doing calls, and he knew that she had been avoiding him because of it. "Kim's afraid to call me," he said, "because it's been about seven months, eight months. If you get the chance and see her, tell her to give me a call. Tell her I ain't gonna fuss at her. She don't know how many nights I couldn't sleep, wondering."

But then he brightened. Kim, he said, was always the stronger of the two girls. "Kim's a worker," Al said. "Not talking about the escort service, but any job she's ever had, they loved her to death. Because she's got a good personality."

Amber, he worried about more. "Amber was raped when she was young," he said. "It messed her mind up. And then when her mother died, she was mama's baby, so she just . . . broke down. She was hooked on heroin. Otherwise, she was a real nice person."

When the FBI filed to seize Akeem Cruz's laptop, they found it at the South Portland home of Ashley Carroll, the girl Vybe had been seeing behind Megan's back. When Ashley relinquished the laptop, Vybe's friends assumed she'd turned against him. "That turned into a shit show," Ashley said. "I had to do it, but in his pea brain, he didn't understand I had to do it. He doesn't understand what a search warrant means?"

Vybe started making menacing calls to Ashley from prison. "He'd be saying, 'Why don't you like me?' And he'd ask about my son." The last time he called, she said, "he told me he was going to kill me and violate me. He said he was going to break my jaw and break my ribs. Because it doesn't leave marks when you break ribs."

Weeks before Vybe's scheduled release date in early 2012, prosecutors found a way to keep him in jail. That April, Akeem Cruz pleaded guilty to violating the Mann Act, transporting Megan several times across state lines, and eventually received a sentence of three years. In jail, Vybe still wasn't saying a word about what he might have seen the night Megan vanished. While the police have never officially connected him to her disappearance, that didn't stop some members of Megan's family from laying the blame at his feet.

A few months later, when Lorraine finally scraped together the money for an eight-hundred-dollar headstone for Megan, Greg complained that it wasn't good enough. "She deserves one with a vase and with angels," he said.

Sometime earlier, Greg had a chance meeting with an important person in his sister's life—someone whom, until then, he'd only heard about. Officer Doug Weed of the Scarborough police said they met when Greg had a "law-enforcement contact," though he won't be any more specific. Until then, Weed had only heard of Megan's older brother, Greg. When he noticed Greg's last name, he made the connection. "*Megan* Waterman?" he said.

Greg's eyes widened. "You're Officer Weed? I know all about you!"

The news about Megan's disappearance, and later, her murder, had surprised Weed as much as anyone. He'd never known anything about Megan and prostitution, and he thought he'd known her pretty well. Once he had time to consider it, he thought he should have seen it coming. He knew that she was in the wrong crowd. It made him think about what chance there really is to help a person with such narrow options. Maybe, he figured, if you got to a point in your life where someone comes up to you and says, "I've got money, I love you, you're beautiful," you're just a sitting duck.

A few months after meeting Greg, Weed got a letter in the mail. Inside was a school photo of a kindergartener—a girl with brown eyes and a heart-shaped face that, to Weed, was unmistakably familiar.

Hi Officer Weed,

Its me Lili. Here is a picture of me from school. I hope I get to
see you again someday. My mommy lives in Heaven now she is
an angel. Nana says she is proud of me and she doesn't lie so I
guess she is. I am five years old and I go to J.F. Kennedy School.
I am in kindergarten and I am real smart. Nana says you are real
nice and you knew my mommy, she was nice too. I hope you like
my picture. Nana says I am beautiful just like my mommy.
Love, hugs and kisses,

Liliana R. Waterman

Doug Weed usually doesn't cry. But that letter put him over
the top. "I literally had to stop when I read it," he said. "I told my
wife, if we get the chance, we'd adopt her. I'm not kidding. My
wife said, 'That's fine, absolutely.' Because she knows."

Maureen's family was Catholic, but no one ever went to church.
"With Catholics, it doesn't matter," Missy said as the car, driven
by her husband, Chris, approached the cemetery. "As long as you
believe there's a God and the mother Mary, you go to heaven.
You believe in Jesus, all that stuff."

Life was continuing even while Missy wasn't paying attention. Missy was pregnant again—a boy, due in September. On
the ultrasound, it looked like he was already flexing his muscles.
The pose in the printout reminded Missy of her brother. She
thought of naming him Liam—like Will's name, William, only

shortened—but she'd told Chris he could name the baby, so his name would be Dominic.

It was windy and cold with a light drizzle as Missy got out of the car at St. Mary's in New London. Maureen and Will were buried next to each other, near a statue of the saint herself. Missy was proud of the location. "Especially in the summertime. If you notice, my brother has all this grass everywhere, and my sister has this perfect grass, too. And everywhere else, it's all messed up."

Will was between two trees. At the other end of the cemetery were Maureen's grandmother and great-grandmother and her uncle Reggie. Missy's father was there, too—the father she and Will barely knew, separated from his son by just two other plots. "It's very, very hard to come here," she said. But Missy, usually so prone to tears, seemed more relaxed at the cemetery than anywhere else. Maybe it was because she got to commune with her past without any self-consciousness, without any guilt that she was neglecting her present-day life. She was mindful as she walked to their headstones. She was, in her way, maternal.

"I was kind of happy when the funeral parlor told me there was a law in Connecticut that states that you cannot cremate a homicide victim," she said. "I didn't want her cremated. I felt like she went through so much that I didn't want her . . . " She trailed off. "You know what I'm saying? I looked at my mom and was like, 'See, you shouldn't cremate her.' And she didn't get cremated, she was buried. And she's in a casket next to my brother. My brother wasn't cremated, either, he's in a casket."

There were some plants on the graves. Missy's mother had brought them. "She comes here more than I do," Missy said. "It's harder for me, I don't know. It's because I'm the middle child. I lost my older and my younger."

On July 14, 2012, the fifth anniversary of Maureen's disappearance, Sara Karnes reached out to Missy on Facebook:

> **SARA KARNES** I wish I had stayed. I really thought I'd be seeing her again on Wednesday
> **MELISSA CANN** Sara there was no way you could have known that Maureen would be in danger and it would be the last time anyone of us would hear from her was this weekend 5 years ago. Your in my thoughts cause I know this is hard for you as well as my family.
> **SARA KARNES** Yeah but even if I didn't know that I shoulda still stayed. What kind of friend leaves their friend all alone in a big ass city?
> **MELISSA CANN** Please remember it is nobodies fault besides the person who took her life. No one could have predicted that this would have happen. I mean, I can say what kind of sister lets their sister go to a big ass city?

Stunts 4 Justice didn't raise close to the five thousand dollars Missy had hoped. But it was good to be with Lorraine that day, and they met a famous crusader for the families of missing persons: Janice Smolinski, whose son, Billy, disappeared in Connecticut in 2004, and who has been working for the creation of Billy's Law, which seeks to expand online public information on missing people and unidentified remains. Over the summer, Missy's activism intensified. She started looking into how to go about getting the Gilgo Beach killer on the FBI's most-wanted list: Others on the list were unidentified, with only the case details listed. Why not this killer and this case?

Missy kept gathering every piece of data, flagging some

sketches of the unidentified bodies she found in a national database and giving them to the press. "The Suffolk police dropped the ball and never released it to the public," she said. Through the Connecticut victims' advocate attorney, she tried to arrange a meeting with Norwich police to go over what steps they took in Maureen's missing-persons case, and maybe even get a look at the case file. "This should be interesting," she said. Once she delivered the baby, Missy wanted to put together another stunt show and finally meet her goal. Somewhere down the line, she was thinking of moving to Stamford, to be closer to Long Island if and when there was an arrest in the case.

Missy monitored the growing national discussion about online ads for escorts. "Knowingly making money off of girls' bodies—that sounds like a pimp or promoting prostitution to me," she said. "Of course, the girls who do this are also wrong, but if it was not for this online hiding of it, I don't think half of them would be out there doing this."

■

The exchange of sex for money has been a part of life in nearly every human civilization, at times playing an accepted, even respected role. Thousands of years before Christ, the profession was connected to religious practices in the temples of Sumeria, and the rights of prostitutes and their children were spelled out in the code of Hammurabi. Brothels were legal in ancient China and ancient Greece, tolerated by the Israelites, taxed by the early Roman Empire, and openly indulged by royalty during the Renaissance. In practically every era, prostitutes have thrived, and in some, they were recognized and exalted.

In America, commercial sex was more or less tolerated as a

sort of low-grade offense in Colonial times, easy for the authorities to ignore. That continued through the Civil War and only changed about a century ago, when progressive groups like the Women's Christian Temperance Union worked to protect young girls from being forced into prostitution. When the Mann Act of 1915 made a federal crime of transporting "any woman or girl for the purpose of prostitution or debauchery, or for any other immoral purpose," prostitutes in America entered a shadow world, even if their services were as in demand as ever.

While Europe experimented with legalization and regulation after WWII, the practice here was more stigmatized than perhaps it had ever been. It was also dangerous. John J. Potterat, one of the nation's leading epidemiologists, noted in 2004 that the leading cause of death for prostitutes was homicide. He also found that most prostitute murders—64 percent—were committed by johns, with the high body count of killers like Gary Ridgway, Robert Pickton, and Robert Lee Yates skewing that statistic away from onetime killers and toward the serially inclined.

The Internet had promised to bring about the most significant change to the sex trade in years, maybe centuries. Never before had the marketing of prostitution become so convenient and unobtrusive—so easy. No one had to go to a bad part of town to look for what they wanted. Everything could take place behind closed doors, where no one was watching. Craigslist was the great disrupter in any number of industries, transforming the way people shopped for anything, and commercial sex was no exception. The great selling point of Craigslist, and the Web in general, was its anonymity. A person can do practically anything online without even their closest loved ones knowing, from commenting on Yelp or Gawker to selling stolen goods or viewing porn videos. This is as true for the escorts as it was for the johns, who have turned sites like TheEroticReview.com into a sort of Yelp for steady customers of commercial sex.

In 2009, Craigslist earned a reported $45 million a year from Adult Services ads, or about a third of the company's total profits (the site had started charging $5 per posting just a year earlier). Some believed that Craigslist and its competitors were doing well by doing good: In 2006, a research team from Princeton and Columbia said that this new type of prostitute had a "careerist orientation." Three years later, a study and survey by Baylor University economist Scott Cunningham confirmed that the Web was drawing entirely different sorts of people into prostitution—better educated, even thinner. And in 2011, University of Arkansas researcher Jennifer Hafer said people embraced online prostitution "for many of the same reasons that people enter the conventional job market—money, stability, autonomy and even job satisfaction." Thanks to the Internet, it was said, prostitution could become a means of economic empowerment for an entire swath of society. The women and men who walked the street could come in from the cold, becoming free agents, liberated from the system of pimps and escort services that had exploited them for so long.

Few people considered how the Web's anonymity stood to make escort work more dangerous than ever. Sure enough, on-line escorts started to report incidents of violence. Nearly half of the New York City indoor sex workers surveyed by a group called the Urban Justice Center in 2006 said they had been forced by a client to do something they did not want to do, and almost as many said they had been threatened or beaten. When the Craigslist killer, Philip Haynes Markoff, made headlines in 2009, the public got its first sense of the danger. The bodies on Gilgo Beach only reinforced the point: a killer using the convenience of the

Internet to carefully select his victims, and taking advantage of the anonymity of the same technology to elude capture.

By 2009, law enforcement had already targeted Craigslist. The sheriff of Cook County, Illinois, sued the company, calling the site "the single largest source of prostitution in the nation." He was joined in the lawsuit by forty state attorneys general, one of whom, Connecticut's Richard Blumenthal, called online sex ads the new Times Square—an unsavory back alley everyone winked at, but no one did anything about. The pressure forced Craigslist to shut down its Adult Services category on September 3, 2010—as it happens, the day after Amber Lynn Costello went missing. Escorts never stopped advertising on Craigslist; they just posted on the sly in other categories. And when the scrutiny and criticism shifted over to the new market leader, Backpage, it was widely understood that if Backpage shut down its Adult Entertainment page, a dozen more sites like it stood ready to pick up the traffic.

The demand for commercial sex will never go away. Neither will the Internet; they're stuck with each other. It may no longer even matter anymore whether the sale of sex among consenting adults is wrong or right, immoral or empowering. What's clear is that no good can come from pretending that the people who participate in prostitution don't exist. That, after all, is what the killer was counting on.

The frustration with the Gilgo Beach case has tempted all the family members of the victims to target the Web itself as the reason for their loss—a coconspirator, along with the killer. They have argued that anyone running sex ads is doing nothing less than enabling a haven for the trafficking of helpless women. "Most of them get conned and lured into this lifestyle and can't find a way out," Missy has said.

But that, like everything about the issue, was a matter of debate. The mistake may be thinking everyone works as an escort for the same reasons. Not all of them are minors, and not all of them have been trafficked. Shannan, Maureen, Megan, Melissa, and Amber were over twenty-one. They were more or less working alone and of their own volition. Despite what some family members said after the fact, they were not lured or overtly pressured. Some would say this makes them complicit in their fate—in other words, they brought this on themselves by doing something so dangerous. But to suggest they had it coming because they put themselves in a risky situation is disingenuous; no one walks through life thinking they're going to be killed. To blame the girls alone would be just as easy as blaming Craigslist or Backpage alone. To place responsibility on any family member—a mother like Mari, or a sister like Kim—means at least partially acquitting the girls themselves. To suggest that someone should have stopped them is to believe that they could have been stopped.

The issue of blame itself, in the end, may be a trap. They weren't angels. They weren't devils. One was the aimless dreamer of her family until the pressures of adult responsibility became impossible to ignore. Another was both adored and feared by all factions of her warring family, but she placed her hope for the future in the hands of her boyfriend. A third was raised by an older sister, also an escort, whom she worshipped and, at times, tried to free herself from. Another wanted to be a success, and coming home from New York anything less than that would have meant admitting defeat. Another was a self-made woman using her money to win a place back in her family. But to their loved ones, some part of each of the girls remains elusive.

There is an impulse now to have a reason. It's as strong an impulse—maybe stronger—as wanting to know who killed them.

After a while, Missy came around to the broader view. She worried that even if Backpage shut its page down, escorting would move further underground, making it even harder to track missing women. "These girls need to be looked at as human beings," she said. Right or wrong, Missy said, escorting needs to be brought in from the shadows. "They need to be protected as if they were any other profession. But since these sites are not regulated, they enable the rapists and killers."

All the activity might lead to nothing, though it gave Missy something to work for, a reason to keep going. But as summer turned to fall, Missy pulled away from Facebook. Some of her new friends, even Lorraine, would get angry at her for not donating the Stunts 4 Justice money to Crimestoppers right away. All the new bonds Missy had forged, all the friendships, were being tested. Lorraine started planning the next Oak Beach vigil without her. When the day of the next vigil arrived, Missy didn't come. Only ten people met up in the Oak Beach parking lot on a clear, cold Saturday in December 2012, two years after police found the first bodies and a year after they finally found Shannan. Nearly a hundred people had swarmed the parking lot a year earlier. For a little while, it seemed like Lorraine might be the only family member to make it. Then Kim arrived with a surprise: She was seven months pregnant with her seventh child, due on Amber's birthday in February. The ceremony was brief, a ritual designed for a catharsis that never seems to arrive. At the end, the group released heart-shaped lanterns and watched them float high in the air, away from the water and back toward the parkway.

The one thing Missy and Mari agreed on was that as bad as not knowing was, knowing was worse. No matter whom they reached out to, part of them remained alone. "I'm starting to forget little things about her," Missy said. "And my brother, too. Not who they are or what they stood for but the little things, like who their favorite teachers were. I'm starting to forget. It's horrible."

Whenever she thought of them, Missy would try to write down what she remembered. Will getting a patch for his motorcycle club. Maureen and Will and Missy sitting in a field as little kids, and Maureen, with her Barbie doll, picking a buttercup and holding it under Will's chin. The sad song Maureen was singing over and over with Missy and Will a few days before she disappeared, "4am" by a band called Our Lady Peace:

And if I don't make it / Know that I loved you all along.

Just before the start of spring, Missy was taking her kids to a park and saw a little boy playing with his dad. It took a second before she realized that the boy was Maureen's son. She hadn't seen Aidan in almost five years. She finally got the chance, that day, to talk to his dad, Steve, and they all went out for ice cream. Missy couldn't remember the last time she felt so happy.

Less than two weeks later, she was outside the ShopRite when she spotted Steve and Aidan again, walking into T. J. Maxx. She thought of going in after them and orchestrating another chance meeting, but then she thought better of it. She didn't want to seem like a stalker. She came away thinking that God puts you in places for a reason.

AFTERWORD (2019)

> I can not believe all the LIES you wrote about my family,
> and I. You should be ashamed at yourself. How dare you
> write such trash!! May karma slam you when you least
> expect it!!
>
> Do NOT write to me again or I will file harassment
> charges against you!!
>
> —E-mail from Mari Gilbert, June 19, 2013 (one month
> before the publication of *Lost Girls*)

This was not entirely unexpected. Mari Gilbert was a confronta-
tional person, not just brusque but antagonistic even with those
closest to her. In the two years that I'd observed her and the family members of the other victims in this case, I'd seen Mari blow
up relationships more than once without warning. She seemed
uncomfortable with good feelings—ill at ease the moment things
seemed most peaceful. There were any number of possible explanations for why she was this way. Perhaps it was immaturity;
perhaps it was restlessness. But as with her daughter Shannan and
the other women connected to this case, no single reason would
ever explain Mari.

From the moment I met Mari, I found myself struggling to
understand her. She had come, at my invitation, to New York
City from Ellenville on May 2, 2011, to participate in a profile of
all the victims' mothers and sisters in *New York* magazine (a scene
later recounted in *Lost Girls*). Mari was unique among those who
came because her daughter Shannan technically was still miss-

ing. She didn't want to be a part of this group. She felt superior to them in a way, insisting under her breath, more than once, that Shannan was not like those other girls—that she fought back against her assailant, that she wasn't a victim. But, being shrewd, Mari also saw the utility of having allies in the struggle to find her daughter. She had active theories about what had happened to Shannan, and she craved support. Within a few weeks, she participated in a vigil at Oak Beach with the other families, and then she developed her own following—people who had read about the case and seen her on TV. These people—most of them women, but not all—became useful tools. Mari was good at harnessing the energy of others to achieve her goals, even if that sometimes meant pitting her new friends against one another—or vilifying the media that was giving her the attention she needed.

After that first meeting, Mari kept me at a distance. A book about her and her daughters was not the kind of exposure she wanted. The circumstances of her family's life before Shannan disappeared might have been the last thing in the world she would want to make public. As she'd said on the day we met, "I told my kids what happens in the house stays in the house. That's, like, a basic given rule." I couldn't begrudge Mari that. It was so clear, beyond everything else, that she was in terrible pain. To shout from the rooftops that your daughter is missing when everyone in law enforcement is saying she's dead has to be one of the most anguished things any parent could endure. This emotional dilemma was what drew me to write about Mari and every mother and sister linked to this unsolved case—Sherre, Lorraine, Muriel, Melissa, Lynn, Kim—as much as the murder mystery. What must it have been like to have been ignored for so long, only to now be at the center of a huge news story—but in danger of being ignored all over again? What must it have been like to have strangers calling your daughter a prostitute, when you knew she was more than that—that she could have been anything, that if she were still alive she could prove to everyone how that word meant nothing, had nothing to do with who she was?

I shadowed the families of the missing women for a year, and in all that time, Mari communicated with me only through intermediaries. She finally agreed to be interviewed on August 3, 2012, a few weeks after I completed the first draft of *Lost Girls*. Mari's lawyer, John Ray, was present for the interview. Shannan's remains had been found months earlier, and that event had seemed to change her. Mari was still guarded, but also strangely sanguine, ready to let the chips fall where they may. What she told me that day went a long way toward helping me understand her better: her vagabond childhood, tragic relationships with men, determined self-sufficiency as a mother, and troubles raising Shannan. An interview eleven days later with Shannan's sister Sherre shed even more light on Mari and the family, what they went through, why there was so much conflict in Shannan's life.

Mari had alienated so many people that I hadn't deluded myself into thinking that I'd be spared. When she e-mailed me a few days after I sent her a copy of the book, I knew this would be the last time we would communicate. She never explained what she found objectionable. Neither Sherre nor a close friend of Mari's ever mentioned any inaccuracies, either. I pushed on. I told myself that I wasn't writing *Lost Girls* to please Mari Gilbert. I was writing it to help the world know her daughter.

So, I wasn't surprised. But pretty much everything that happened after that did surprise me.

Of Mari's four daughters, it was Sarra Gilbert—third in the birth order, after Shannan and Sherre but before the baby, Stevie—

whom Mari had always considered the reliable one. She was the rock, the unfussy one, the child who parented the other children when Mari wasn't around. The Sarra I saw during the reporting of *Lost Girls* was a quiet presence, uninterested in publicity. She was the family's archivist, the one gathering notes and following the particulars of the case with a hungry eye for detail. I didn't know then that she had experienced the same terrible abuse as her sister Sherre: She too had been molested by her mother's boyfriend, and she too was simmering with resentment and torment over it. Shannan had been in foster care at the time.

I had no idea how, once that boyfriend of Mari's was out of the picture, Sarra's difficulties only intensified. She had an abortion at the age of fourteen, dropped out of school at sixteen, and moved in with her boyfriend, a twenty-two-year-old drug dealer named Manny. The two had a son in 2009, a boy named Hayden. Things weren't the same after the baby. The couple would serially break up and reconcile. Manny served time for drug arrests. At least once, Sarra ended up in a shelter for victims of domestic violence. In the years following Shannan's disappearance, Sarra became more dependent on her family, and on Mari especially, than ever before. Mari stepped up by all accounts, taking in the baby when needed and becoming Sarra's emotional support system.

But by the time the bodies were uncovered at Gilgo Beach, Sarra was hardly in a position to sustain another trauma. At least one psychiatrist who examined Sarra, a forensic specialist named Alexander Bardey, said the discovery of the remains—including, eventually, those of her own sister—re-traumatized her, activating what until then had been largely suppressed vulnerability and rage. It didn't take long, several months after the second examination of Shannan's remains questioning the cause of her death, for Sarra to experience her first profound mental collapse.

In late 2013, Sarra was watching the American Music Awards on television and became consumed with the belief that she and Shannan had cowritten several hit songs for Rihanna, Beyoncé, and Jay-Z. Not long after that, she developed a second, more ominous set of delusions, involving the people she loved becoming possessed by demons. She would insist that Shannan wasn't dead, and that she could tell by looking into someone's eyes if they were possessed. She told people she was a god, and her job was to defeat all evil gods, and that quite often the evil gods took the form of her sisters and mother.

In January 2014, Mari and Sherre visited Sarra at her house. Sarra announced that they both were demons and tried to attack Mari before the police came and hospitalized Sarra at Orange Regional Medical Center. She returned there in February, and again in July after she'd become convinced that her son was a demon. Sarra spent a summer at that hospital before being transferred to Rockland Psychiatric Center, where she stayed until December. Diagnosed with paranoid schizophrenia and compelled by a court order, she began receiving a long-acting injectable antipsychotic medication called Haldol Decanoate. That kept her out of hospitals for all of 2015. But soon enough, she was failing to comply with her mental-health treatment and regularly using illegal drugs, mostly pot but also ecstasy. The demons were back, too.

On February 19, 2016, with her son in the house, Sarra drowned the family dog in a bathtub, and then called Mari and said Mari was the reason why the dog had to die. Mari lived just a few minutes away. She rushed over and grabbed Hayden; then she called the police, who brought Sarra to another hospital, St. Mary's, where she was so combative that the police took her to Mid-Hudson Forensic Psychiatric Center, a law-enforcement facility. Hayden stayed at Mari's, and while Mari visited her daughter in the new facility, she decided not to intervene on her behalf for an early release. "Sometimes a mom has to be tough in her love," she said. The mother and daughter embraced. But that spring when she was released, Sarra found out that for the foreseeable future her son would live with Mari. The state would no longer allow Hayden to be in her care.

Without Hayden at home, Sarra no longer received government checks to help her pay the bills. She was angry, broke, and stubborn, refusing to take her medication. At the beginning of July, she overdosed—she believed she was taking ecstasy, while others say it was likely LSD—and landed at Albany Medical Center. The drug had brought her body temperature up to 107.1°F, forcing doctors to pack her in ice. Once awake, Sarra was so delirious and combative that the staff induced a coma to prevent her from harming herself. By the time she was released, Sarra had skipped her monthly Haldol shot. There was nothing to keep her now from becoming actively psychotic.

Mari and Sherre tried visiting Sarra at home, but Sarra wouldn't open the door. Mari left a cup of coffee for her. Sarra believed it had been poisoned and dumped it in the trash. And as July progressed, Sarra became increasingly isolated. Between court-supervised visits with her son, she realized what she had to do next.

On the morning of July 23, 2016, Sarra, after a sleepless night, texted Sherre to say she was hearing voices again. Sherre told her sister to call 911, or at least to call her mom for help. Unwilling to go back to the hospital, Sarra decided to call Mari, who said she was coming right over. But sometime between the end of that call and Mari's arrival, Sarra became convinced that Mari wasn't coming to help her. She grabbed a fifteen-inch kitchen knife she'd bought at Kmart and placed it beside her on the sofa, under a pillow. She also placed a fire extinguisher within reach. Then she waited.

Mari walked in at about 10:30 A.M. and sat down next to Sarra on the couch, where the two would have their last conversation. Sarra would later recall asking her mother if she was an evil god. In some of her explanations of what happened, Sarra said her mother denied it; in others, Mari admitted it. But in every version, Sarra remembered that as they talked, Mari noticed a nearby photograph of Sarra and Hayden. It was when Mari smiled and reached for the photo, Sarra said, that she first stabbed Mari in the chest.

Mari tried to stand. Sarra kept stabbing. Mari grunted for her daughter to stop, then bent over, fell to the floor, and tried to inch under a coffee table to protect herself. Sarra pulled Mari out from under the table, sat on top of her, and kept stabbing, aiming for Mari's heart, lungs, midsection, everywhere where Sarra thought it would be lethal.

Mari's phone buzzed. It was Sherre. Sarra shut off the phone. Then she picked up the fire extinguisher and struck Mari in the head, more than once. Sarra became convinced Mari was still breathing, and so she sprayed the extinguisher into Mari's mouth, too, trying to drown her. Then she stabbed at Mari's neck, perhaps trying to decapitate her, though she was most certainly dead by then.

Sarra was soaked in blood. She took off her pants and went to her bedroom to lie down. She smoked a cigarette and listened to music before the police arrived at 1:45 P.M.—summoned by Sherre, who had come to the house, pounded on the doors and windows, and tried to look inside. Sherre told the police that her sister had been hearing voices. But Sarra's first words upon being discovered inside the apartment showed she knew why they were there: "I am under arrest."

The knife's tip had snapped off, its end bent at a 90-degree angle. The medical examiner would count 227 different stab wounds on the body, many of them defensive wounds on the hands and arms. Mari's life, transformed by the death of one daughter, had been ended by another.

John Ray, the lawyer mounting Shannan's family's ongoing civil suit against Dr. Peter Hackett, represented Sarra at her murder trial at the Ulster County courthouse in spring of 2017. Ray mounted an insanity defense, and everything about his opening statement suggested that Sarra's actions made mental illness the obvious explanation for what had happened to Mari. He made it clear that Sarra hadn't taken her antipsychotic medication for close to eight weeks before the killing took place. And then there was the killing itself. "Two hundred twenty-seven stab wounds," Ray said. "Does that sound like something that somebody is responsible for? If you think that, I guess you can think anything."

The American legal system, however, sets an extraordinarily high bar for proving insanity. To acquit Sarra, the jury would have to believe not just that she was delusional (which she most certainly was) and that she suffered from schizophrenia (which her doctors generally agreed was the case); they would also have to believe, unanimously, that Sarra had no concept of right and wrong, and therefore could not have been responsible for her actions.

The prosecutor, Emmanuel Nneji, wasted no time attacking that notion. How could Sarra not know right from wrong, Nneji said, if, over many years while her illness was at a crescendo, she walked her son to school every day, cared for him, fed him, paid the rent for their home? How could she be completely unstable, he said, if she went to the same place every day for coffee, never causing the slightest commotion? How could she be uncontrollably homicidal, he said, if she never once tried to kill Sherre or Stevie—even though they, too, were supposedly demons in disguise?

In the prosecutor's view, the killing of Mari Gilbert was a crime of passion, quite likely drug-fueled, against a mother whom Sarra resented for years. Mari had engineered the taking of Sarra's son, and with him the government support payments. Mari had committed historical sins, too—her absentee parenting, allowing Sarra and Sherre's abuse, letting Shannan be raised elsewhere. What happened on July 23, 2016, was a reckoning Sarra had been planning in advance, the prosecutor said. It couldn't be anything other than that, he argued, when she had placed that knife and fire extinguisher within reach *before* having asked her mother if she was good or evil—before, in fact, Mari even walked through the door.

Mari's answer to that question hadn't mattered. Her fate was sealed. Sarra said as much on the witness stand. "My intention was to kill my mom," she said coolly. "She's evil."

The jury heard a recording of a jailhouse phone conversation between Sarra and Stevie, revealing Sarra's tone to be even, her mood controlled, perhaps even calculating. Sarra seemed the same way on the witness stand—unmoved by the most upsetting questions, defiant in the face of the prospect of life imprisonment. Such impassiveness could also be a sign of the antipsychotic drugs she was now taking. But aside from a psychiatrist, she had no one testifying to her character, not even her sisters. Sherre was too distraught to take the stand. And Stevie appeared for the prosecution, testifying that she believed it was drugs, not mental illness, that drove her sister to kill their mother. She called the act "the result of long term hate and not a mental breakdown."

In his summation, Ray made one last plea for Sarra, whom he called "a true psychotic," let down by a mental health system that should never have allowed her out without her medication. "None of these poor people in this case deserve this," Ray said. "Certainly not Mari, certainly not Stevie, not Sherre, certainly not this broken, poor psychotic little girl."

The jury found Sarra guilty. The judge, Donald Williams, declared Sarra's sentence to be motivated by "an overwhelming desire to protect other people by taking you off the streets for as long as I can." Sarra is currently serving twenty-five years in state prison, and her son is living with relatives of his father. Ray is appealing the case.

In the years since the publication of *Lost Girls*, the Suffolk County Police Department has found itself mired in scandal. The chief, James Burke, Suffolk's highest-ranking uniformed officer, was brought down in a federal corruption probe. Long the subject of scrutiny, Burke finally served time for beating up a man who had stolen a duffel bag from his SUV, and then taking steps to cover up the crime. At least one report suggested it was Burke who had kept the FBI away from the serial-killer case for so long, out of concern that the federal agents would see what he was up to. Ever since his scandal made the news, the Internet rumor mill has accused Burke, without any substantiation, of everything from attending Joe Brewer's parties at Oak Beach to being the killer himself.

There has been one arrest, albeit not in this case. In 2017, John Bittrolff, a longtime resident of the pine barrens of outer Long Island, was convicted of the murders of two escorts, Rita Tangredi and Colleen McNamee. The murders were in the mid-1990s, several years before the disappearances and deaths of the women in *Lost Girls*. Tangredi and McNamee's bodies were found not far from where police discovered body parts of victims whose remains also turned up along Ocean Parkway—a link, however tenuous, to the current serial-killer case. At Bittrolff's sentencing, a prosecutor suggested that Bittrolff might be the Long Island serial killer. But there has been no follow-up to that statement, no indication that that was anything more than wishful thinking—a zealous DA floating a theory to sway a judge. Bittrolff himself is not talking.

The district attorney, Thomas Spota, is no longer in office, pressured out after his own role in helping Burke's cover-up became public. Richard Dormer, the former police commissioner, died of cancer in 2019, insisting until the end that the department did what it could for the girls, for Shannan, for Mari. But the case remains unsolved, a stain on Suffolk County law-enforcement. This much is obvious, given how hard the police have worked not to release Shannan's 911 recording. In October 2018, the judge overseeing Shannan's estate's lawsuit against Hackett ruled that the recording should be made public—something that would seem sensible enough, given that the police have said that Shannan's death was accidental. Since then, the department has tied up the order in the courts. Through back channels, John Ray says he has been told that the police will never give it up. He sometimes wonders if the recording has been destroyed—gone forever, like Shannan herself.

Oak Beach isn't what it used to be. Gus Coletti is deceased, from natural causes. Joe Scalise, Jr., has served time for running a marijuana farm. Joe Brewer moved away long ago, and so has Peter Hackett. The remaining neighbors who may know more about what happened to Shannan in the early hours of May 1, 2010—Tom Canning, Barbara Brennan, and Bruce Anderson—still aren't talking.

But the case's notoriety, its legacy, speaks volumes. Whether she was a victim of the serial killer or not, Shannan Gilbert has accomplished something extraordinary in our society. Few people can name one of the victims of Joel Rifkin, or of Jack the Ripper, for that matter. But from the Green River Killer in Washington and Oregon to the Southside Slayer in Los Angeles, the victims in serial-killer cases are escorts—people overlooked by police. As far as the authorities are concerned, their profession still seals their fate.

Shannan puts a face on these women. She lives on as a symbol of a system that lets down those who are vulnerable. For that, we have many people to thank, but chief among them is Mari Gilbert.

I had hoped to make a few points about human nature, justice, and class in *Lost Girls*. But the lesson I learned was one I mistakenly thought I understood all along: There is more than one thing to know about a person. We all contain multitudes; we all are good and bad, wise and foolish, noble and self-defeating. Mari lived more loudly than many of us, but she was no exception. Of all the family members, she was the one who got the most out of the police, forced them to do things they otherwise wouldn't. And she didn't just make a lot of noise; the experience of fighting on behalf of her daughter Shannan transformed Mari, too.

I spoke with two people who knew Mari—one a close friend, another someone who knew her well but never liked her—and they both had the same impression of her in her final years: She'd found purpose, coherence, a cause. She mended fences with the daughter with whom she had the most fraught relationship,

Sherre. And she divided her time between helping the daughter who was struggling the most, Sarra, and the daughter whom she'd lost, Shannan, continuing the court battle to get the police to recognize her death as a homicide.

"I think the fact that Mari was trying to find the killer—or trying to get justice—actually stirred a certain virtue with her," John Ray told me. "By any human standard, she redeemed herself in the end."

It's quite a thing to contemplate—a truth too painful and powerful to ignore. But Mari spent the last years of her life becoming the person she'd always wanted to be.

New York, October 2019

EPILOGUE (2023)

So many dates and details, so many theories, so much ~~...~~
tion. Only in hindsight is it clear how the case could have been
solved so much sooner.

Monday, July 9, 2007. Maureen Brainard-Barnes is in a bind.
She'd come to New York on Friday, but three days in, she isn't
even close to making the $1,200 she needs to keep her apartment.
She tells her friends to leave without her, and she stays an extra
day than she'd planned. At 11:30 P.M., she calls her sister, Missy
Cann, and learns no one can come get her. Then she calls again a
half hour later, saying she'll be all right. Then she's gone.

For the longest time, that was all anyone knew about what
happened to Maureen. But we now know that she had one last
business prospect. The entire weekend, she'd been in touch sixteen times with someone on her cell phone—a person with a
burner phone with no name attached to it. Whether these were
calls or texts, the available record does not say. But with that
much back and forth, it stands to reason that Maureen was negotiating with a potential Craigslist client, and the client in question
seemed to be demonstrating interest. Sure enough, at 11:56 P.M.,
Maureen's mobile phone signal registered with a cell tower in
midtown Manhattan, east of Penn Station near the Queensboro
Bridge—the route a person would take if they were heading to
Long Island.

July 10, 2009. Melissa Barthelemy is last seen sitting on the
curb outside her building on Underhill Avenue in the Bronx. A
friend later said she'd arranged a Craigslist appointment on Long
Island. We now know that like Maureen, Melissa had been in
steady touch with a caller who was using a burner phone—four

399

...ts on July 3, 6, 9, and 10. The day she vanished, that ...her phone's signal pinged off a cell tower in Massapequa, followed by a tower in midtown Manhattan.

June 6, 2010. Megan Waterman leaves a Holiday Inn Express in Hauppauge, Long Island, never to return. Police later learned that Megan's phone registered its last ping at 3:11 A.M., off a cell tower in Massapequa Park.

September 2, 2010. Amber Costello walks out of her rented house in West Babylon, Long Island, to meet a man no one sees. We now know that Amber also had been communicating with a caller with a burner phone for two days.

Four lost women.

Four different burner phones.

An unknown but significant number of pings in central Long Island and midtown Manhattan.

And a man who lived in one place and worked in the other, staying exactly where he was for years, not once arousing interest. Hiding in plain sight.

In the years that the women disappeared, Rex Heuermann was in his forties and living with his wife and two children in the house he'd grown up in, a ramshackle place that stood out among the tidier homes along First Avenue in Massapequa Park. Heavyset and six-foot-four with a squinty glare, Heuermann had a rough, confident bearing. Massapequa Park is a small but busy town of commuters, an hour from the city, and Heuermann was among them, an architect with his own business, R H Consultants & Associates, with an office in midtown Manhattan, a block from Penn Station.

Certain suburbs make a big show of being tranquil. But the towns of central Long Island passed the tranquil exit a long time ago. These are densely packed bedroom communities with skyrocketing real estate values—the American dream, pressure-cooker style, where middle-class striving and social anxiety go hand in hand. In his career, Heuermann seemed to thrive under that pressure. His business focused on the regulatory maze of building renovations and construction—installing a new fire escape, repointing the bricks of a facade. His clientele included large condo and co-op buildings, often with residents who ran their own companies and were accustomed to being in power. For a very brief period of time, Heuermann would be the most important person in their world—the guy standing in the way of the job. If and only if they paid attention to him, then maybe they'd get what they wanted.

The people who talked with Heuermann, did business with him, worked alongside or down the hall from him, remember someone with a certain air of self-importance—the only competent person in a world of incompetent people. He believed in his own indispensability—a confident fixer with main-character energy. At work, he was gregarious, even jovial when it suited him, even to the point of inviting colleagues to go hunting or shooting at a gun range.

At home, it would have made sense for things to be the same. He was a family man, after all. But on the sidewalks and in the shops of Massapequa Park, Heuermann was diffident and wordless, not explaining himself to anyone. He was the sort of neighbor you might live next door to for years, but never really get to know.

July 14, 2023. Maureen's sister Missy Cann is back on Long Island, standing with her husband Chris at a news conference—onstage, facing the cameras, once again back in the limelight because of the case that had haunted her for sixteen years.

Next to her is Melissa Barthelemy's sister, Amanda—married now and a mother, no longer the sixteen-year-old in Buffalo listening to a killer taunt her on the phone as the police tried in vain to trace the calls.

And next to Amanda is Megan Waterman's daughter, Lili—now a high schooler, raised under the care of a great-aunt. Lili's grandmother, Megan's mother Lorraine, had died less than a year earlier, after many years of chronic health problems.

And now, onstage with Missy and Amanda and Lili, is the district attorney of Suffolk County, Ray Tierney, saying that while the man in custody for the murders represented the worst of humanity, the families of the victims seemed to him to embody the best of all of us. And then, after Tierney, comes the police commissioner, Rodney Harrison, who gives Missy and Amanda and Lili each a long hug.

It's a big difference, twelve and a half years: The victims seem to matter.

They are all there to announce a long-awaited arrest in the Gilgo Beach murders: Rex Heuermann, a fifty-nine-year-old architect and married father of two who commuted to Manhattan from his home in Massapequa Park. Heuermann had been in plain sight the whole time in a number of ways. According to prosecutors, he had ninety-seven gun permits—an astonishing number, by any standard, that you would think would raise a few eyebrows in any cursory search. Police searches of his email accounts showed he was far from lying low. He was actively patronizing escorts—raising questions if he harmed others, if these victims were just the start. While the families of the victims, who had been waiting for this moment, were overwhelmed by the news of the arrest, they also wondered why it took so long.

Since the case's early days, law enforcement officers have rarely spoken to the media. When I was reporting *Lost Girls*, the police were largely silent. But in the months after Heuermann's arrest, some were willing to discuss the investigation with a greater degree of detail and candor. I spoke with people close to the case during every chapter of its bizarre thirteen-year timeline. (Several sources asked for anonymity, concerned that public statements by insiders might undercut the case against Heuermann before the trial.) The story they tell—at times self-serving and at other times soul-searching—demonstrates, inadvertently and otherwise, how institutional rot helped contribute to the delays and paralysis of the investigation. What started out as indifference and apathy soon curdled into obstinance, willful ignorance, and corruption. From the moment those women were found at Gilgo Beach, the law-enforcement culture of Suffolk County seemed so preternaturally ill-suited to handle this case that a killer was allowed to roam free. Which was all the more galling, given what we know now—that everything the police needed to solve the case, they had almost on day one.

To understand what went wrong with the Long Island serial killer case, it helps to have a passing familiarity with the dark, contradictory nature of Suffolk County—encompassing some of the most rarefied communities in the world, including the Hamptons and Fire Island, as well as struggling towns like Brentwood, Wyandanch, and Central Islip. It's a place full of sophisticated, powerful people, where time and again, law-enforcement has closed ranks and done things their way, often with little oversight.

In the 1970s, to take one notable example, the Suffolk County Police Department's homicide unit was known for an impossibly high confession rate of 97 percent, which almost certainly meant they engaged in coercion. When that statistic made the news, officers in that unit proudly took to wearing T-shirts with the insignia 97%. Prosecutors have, at times, ignored and even enabled those excesses. In 1988, a teenager named Martin Tankleff was driven to confess falsely to the murder of his father; it would take almost eighteen years for him to be exonerated and released. And a year later, in 1989, New York's Commission of Investigation issued a report lambasting the Suffolk Police and the district attorney's office and citing evidence of more coerced confessions, plus illegal wiretaps, preferential treatment for people close to public officials, and "the practice of sweeping law enforcement misconduct under the rug."

The police often went unchecked because in Suffolk County, their union is a powerful source of campaign contributions with its own super PAC. The union's political clout helps explain why the Suffolk Police Department is one of the nation's largest, with about 2,500 sworn officers, and their salaries are among the highest. A politician who supports the police can earn the union's backing and ensure a swift rise to the top. And for many decades, any district attorney with ambition would not look too closely at police indiscretions, and even use the police to their advantage to consolidate political power.

When Thomas Spota became district attorney in 2002, he was perceived as a white knight, largely expected to clean house after an era of corruption. But Spota, it became clear later, found ways to install his own allies in police leadership positions, which, in turn, would secure the union's support. When the Gilgo case emerged eight years into Spota's tenure, he was publicly second-guessing Police Department decisions and lining up personnel he wanted to move in to run things—even as the body count around Gilgo Beach rose, the media took up residence on the South Shore, and investigators struggled to handle an unprecedented case involving at least one serial killer.

The Suffolk detectives had more than enough to deal with in those first few months. Ten possible victims meant ten different sets of evidence—not just bodies, but also physical evidence and phone records. The police knew the killer targeted women who posted ads on Craigslist. They knew he used camouflaged burlap straps to bind them, the kind a hunter uses. They knew he used hard-to-trace burner phones to contact each woman, a different phone for each victim: sixteen calls or texts to Maureen before she vanished, and four before Melissa Barthelemy disappeared. At the time, the burner phones made him seem clever—a loyal watcher of certain police procedurals, perhaps.

But the killer made mistakes, too. Police knew he used tape to wrap the victims and found at least a few hairs on the tape. With the right technology, furnished by the FBI or an outside lab with expertise, they might be able to extract DNA and find a match, provided they had a suspect's DNA to compare it with. They also recovered a belt on the scene with initials, either HM or WH.

The police started to understand where this killer might operate—where he lived and maybe where he worked. They learned how in the summer of 2009, the killer made taunting phone calls from midtown Manhattan to Amanda, using Melissa's phone. Maureen's phone also connected to a cell tower in midtown, near the Queensboro Bridge, before she vanished in 2007. Megan's phone last registered at a cell tower in central Long Island, near Massapequa Park. So did Melissa's. Early on, they understood that pattern: a killer who potentially commuted between central Long Island and midtown Manhattan.

These were densely populated areas, where it might seem impossible that he could ever be traced. And yet during the first year of the Gilgo case, in 2011, the FBI started to provide help on that front: technology that might track those burner phones by seeing if their numbers appeared in the records of certain cell towers on Long Island. Cell-tower data is voluminous, a haystack full of needles: Think of all the signals from all the phones that ping at various cell towers every second. But if any of the killer's burner phones pinged at the same towers, they would have a sense of where, perhaps, he spent most of his time.

If this seemed promising, Suffolk's investigation for most of 2011 was essentially at a standstill, in part because the district attorney, Spota, was stepping up his efforts to orchestrate a soft takeover of the police. He went public with his fury at the existing police leadership in May after senior officials under Police Commissioner Richard Dormer suggested that a single killer might be responsible for all the murders. Spota "was so incensed by the one-killer theory," a former senior police officer told me, because he believed it encouraged panic. "That heightens the alarm to everyone that we have an active killer—that it could happen again."

Days later, Spota held a news conference of his own. He made sure Richard Dormer, the police commissioner, was standing there as he spoke—a public defenestration. "Dormer has no idea what Spota is going to say," the former senior officer recalled. "And Spota runs the whole show. He's got the clipboards up, and he shows where all the bodies are laid out. It's very telling." Spota announced that there could be as many as three killers at work on Long Island—that the South Shore might have been a dumping ground. "It is clear that the area in and around Gilgo Beach has been used to discard human remains for some period of time,"

406   Epilogue

Spota declared. "As distasteful and disturbing as that is, there is no evidence that all of these remains are the work of a single killer."

Among the police and the media, those watching the case were baffled. Isn't an open disagreement between the police commissioner and the district attorney a gift to any future defense lawyer handling the case at trial? But insiders understood that this wasn't so much about solving this case as it was about Spota's larger ambitions. They knew that Dormer was an appointee of Steve Levy, the county executive and Spota's political foe, a rival for power within the county's Democratic Party organization. Spota was going after them both. Publicly, he excoriated Dormer, while privately, he had Levy investigated for campaign-finance improprieties. In March, two months before this news conference, Spota pressured Levy to drop his bid for reelection in return for not being prosecuted. Dormer was out as commissioner before the end of the year.

The public would never learn exactly what Levy supposedly did—a classic Suffolk County backroom deal. And his successor, Steve Bellone, having just witnessed a demonstration of Spota's clout, was happy to sign off on a new chief of the Police Department, who happened to be a longtime protégé of Spota's—and who, to the eternal detriment of the Gilgo investigation, would go on to become widely known as the most corrupt police official in modern Suffolk history.

Shortly after the bodies were identified by DNA in early 2011, the police visited the house on America Avenue in West Babylon where Amber lived with Dave Schaller and her boyfriend, Björn "Bear" Brodsky. The place was a drug pit, well known to neighbors, who had been watching cars coming and going for months. All three housemates spent most of their days doing heroin, with

Amber's sister Kim popping by for visits. The money for the heroin came from Amber's escort work, starting at $250 a call.

Dave said at the time that during Amber's last night at the house, she was on the phone with a potential client and arrived at an unusually high fee: $1,500 for the whole night. She asked to meet him outside the house. Dave walked Amber out the door, but he didn't see Amber's client. He wrote in a 2012 Facebook post that he was too high to remember him. But the police had access to Amber's phone records, and they saw that the same man she was talking with had also been texting her the night before. They even saw a text message suggesting he had met with her in person that first night: The client seemed mad that something had gone wrong, and he wanted to see her again.

The police learned that on the first night, the client wanted to hire Amber, but as soon as he paid, Dave jumped out of the shadows and chased him away. This was a scam Dave and Bear pulled whenever they could that summer—accosting Amber's clients and taking their money before she had to follow through with the job. But this time, the client seemed to want another chance.

Police started looking for anyone who could remember seeing the client on that first night. They found a witness who saw a large, white male, six-foot-four or taller—resembling an "ogre"—in his mid-forties, with "dark bushy hair" and big glasses. The witness also spotted the car this man drove: a green Chevrolet Avalanche with a distinctive rear door, like a truck's. At that moment, with the description of a man and a make, model, and color of a car, the police were closer to targeting a suspect than they had ever been.

And then the lead withered away. The initial database search for the car went nowhere. A source close to the Gilgo investigators told me that the detectives were using a program known as LAWMAN—a product of 1990s database technology, accessing millions of New York State's paper DMV records. When it first became available, the LAWMAN search seemed like a godsend. Pretty much everything that sat in the DMV archives was instantly searchable. But over the years, as databases age, their data becomes harder to navigate. New cars like Avalanches, which are a blend of a truck and a car, could be misfiled by the DMV—and what gets mangled by the DMV can disappear entirely in the LAWMAN searches. In retrospect, the source told me, the car must have been miscategorized.

It's hard to imagine that the police would not at least have tried to continue pursuing eyewitness information about the last man to see Amber alive. But that did not happen. Just like that, the police seemed to stop talking about the "ogre" and the Avalanche—not with their superiors in the department and not with an outside agency like the state police or the FBI. A senior police official with close knowledge of the investigation's first year told me that he had no recollection of the Avalanche tip. The chief of detectives at the time, Dominick Varrone, has also said he heard nothing about it. For a decade, the lead sat at the bottom of a growing case file, with no sign that it might ever be discovered again.

Around the same time, the department was adrift, waiting for Spota's handpicked police chief to arrive. James Burke was a former Suffolk narcotics detective whose alliance with Spota spanned decades, almost like a blood tie. In a 1979 case that brought him recognition as a young prosecutor, Spota secured the convictions of two teenage defendants for the murder of a thirteen-year-old boy named John Pius. A key witness was Burke, who at the time was just fourteen. A decade later, participants in the case claimed that witnesses had been coached to lie on the stand. Spota was never charged with, and has denied, any wrongdoing. And his bond with Burke never wavered—even years later when Burke ran into trouble.

As a police officer, Burke lost track of his firearm more than once. And in 1993, an internal affairs investigation accused him of patronizing and smoking crack with a sex worker. Spota, who was in private practice at the time, offered to represent Burke. Burke eventually was punished with the loss of fifteen vacation days. Once Spota became district attorney in 2002, he gave Burke a senior role overseeing a group of detectives in his office. It was clear back then to Spota's staff that one day, when Spota had the chance, he would put Burke in charge of the Police Department.

With Burke arriving as chief in 2012, Spota managed to do what even in Suffolk County once seemed impossible— consolidate political power between the police and the district attorney's office. There was nothing to hold back the impulse to close ranks and remove all outside scrutiny. "It was: 'Hey, we run our own shop. Stay out,'" Bellone, the county executive during much of Spota's tenure, told me.

When, in early 2012, staff members from the FBI's celebrated Behavioral Analysis Unit arrived in New York from Quantico, Virginia, to help with the case at the invitation of the previous leaders of the Police Department, Spota had them turn around and fly back home, declaring their work unnecessary.

The loss of the FBI's help was a severe blow to the Gilgo investigation, impeding any meaningful progress in the case. Before being shut out, the FBI handed the police a raft of cell-tower information that they had collected over the past several months. Their analysis traced the signals from the killer's burner phones to two regions on a map—geographic "boxes," they called them—one in central Long Island (including Massapequa Park), and one in midtown Manhattan. As a next step, the FBI was willing to help search cell-tower data in central Long Island for other cell phone numbers that registered with those towers at the same time as the killer's burner phones. In theory, whoever used those burner phones also carried a regular phone that pinged the same towers at the same time. That number, unlike the burners, would be traceable.

Spota abandoned this entire approach. He refused to petition the courts to search any more cell-tower data on Long Island. Spota's staff members, who would have had to request the warrants for that data, waved off the idea as a fishing expedition. "They didn't understand it, and they didn't want to litigate something that they didn't understand," the source close to the Gilgo investigators told me. In truth, cell-tower data was hardly novel; in 2004, it helped disprove the alibi of the accused California wife-killer Scott Peterson. A different district attorney might have seen where the data led.

There were other ways for Spota to rationalize not squandering time and resources on cell-tower data. Just because the killer made some calls from central Long Island didn't mean he had to be living there. Clearly the killer was good at avoiding detection. He seemed too smart to continue living a few miles from where the bodies were found. By now, he had to be a ghost. The problem with that argument was that every lead they had, upon examination, could be written off as a long shot. A police source who was part of the early investigation told me that they had been pulling hunting licenses in the area because the burlap found on the bodies suggested the killer was a hunter. They appeared to drop that strategy, but Rex Heuermann, it turns out, was an enthusiastic hunter. "I find it hard to believe his name isn't somewhere," the source told me.

Despite that initial interest in hunting licenses, the team hadn't concentrated on gun permits. "The victims weren't shot," the source close to the Gilgo investigators told me. This was technically true—the bodies had no signs of gun trauma, causing many to speculate that they were strangled. But a different set of investigators, one that closely partnered with other agencies like the FBI or the Bureau of Alcohol, Tobacco, Firearms and Explosives, might have looked at gun permits and noticed the man in Massapequa Park with ninety-seven.

In the four years that Burke ran the Police Department, from 2012 to 2015, the "Gilgo room" at Suffolk Police Headquarters became a place for part-time work, with little urgency dictated from above. Under Burke, the police were in what would later be characterized by federal prosecutors as a complete ethical free-fall: His staff served drinks in his office every night. He ordered officers to spy on his girlfriend, her exes, and her son and follow his perceived adversaries, including Steve Bellone, the county executive. He turned the police force into his own empire, punishing anyone he deemed disloyal and then celebrating with friends after their demotion.

Instead of prioritizing the search for an at-large serial killer, Spota, too, seemed more interested in investigating his rivals, including Bellone, who recalled being approached more than once by Spota's staff, apparently just to let him know they were watching. "DA is the most powerful office that we have," Bellone told me. "If you're willing to target people and go after people—that is an awesome power. You don't even have to indict somebody to ruin their life. Just starting to investigate someone can cause people to lose jobs."

For about a year, things went smoothly for Spota and Burke, until Burke spoiled everything with an unchecked explosion of violence inside a Suffolk Police precinct house. In December 2012, a witness in a drug case, who also happened to be pilfering from police vehicles, grabbed a duffel bag from Burke's car that contained pornography, sex toys, cigars, a gun belt, and ammunition. (Federal prosecutors would later call this duffel Burke's "party bag.") When Burke found out, he attacked the witness in full view of several other detectives, some of whom took part in the beating, and even bragged about it later. Federal agents started investigating Burke in April, and Burke spent the next year or so pressuring witnesses to take part in a cover-up.

He had help from Spota's staff, who used wiretaps and car-tracking devices to monitor police detectives he distrusted, searching for blackmail material. Instead of filing subpoenas for more cell-tower data in the Gilgo case, Spota's staff were wiretapping a police detective they suspected of leaking information about a gang case to *Newsday*, the Long Island newspaper. The tapes included calls between the detective and FBI agents—as well as the federal prosecutors involved in the investigation into Burke.

By law, Spota needed to notify Loretta Lynch, then the US attorney for the Eastern District of New York, when federal agents appeared on police wiretaps. When he did, federal officials immediately saw how far afield those wiretaps went—and how, perhaps, the whole point may have been to learn how close the FBI might be to taking down Burke. "The problem for them," Bellone told me, "was that they didn't know that President Obama was going to nominate Loretta Lynch to be the attorney general of the United States." Once that happened, the federal investigation into Burke expanded into an inquiry of all of Suffolk County law enforcement.

Lynch's office issued "immunity orders," or a requirement to testify, to witnesses in the department who had seen Burke in action. Burke was indicted and pleaded guilty in 2016 to conspiring to obstruct justice and violating the civil rights of the witness he had beaten. He served a sentence of forty-six months. Back home on Long Island, he still receives a pension. (In a bleak but strangely resonant moment, Burke was arrested just a few weeks after Heuermann for soliciting sex in a public park.)

Spota resigned in 2017, the day after he was indicted on charges of conspiracy, obstruction of justice, witness tampering, and other crimes. Bellone, finally free of Spota's surveillance and intimidation, said during a news conference that Spota and Burke had been running a "criminal enterprise." In December 2019, Spota was convicted in federal court and later sentenced to five years.

Spota and Burke were gone, but the bunker mentality remained. No one collided with that culture more directly than Tim Sini, who became police commissioner in 2015, just after Burke's indictment. Sini, a senior prosecutor in Manhattan under the US attorney, Preet Bharara, was hired to clean up the mess Burke left behind. The problem was that those very credentials made Sini suspect to many in the department, never mind that he was commissioner of a police force without ever having been a police officer himself. Sini sensed pushback from the start. "There's this culture of, you know, this is our town and we do it our way," he told me.

Sini wanted to modernize the Gilgo investigation. He brought the FBI back in, asking for help with the cell phone piece of the case. He invested in new equipment, including the Gladiator Autonomous Receiver, or GAR. A burner phone's signal from a tower suggests a huge geographical area, but the GAR can make that area smaller. "So essentially, what that did was reduce your number of persons of interest," he said. But these efforts were met with resistance from the detectives handling Gilgo.

That disagreement came to a head in 2018, when Sini was elected as the district attorney and started pushing the police to find two specific suspects in those geographic areas, one of them a former police officer. A source with knowledge of the investigation told me that Sini was treated as if he had somehow broken protocol and failed to understand that the Police Department decided who did and didn't receive subpoenas.

Both of Sini's suggested targets were ruled out as suspects; the source close to the Gilgo investigators told me that the detectives felt that Sini, an outsider using Suffolk County as a step on his political ladder to higher office, was more interested in looking busy than getting results. "We made them look foolish" by knocking out their potential suspects, the source said.

Some police were also upset that Sini was diving into Suffolk County's history of botched murder cases. As soon as he became district attorney, he opened the county's first conviction-integrity unit, an office that reviewed past cases in which police malfeasance led to gross injustices. In 2019, that unit successfully exposed wrongdoing in a legendary case from Suffolk's past: the beating and confession of Keith Bush, who was convicted in 1977 and spent thirty-three years in prison for a murder he didn't commit. The Bush case now stands as the longest wrongful incarceration in New York State history. But the past is never past in Suffolk County. At least one senior Gilgo detective knew some of the players in the case personally—officers discredited by the exoneration. Sini said that he may not have appreciated at the time that reopening the Bush case "was a declaration of war on the establishment."

The conflict between the police and Sini seemed to have a direct effect on the Gilgo case. Sini's office kept narrowing the data that police needed to investigate, and the police kept not doing anything with that data. By the summer of 2021, the source with knowledge of the investigation told me, the geographic areas had been reduced to the smallest yet on Long Island and in midtown Manhattan. This source suggested that fewer than one thousand men lived in the Long Island area. All that was left was to see which of them worked in that tiny sliver of Manhattan. "It was eminently doable," the source said. "But it just didn't happen."

Sini's team reached out to neighboring Nassau County, where Massapequa Park is, to help create a list of homes within the geographic area. Nassau isolated several hundred houses— including on First Avenue, where Heuermann and his family lived. They provided short dossiers of each home. Heuermann, the source told me, was on that list. Again, the police seemed to do nothing.

The FBI was as frustrated with the police as Sini was and threatened to leave the investigation. Police leadership responded by pulling a longtime lead detective off the Gilgo case. It was taking time, but in certain ways, the law-enforcement culture was changing. Sini had some help from the police commissioner who succeeded him, Geraldine Hart, another outsider, who spent more than twenty years with the FBI. Inspired by the breakthrough in the Golden State Killer case in California, Hart commissioned an outside lab that could use genetic genealogy—matching DNA evidence to genetic material collected by private companies, like 23andMe—to successfully identify a victim found during the

Gilgo Beach search in 2011 as Valerie Mack. She disappeared in 2000 and, like the other four women, worked as an escort.

Hart also made public an intriguing piece of evidence that the police had not disclosed: the leather belt with imprinted initials. Hart said the police believed the killer had handled the belt. (Police are still trying to extract DNA from a hair that was found near the belt buckle.) There's always a risk when revealing sensitive information about a case—it could tip their hand to the killer, for example. But enough time had passed. The case was now convincingly alive again.

It took until 2022 for the Gilgo case to get what it needed all along—an interagency task force with full-time investigators sharing information, resources, and ideas. There's a certain poetry in the fact that the Suffolk district attorney who helped make it happen, Ray Tierney, had been pressured out of Spota's office in 2008. Then a junior prosecutor, Tierney ran into trouble when he started questioning some corner-cutting in Spota's political-corruption unit. Quite abruptly, Tierney was transferred to rackets, throwing his future into jeopardy. "They took my car, they took the phone," Tierney told me. "I certainly got the message. I said, 'My career in the DA's office is effectively over.' I was way outside the circle of trust."

Tierney left that office, but he never stopped working as a prosecutor—first in the US attorney's office on Long Island and then for the Brooklyn district attorney. In both jobs, Tierney mounted cases against violent gangs that relied heavily on cell-tower data. Like Sini, Tierney understood that when witnesses aren't helpful, the data is essential. During the thirteen years that he was outside Suffolk's closed universe, he heard plenty about the troubles in the Burke era, and he never stopped watching to see if there was a break in the Gilgo case. In 2021, when he ran for Suffolk County district attorney, Tierney made cracking the Gilgo case part of his platform.

While campaigning, Tierney met with some of the Gilgo victims' family members face to face, watching their expressions harden as they talked about the decade of frustration. At that moment, Tierney found himself trying not to make promises he was not sure he could keep. "I didn't know if it would be possible to solve," he told me. After all this time, it still seemed like a needle in a haystack. Even if the killer was from Long Island and commuted to New York, did that really narrow things down? "I grew up in Commack," Tierney told me. "Everybody who lived in Commack, you either owned your own business or you were a cop or fireman—or your dad or your mom or both of them got on the train, went into the city, and came home. How many other people do that?"

Soon after Tierney won the election, Rodney Harrison became the new police commissioner. He had spent twelve years in investigations for the NYPD and worked a number of gang cases with Tierney. Harrison told Tierney that he wanted a task force, this time not just with the FBI but with everyone: Nassau County police officers, state police officers, and the local sheriff's office all in a room, working daily and talking constantly. Tierney had been saying the same thing on the campaign trail. It seemed strange to each of them that nothing quite like this had happened before.

In his first days as commissioner, Harrison visited the site on Ocean Parkway, met with the detectives, and held a news conference saying he liked his chances. Privately, though, Harrison was shocked to see that, after ten years, the mountains of witness statements, interview transcripts, and investigation notes had never been digitized. All the work Suffolk detectives had done on the case was unsearchable—accessible only to a few detectives who were relying on their own limited memories of the case. "We had to collect everything and send it down to Quantico," Harrison told me. "So that was big."

They didn't even know what they had. The task force was announced on February 15, 2022. On March 14, they learned about the Chevy Avalanche.

It was simply a matter of which search tool they used. In the early days of the investigation, the DMV record search used by Suffolk detectives to find the Avalanche came up short. But in 2022, a member of the new task force from the state police used a service called TLOxp—a private, subscription-based database that accesses more records in more places, all around the country. (The database was available in 2011, when the police first learned about the Avalanche.) This search had none of the filing issues of the previous search. A car turned up right away: an Avalanche owned by Heuermann at the time the bodies were first found. Since then, the ownership had transferred to Heuermann's brother, Craig, in South Carolina. "The state police were the game changers," Harrison told me. They had never been part of the investigation. "Once we brought them to the table, they made the difference."

As soon as they saw a car record linked to Rex Heuermann—a man the size of an ogre, living and working in the exact geographic area that the data had been suggesting and resuggesting for ten years—the team locked in on him as a potential suspect. There was even an archived Google map photo from November 2011, showing a Chevy Avalanche parked outside Heuermann's house in Massapequa Park.

For much of 2022, the task force used cell-tower data furnished by the FBI and refined by Sini to match Heuermann's movements to the movements of the victims and the killer. Tierney's office filed about three hundred subpoenas and search warrants. Sure enough, wherever Heuermann's personal cellphone went, the burner phones attributed to the killer seemed to follow. None of this explained how a married father of two in a densely populated neighborhood might operate unnoticed. But then they used more conventional Web searches to piece together Heuermann's life and the life of his family. When Megan disappeared, Heuermann's wife, Asa Ellerup, was away, in the middle of a four-day trip to Maryland. When Amber vanished, Ellerup was spending a week away from home in New Jersey.

And in the summer of 2009, two days before Melissa disappeared, Heuermann's wife left the United States on a trip to Iceland. She was not in town when Melissa vanished nor was she in town a few days later when Amanda started getting harassing calls from a man using Melissa's phone. Heuermann did appear to be in town then, but he left for Iceland several days later, and for the length of his time out of the country, Amanda received no calls from her sister's phone. Those calls resumed the day after Heuermann came home.

Scouring Heuermann's email, the police found accounts for burner phones. None were the ones connected to the women's disappearances. But with one of those burners, they found something significant: an email account he used to conduct Google searches. The content of these searches was everything the police had hoped and dreaded it to be. He was interested in violent porn. He was interested in child porn. He wanted to know what this new Gilgo task force was up to. And from other record searches, they learned he was using Tinder and contacting escorts. And he had guns. Lots and lots of guns.

With this new insight into Heuermann, Harrison knew the clock was ticking. Who's to say if he'd already hurt other people or was about to? From there, Harrison said his thoughts turned even darker. All those gun permits—ninety-seven of them. How would someone with that many guns react if he knew he was being investigated? What would a person like that do if someone tried to arrest him? "Honestly, I was nervous," Harrison told me. "What's his mind-set? Is he somebody unstable that can do a mass shooting incident or something like that? You know, your mind starts racing all over."

They needed DNA to confirm everything else they had found, including the hairs on the tape used to bind the bodies. Tailing Heuermann, they picked up their sample from a pizza box he tossed into a garbage can on Fifth Avenue in Manhattan—one more indelible image to make this case notorious, like the burlap and the bramble. The hair follicles from the tape contained trace genetic samples requiring a special process called mitochondrial analysis. The FBI matched Heuermann's DNA to one hair. Two other hairs matched Heuermann's wife, whose DNA the police found on two bottles left outside their home. The theory is that Heuermann used a roll of tape that had been lying around the house.

On Thursday, July 13, 2023, a group of officers approached Heuermann as he was walking along Fifth Avenue, near his office. As one stopped him, the others formed a circle, tightening around him. There was not a hint of violence—an arrest so smooth that pedestrians kept on walking past them.

After all this time, the police had a win. They built their case, found a plausible suspect, and apprehended him without bloodshed. Tierney and Harrison held a news conference with the victims' families squarely behind them—another change from the old days, when the families were told to keep their distance. But this is Suffolk County, and so that same day, Steve Bellone, whose term as county executive ended in 2023 and whose legacy will be forever entangled with the Burke-Spota era, held his own news conference. The governor, Kathy Hochul, made her remarks separately, too, during an unrelated media event at Jones Beach. They weren't invited to Tierney and Harrison's news conference, Tierney said later, because "this wasn't about politics."

Heuermann has been charged in the murders of Maureen, Megan, Melissa, and Amber, the four women the police first found on Gilgo Beach in December 2010. There are six more sets of remains with no suspects attached—not counting Shannan Gilbert, whose death police continue to maintain was unrelated, a cruel coincidental tragedy that set this case in motion. While Joel Rifkin, a prolific Long Island serial killer of an earlier era, confessed right away to seventeen murders, Heuermann is maintaining his innocence, and for the time being his silence.

In all the time this case went without an arrest, what chance would there be that the killer never tried something else like it? Would someone like him just stop at four? Tierney has seen all the suspect's Web searches and has his own assessment of the man. "I would say that the interest and the obsession never left," he said.

Tierney has announced he will try the case against Heuermann personally—a district attorney going into court to argue before a jury the most notorious serial killer trial in a generation. All eyes will be on Suffolk County again. What happens next is a chance to make up, at least partly, for the years when this case was in such disarray—and Suffolk County's law enforcement culture seemed all too willing to forget it ever happened.

It's been thirteen years since the bodies were found in the bramble beside Ocean Parkway. For the family members, that's an eternity of wondering and waiting, and feeling every bit as discarded as the loved ones they lost.

Ocean Parkway

The Gate

Ocean Beach Rd

The Fairway ☐ **Gus Coletti's house**

Shannan's body fou

☐
Joe Brewer's house

Oak Beach

Anchor Way

The Bayou

○ **Shannan's purse, cell phone, jean
shoes, and lip gloss found**

Dr. Hackett's house

Circle D

☐
Larboard Court

CAPTREE ISLAND

Robert Moses Causeway

JONES BEACH ISLAND

FIRE ISLAND INLET

CONNECTICUT

LONG ISLAND
SOUND

NEW YORK

John Doe, Asian male
April 4, 2011

Skull, hands, forearms of
Jessica Taylor (Manorville)
March 29, 2011

Melissa Barthelemy
December 11, 2010

Maureen Brainard-Barnes
December 13, 2010

Remains of Valerie Mack
(linked to torso in Manorv
and unidentified toddler
April 4, 2011

Megan Waterman
December 13, 2010

Amber Lynn Costello
December 13, 2010

Shannan Gilbert
December 13, 20

Skull of Karen Vergata
April 11, 2011

Unidentified human bones
April 11, 2011

Oak Beach

W. Gilgo Beach

Jones Beach

Dates when remains found

Torso of Valerie Mack
(linked to remains found near
Oak Beach on April 4, 2011)
November 19, 2000

Torso of Jessica Taylor
July 26, 2003

Manorville

LONG ISLAND

ATLANTIC
OCEAN

CHRONOLOGY

April 20, 1996
Two female legs, wrapped in a plastic bag, are discovered on Fire Island west of Davis Park Beach.

December 19, 2000
The first of two human torsos is discovered by hikers in the Long Island Pine Barrens in Manorville, off of Halsey Manor Road.

July 26, 2003
The second human torso is discovered in the Pine Barrens, not far from the first. The remains are identified as Jessica Taylor, a twenty-year-old escort from Washington, D.C., last seen days earlier at the Port Authority Bus Terminal in Manhattan.

July 9, 2007
Maureen Brainard-Barnes is last seen in her room at the Super 8 Hotel in midtown Manhattan. Her last known call that night is to her sister, Missy, during which she says she is at Penn Station.

July 12, 2009
Melissa Barthelemy is last seen outside her apartment in the Bronx. In the next month, her sister, Amanda, will receive seven phone calls from a man claiming to be her killer.

May 1, 2010
Shannan Gilbert disappears at sunrise after being seen running out of Joe Brewer's house in Oak Beach, Long Island. Neighbors Gus Coletti and Barbara Brennan are among the last to see her, in the vicinity of Anchor Way.

June 5, 2010
Megan Waterman disappears from the Hauppauge Holiday Inn Express, last seen heading toward a nearby convenience store on foot.

September 2, 2010
Amber Lynn Costello leaves her home in West Babylon to meet a client, never to be seen alive again.

December 11, 2010
Police discover a full skeleton, wrapped in burlap, in the bramble beside Ocean Parkway near Gilgo Beach, three miles from Oak Beach. The remains are later identified as Melissa Barthelemy.

December 13, 2010
Near where Melissa was found, police find three more sets of remains, also skeletons wrapped in burlap, later identified as Megan Waterman, Maureen Brainard-Barnes, and Amber Lynn Costello.

January 25, 2011
Suffolk County Police Commissioner Richard Dormer and Suffolk County District Attorney Thomas Spota publicly acknowledge that the police are looking for a serial killer.

March 29, 2011
Police find a skull, hands, and forearm, later verified to be additional remains of Jessica Taylor, the woman whose torso was found in Manorville in 2003. These remains are also found along Ocean Parkway, three quarters of a mile east of where the first four bodies were discovered.

April 4, 2011
Three more sets of remains are found along Ocean Parkway: an unidentified Asian male dressed in women's clothing; the skull, hands, and foot of the first Manorville Jane Doe; and an unidentified girl between sixteen and thirty-two months old.

April 11, 2011
Police uncover two more sets of remains in two separate locations. The first discovery, female bones and jewelry found near the Jones Beach water tower, is later suggested by DNA to be the likely mother of the girl found eight days earlier along Ocean Parkway. The second, a skull discovered west of Tobay Beach in Nassau County, is later determined to be that of the Jane Doe torso found in 1996 on Fire Island.

April 12, 2011
The first news reports air about Mari Gilbert's claim that she spoke with Oak Beach resident Dr. Peter Hackett in the days after her daughter Shannan's disappearance. Hackett and his wife deny that the conversations took place.

May 9, 2011
In light of the six latest discoveries, Spota revises his theory of the case, announcing, "There is no evidence that all of these remains are the work of a single killer."

June 14, 2011
Family members hold the first of several vigils at Oak Beach.

July 11, 2011
Peter Hackett tells CBS News he indeed spoke with Mari Gilbert on the phone days after Shannan disappeared.

November 29, 2011
Dormer revises the case theory yet again, announcing he believes a single serial killer is to blame for all ten victims, and that Shannan's disappearance is a separate case, perhaps not even a murder.

November 30, 2011
The Suffolk County police announce they will reopen the search for Shannan along Ocean Parkway.

December 6, 2011
On day two of the new search, the police move from Ocean Parkway to Oak Beach. That same day, they find Shannan's pocketbook, ID, cell phone, jeans, and shoes in a marsh, steps from where she was last seen on Anchor Way.

December 13, 2011
Shannan's remains are found on the far side of the Oak Beach marsh, a quarter mile from her belongings. Before an autopsy is performed, Dormer refers to her death as an accident.

December 15, 2011
Spota decries Dormer's single-killer theory. The same day, County Executive–elect Steve Bellone names Dormer's replacement as police commissioner, effective January 1.

December 20, 2011
Mari Gilbert and her attorney publicly call for the FBI to take over the case.

January 3, 2012
Suffolk County Interim Commissioner Edward Webber announces, "There's no fixed theories at the moment" about the Gilbert case or any of the Ocean Parkway cases.

May 1, 2012
Shannan's autopsy results are shared with her family. The cause of death is "undetermined."

November 15, 2012
Shannan's family files a wrongful death lawsuit against Peter Hackett.

February 26, 2016

Former Suffolk County Police Chief of Department James Burke pleads guilty to conspiring to obstruct justice and violating the civil rights of a witness he had beaten. Burke is blamed for keeping the FBI and other agencies from helping with the Gilgo Beach investigation for several years.

May 28, 2020

Suffolk County Police Commissioner Geraldine Hart announces the identification of a Jane Doe: Valerie Mack's remains were found in Manorville, Long Island, on November 19, 2000 (the same year she went missing). More of her remains were found along Ocean Parkway on April 4, 2011 (see map on pages 424–425).

February 15, 2022

Suffolk County Police Commissioner Rodney Harrison and District Attorney Ray Tierney convene a new interagency task force to investigate the Gilgo Beach case. Three months later, Shannan Gilbert's 911 tape is finally made public.

July 13, 2023

Architect Rex Heuermann is arrested and later charged with the murders of Melissa Barthelemy, Megan Waterman, and Amber Costello, and remains the prime suspect in the death of Maureen Brainard-Barnes. He pleads not guilty.

August 4, 2023

Tierney announces the identification of another Jane Doe: Karen Vergata's legs and feet were found on Fire Island in 1996. Her skull was found during the Gilgo Beach case on April 11, 2011 (see map on pages 426–427).

January 16, 2024

Rex Heuermann is charged with the murder of Maureen Brainard-Barnes. He pleads not guilty.

ACKNOWLEDGMENTS

This project never would have been possible without the generous participation of the mothers and sisters of the women whose lives I have tried to present here. My deepest thanks go to Melissa "Missy" Cann, Lynn Barthelemy, Amanda Funderberg, Mari Gilbert, Sherre Gilbert, Lorraine Waterman, Muriel Benner, and Kim Overstreet. Many others contributed invaluable insights; with apologies for not mentioning everyone, I'm particularly indebted to Sara Karnes, Jason DuBrule, Jeff Martina, Kritzia Lugo, Elmer Barthelemy, Anthony Sims, Liz Meserve, Alfred Overstreet, Melissa Brock Wright, and Dave Schaller. This book is a tribute to their candor and sensitivity and to the love they feel for those who were lost.

A great many others offered expertise and opened doors. On Long Island, thanks to Steve Barcelo, Brendan Murphy, Jim Jones, Michele Kutner, Joe Scalise, Jr., Mary Cascone of the Town of Babylon's Office of Historic Services, Babylon Chief of Staff Ronald Kluesener, Babylon Waterways Management Supervisor Brian Zitani, and State Parks ecologist Julie Lundgren of the New York Natural Heritage Program. Beyond Long Island, thanks to Neale Duffett and Jim Cloutier in Portland, Maine; Doug Weed in Scarborough, Maine; Aaron Bartley in Buffalo, New York; John Jeremiah Sullivan and Ben Steelman in Wilmington, North Carolina; and Charlie Hannon in Jersey City, New Jersey. The forensic pathologist Michael Baden provided great insight into his field, as did Sienna Baskin of the Urban Justice Center's Sex Workers Project and several employees at Safe Horizon, a social services organization in New York. Thanks also to John Connolly, Robert D. Ryan, and Susie Sampierre.

For historical material, I relied heavily on two essays from the dearly departed journal *Long Island Forum:* "The Old Time Ma'shin' Season" by Julian Denton Smith (1957) and "By-gone Days At Oak Beach" by Ulla S. Kimball (1968). The personal remembrances of Ed Meade, Sr., written in 1983, were also invaluable. My account of the search for bodies owes a debt to the work of a number of reporters: Andrew Strickler and Michael Amon broke news constantly in *Newsday*; Manny Fernandez and Tim Stelloh of *The New York Times* wrote the definitive piece on Officer John Mallia and his dog, Blue; Jaclyn Gallucci of the *Long Island Press* reported comprehensively on the case; and Christine Pelisek and Roja Heydarpour of the *Daily Beast* published the first major report on the relatives of the victims forming a "sisterhood."

I would like to thank my talented and caring editors at Harper-Collins, David Hirshey and Barry Harbaugh, for believing in the book and improving it tremendously; Bill Ruoto for designing a beautiful finished book; Beth Thomas and Lydia Weaver for a skillful copyedit; and my agents, David Gernert and Chris Parris-Lamb, for their faith, encouragement, and expertise. Jon Gluck has been my great friend and editor at *New York* magazine for ten years. The article from which this book evolved, "A Serial Killer in Common," is just one example of Jon's editing skill, story sense, and boundless enthusiasm. I've treasured our partnership. Editor in chief Adam Moss and managing editor Ann Clarke were very gracious and supportive while I took time to complete this book. Several skilled reporters from the magazine and elsewhere assisted me with transcription and research: Bianca Male, Taylor Berman, Thayer McClanahan, and Rachel Arons.

Through countless discussions over a great many salads, Jennifer Senior helped me figure out what to say and when and how to say it. She and Mark Levine, Emily Nussbaum, and Clive Thompson never failed to offer moral support. Amy Gross and Kenneth Mueller helped me through some of the worst of it. Thanks also to Chris Bonanos, Juliet Lapidos, and Cristine Cronin. Other good friends contributed not just encouragement but much-needed child care: Josh Goldfein and Yvonne Brown, Michael Kelleher and Shari Zisman, and Doug McMullen and Corinna Snyder. My family, the Kolkers and Hallocks of Maryland and Illinois and the Danises of Massachusetts, North Carolina, and Georgia, have always been so very supportive, and I can never thank them enough.

A few months before *Lost Girls* was completed, our family experienced the loss of Henry L. Danis, Jr. We'll always cherish his memory. This book is for him, and for Audrey and Nate, and for my wife, Kirsten. I am so glad to have this chance in print to thank her not just for encouraging me, but for her beauty, understanding, and love. She means the world to me.

ABOUT THE AUTHOR

ROBERT KOLKER is also the author of *Hidden Valley Road: Inside the Mind of an American Family*, an instant #1 *New York Times* bestseller, a selection of Oprah's Book Club, and one of President Barack Obama's favorite books of 2020. He is a National Magazine Award finalist and a recipient of the John Jay College of Criminal Justice/Harry Frank Guggenheim Award for Excellence in Criminal Justice Reporting. His journalism has appeared in *New York* magazine, the *New York Times Magazine*, *The Atlantic*, *Bloomberg Businessweek*, *Wired*, *O, the Oprah Magazine*, and the Marshall Project. He lives with his family in Brooklyn, New York.